The Road to Croke Park

Great GAA Personalities

Séamus McRory

BLACKWATER PRESS

Editor
Aidan Culhane

Design & Layout
Paula Byrne

Cover Design
Liz Murphy

ISBN
1841314463

© – Séamus McRory 1999

Produced in Ireland by
Blackwater Press
Hibernian Industrial Estate
Greenhills Road
Tallaght, Dublin 24.

Acknowledgements

I would like to thank, most sincerely, all those who contributed to the production of this book. In particular I wish to express my deep appreciation to the following: all the staff at Blackwater Press, especially managing director, John O'Connor and editor, Aidan Culhane for their advice and assistance; the GAA personalities themselves for sharing with me their days of glory, moments of disappointment and their hopes for the future – their spirit of generosity and amicable co-operation greatly simplified my work; the President of the GAA Joe McDonagh for, so willingly, contributing the foreword despite the many and varied constraints on his time; Fr Liam Devine PRO of Sligo County Board; Paddy Flanagan PRO of Westmeath County Board; Gerry Donnelly PRO'of Derry County Board; Seán O'Sullivan Leitrim County Librarian; Micheál McGeary, *Sunday Life* Belfast; Brendan McRory Lissan; Brigid Mulvihill, Kenagh, Co. Longford; all the staff at Croke Park especially PRO, Danny Lynch and financial controller, Frank Tierney – Frank deserves a special word of praise for his diligent and time-consuming research; Cahal McWeeney and Pat Lynch of Longford for their extensive assistance with general research; my wife Olive for her patient endurance during the whole process and my family Mairéad and Diarmuid for their meticulous transcription of tapes; Joe Hunt, Legan, for the thoroughly efficient way in which he undertook the arduous task of proofing; Noel O'Connor, Newsround, Longford; Larry Mitchell, District Manager Longford/Roscommon Bank of Ireland; Tim Shanley, Manager, Ulster Bank Longford; Kieran O'Regan, Manager, TSB Longford; John Murphy, Manager, Irish Permanent Building Society, Longford and Betty Martin, Area Manager of the Educational Building Society for their kind contributions to the personal preparation of the book; James Reynolds, Longford Arms Hotel for the arrangements he made to facilitate interviews. A particular word of gratitude is especially due to the publishers of leading GAA magazine *The Hogan Stand* for the use of photographs and *The Examiner* for the cover photograph of Jimmy Barry Murphy. I would also like to record my sincere appreciation to Eamonn Brennan, Longford for his invaluable suggestions and constant encouragement. Most of all, I thank John Barry, not only for his computer expertise, but also for his patience, advice and his availability at all times. No one worked harder to ensure that this book progressed satisfactorily from the embryonic stage to that of final production. John deserves my greatest thanks.

DEDICATION

To Olive, Mairéad and Diarmuid

With sincere thanks for their constant support, help and encouragement.

Contents

Foreword

Teachtaireacht ón Uachtarán

For everyone involved in Gaelic Games, one of the greatest thrills is meeting the great personalities, be they players, supporters or officials. It is they who provide the colour, the drama and the excitement that is quite unique to the national sports of this country.

Over the last decade we have enjoyed an explosion in the number of books written about Gaelic games and the people central to the GAA. The library is a veritable treasure trove of memories for all of us to cherish. And now we have the latest addition to that library to bring with us into the new millennium.

The author, Séamus McRory, in what was clearly a labour of love, has done us a great service by allowing us meet some of the legendary figures, to re-live their great moments and discuss the many aspects of Gaelic games that constantly arouse our passions. The stories of the 26 personalities interviewed by the author give us a clear picture of the culture of Gaelic games.

A half-century of people and stories is covered in this book and it is great to see some of our current players like Anthony Daly, Peter Canavan and Glenn Ryan feature alongside Enda Colleran, Eddie Keher and Jimmy Smyth.

It is very important that we constantly celebrate the achievements of our players. Séamus McRory has certainly done that in this book.

Seamah Mac Donncha

Joe McDonagh, President, GAA

Séamus McRory

Introduction

Travelling through the countryside of Ireland on my way to interview the famous GAA personalities in this book provided me with a host of enriching experiences. When I met those men whose names are indelibly linked with hurling and football and shared so many memories of past glories and frustrating disappointments, I became acutely aware of what Gaelic games meant to them. They all possessed a natural love of the games which was deeply ingrained in their consciousness.

From those pleasant days and balmy evenings of recall, discussion and future hopes, four major influences as to how each of them became interested in Gaelic games in the first instance, emerged. While these are unsurprising in themselves, it is perhaps worth recounting them for the sake of present and future generations of GAA enthusiasts. The persuasive influence of family and friends and the considerable impact of the local GAA club either in a rural area or an urban district were the two most dominating factors. However, two other issues are increasingly playing a more central role in determining the direction of future sporting stars. The magnetism engendered by all sections of the media, especially television, and the pressing necessity for each young person to have a sporting hero to serve as a role model are beginning to dictate more and more the preferred sporting allegiances of young players.

All of the personalities in the book have had similar beginnings. For example, Wexford's magnificent hurling sides of the 1950s inspired Liam Griffin in the same way that Frank McGuigan's glorious eleven points from play in the 1984 Ulster final made Peter Canavan determined to be Tyrone's next hero. The positive words of encouragement by Seán Purcell in 1960 to Enda Colleran and the emphasis on continual practising of skills by Fr Tommy Maher to Eddie Keher had the same effect. When Kerry legends Mick O'Connell and Mick O'Dwyer went to Cahirciveen to practise their ball skills they had a very willing and regular ball boy in Jack O'Shea. No one listened as carefully or watched as intently as Jack did with such obvious results.

The people featured in this book have successfully passed on their love of Gaelic games to all of us. It is up to each coach and administrator at club, county, provincial and national level to ensure that the children of today will be as enthusiastic and as dedicated to the games of the Gael as those GAA 'Greats' have been. They deserve no better.

Séamus McRory
20 October 1999

About the Author

Séamus McRory was born in the parish of Lissan in south Derry. Having taken a teaching position in Co. Longford in the mid-1970s, he became interested in coaching and was one of the mentors with the Co. Longford Vocational Schools side which reached the 1976 All-Ireland final.

A former chairman of his native Lissan with whom he played football in the 1960s and 1970s, he currently represents his adopted club, Longford Slashers, on Longford County Board. Over the past 30 years, he has contributed many articles to various GAA publications. He is also the author of *The Voice from the Sideline – Famous GAA Managers* (Blackwater Press, 1997). He lives in Abbeycarton, just outside Longford town, with his wife, Olive and children Mairéad and Diarmuid.

Jack O'Shea

ONE SPRING EVENING IN 1975 a knock came to the door of a neat, semi-detached house in Dublin's Drumcondra. The lady of the house answered the visitor. 'Could I please speak to a young lad called Jack O'Shea?' the familiar looking man with the dulcet voice enquired. A tall, strapping, shy, youth came to the door. He stared in awe at the legendary figure before him. 'Your county minor trainer, Séamus Fitzgerald, asked me to look after you in Dublin.' None other than well-known radio commentator, Micheál Ó Muircheartaigh, had been assigned to look after Kerry's most promising Gaelic footballer. Young Jack, who had come to Dublin to undertake an AnCO training course, may have been very far away from home but he was now in the safest of Kerry hands. The die for future glory was well and truly, securely cast.

Jack O'Shea comes from a stronghold of Gaelic football in Cahirciveen, Co. Kerry. He lived opposite the local St Mary's Club football field, known as the Con Keating Memorial Park. It really was the young O'Shea's playground. Every spare moment he had, he spent on that field watching and playing with local and county stars. During his formative childhood years in the 1960s, O'Shea was privileged to have two of the all-time stars of Kerry football visit his local pitch on a regular basis. The great Mick O'Connell, who lived in Valentia Island, used to row his boat over to the mainland and disembark two miles from Cahirciveen. Then he would take his bicycle out of his boat and cycle to Con Keating Park. Meanwhile, his friend and fellow South Kerry county 'great' – Mick O'Dwyer – would drive up from Waterville and the two footballing legends would then spend two to three hours, three or four evenings per week practising their catching and kicking skills. They came to Cahirciveen for extra practice when there were no scheduled county training sessions. In essence, their skills were sharpened and perfected before the eyes of a very young, shrewd observer. Acting as regular ball boy to the two maestros, O'Shea stood behind the goals, observed their techniques and imitated them when he retrieved the ball. Without realising it, O'Shea had developed his own natural ability and could not wait until he could find a proper platform to display those skills. No aspiring footballer could have asked for a more fruitful apprenticeship.

Under the guidance of the Christian Brothers at his local primary school and town curate, Fr McSweeney, O'Shea played both in school leagues and street leagues. By the age of 13, he was deemed good enough to play at wing back for the Kerry U-14 team in a challenge game against Cork on the morning of the 1971 Munster senior football final. Thus, for the first time the two Micks and their ball boy represented their county, at different levels, on the same day.

Jack O'Shea made his first competitive appearance for Kerry against Waterford in the first round of the 1974 Munster minor championship. Having scored 1–5 from the corner forward position in that initial round, O'Shea was very disappointed not to be selected for the Munster final against Cork, which Kerry lost. In 1975, he was selected at full forward on that year's team. In a brilliant side that not only won the Munster title but the All-Ireland as well, Jack was in exalted company. Charlie Nelligan, Mick Spillane, Seánie Walsh, Vincent O'Connor and Johnny Mulvihill were some of the more notable names in a side that easily overcame Ulster Champions, Tyrone.

Jack made his U-21 debut that year as well, winning the Munster title and defeating Antrim in the All-Ireland semi final. Playing for Antrim was future Tottenham and Northern Ireland World Cup star, Gerry Armstrong. Just after Kerry had beaten Dublin in that year's All-Ireland senior final, the two counties met again in the U-21 final in Tipperary town. With O'Shea again starring in the full forward position and supported by established senior players like Tim Kennelly, Ogie Moran, Mike Sheehy and Pat Spillane, Kerry coasted to victory by a margin of six points. 1975 had presented Jack O'Shea with two All-Ireland medals. His U-21 final appearance was the first of four successive finals at this level. In the 1976 final, Kerry defeated Kildare while in the 1977 decider, they overcame Down. However, they were prevented from recording an unprecedented fourth U-21 success when Roscommon pipped them by a point in the 1978 final. What was most significant about the 1976 success was that Jack O'Shea was now playing centre field along with Seánie Walsh. This was to be the midfield combination that was to achieve many great honours for the Kingdom.

In the early summer of 1976, many pundits in Kerry were saying that Jack O'Shea should be on the senior panel. Having played impressively in some county trial games he sat on the bench as an unofficial sub in that year's Munster final. Nevertheless he did not feature any further in that year's championship campaign. He himself did not mind as he was just a month over age for the minor side and was, as yet, very light in stature. His first senior breakthrough came in October 1976 when he was selected as a substitute against Meath in a National Football League game in Navan. As a car containing some of the regular team members broke down, leaving the occupants late for the start of the game, O'Shea was drafted into midfield from the beginning. For the next 16 years, Jack O'Shea was to be a permanent member of each Kerry side. During that year's league campaign O'Shea impressed everyone with his fetching, long-range point scoring and, more than anything else, his mobility. Possessing phenomenal stamina and great positional sense, Jack always seemed to be where the ball was. This was to be the hallmark of O'Shea's many outstanding performances in the green and gold for the rest of his career. That 1976–1977 league was the time that the great, young pretender to football fame actually became accepted as being a brilliant all-round player. His and Kerry's efforts were rewarded when they defeated old rivals Dublin by two points in the National League final.

When Kerry won the Munster championship in 1977 and qualified to meet Dublin in the All-Ireland semi-final, Jack O'Shea was confident because he now knew he was a competent athlete. This game was destined, retrospectively, to be viewed as a benchmark in the development of Gaelic football. In 1974, Dublin had introduced, to an unsuspecting public, the short passing game. This, allied to an unparalleled level of physical fitness, was primarily responsible for that year's All-Ireland success for the Liffeysiders. In 1975, Mick O'Dwyer and his Kerry team had adjusted to the short passing game as well. Possessing more all-round skilful players than Dublin, they literally surprised and destroyed them as they brought the Sam Maguire cup back to the Kingdom. Dublin, almost incredibly, gained their revenge the following year as they regained the All-Ireland title by defeating Kerry by a seven-point margin. So, before a ball was kicked in 1977, the mental pressure on both sides was immense.

Played at a frenetic pace, this game was a perfect snapshot of the handpassing era at its zenith. In the first half, both teams had their dominant periods with Kerry retiring at half time three points in front. The second half of this enthralling encounter is popularly acknowledged as one of the greatest ever displays of Gaelic football. Within minutes of the restart, a sweeping Dublin movement ended in a John McCarthy goal. The impetus and advantage now appeared with Dublin as Brian Mullins controlled the midfield sector. Nevertheless, the accurate Kerry forward line could live on scraps and this they did to full advantage, going two points ahead with six minutes to go. Then, in a defensive mix-up, Kerry allowed the ball to run free to Tony Hanahoe, who quickly passed it to David Hickey who sent it to the net. Dublin were a point ahead. Three minutes later Pat O'Neill harassed Ger O'Keeffe and the ball broke free to Bobby Doyle who passed it to Hickey. He flicked it to Hanahoe who spotted an inrushing Brogan. From 20 yards Brogan slammed the ball to the net. This whole period of play was orchestrated by schemer-in-chief and now player-manager, Tony Hanahoe, who afterwards admitted that this was Dublin at the height of their power. As Hanahoe fittingly closed proceedings with a point, Dublin had turned imminent defeat into a rather flattering five-point winning margin. All who witnessed this game either in person or on television will never forget the wonderful spectacle of footballing excellence, the fluctuating fortunes of the participants and the ambience of excitement and tension that permeated that whole second half.

Thirty-one counties may have celebrated this momentous occasion but Kerry people were totally, though only momentarily, despondent. For Jack O'Shea it was an inauspicious beginning to his big-stage career. Unable to cope with the magnificence of the experienced Mullins, he switched to the '40' with Paudie Lynch reverting to midfield. However, neither Lynch nor the other midfield incumbent, Páidí Ó Sé, could break the dominance of Brian Mullins and his partner, Bernard Brogan. Ó Sé resolved that day that he would be back a better and a wiser man.

The opportunity for Kerry and O'Shea to redress the balance, which had now tilted most firmly in Dublin's favour, occurred the following year when both sides met for the fourth consecutive championship match. Prior to the All-Ireland final of 1978, manager O'Dwyer, now under pressure from within his own county, intensified the training schedule so much that some players actually got physically sick during sessions. Two successive championship defeats to Dublin were hard to take and O'Dwyer was making sure that there would be no excuse for a third defeat in a row.

In that game, Dublin seized the initiative and after 20 minutes led six points to one before an opportunist goal by Kerry corner forward John Egan steadied Kerry's nerves. When Mike Sheehy chipped goalie Paddy Cullen from a free kick for a spectacular goal before the interval, Kerry were now in the driving seat. In the second half, with Jack O'Shea now lording the midfield exchanges, the wonderful Kerry forward line literally tore the Dublin defence apart, with new full forward Eoin Liston notching three goals in the process. Winning the game by 5-11 to 0-9, no one disputed Kerry's greatness and O'Shea's brilliance. In 1975, Kerry had promised to be a great side. Now, with the addition of O'Shea and Liston, the two missing central pieces of that marvellous Kerry jigsaw were in place. The earlier promise had been delivered with interest. As he left the field, Jack O'Shea was a very contented young man. True, he had his full quota of minor, U-21 and senior All-Ireland football medals but more importantly he realised, though modesty forbade him to say so, that he had made a full contribution to the achievement. From 1978 to 1981, when Kerry won four, successive All-Ireland titles, it is generally conceded that we saw Gaelic football at its very highest standard. Beating Dublin again in 1979, Roscommon, rather luckily in 1980, and Offaly in 1981 simply reinforced the thoughts of those who believed that we were witnessing the greatest side in the history of Gaelic football. The 1981 final was especially pleasing for O'Shea. Having dominated the midfield battle along with Seánie Walsh, he sealed the issue when he scored a spectacular goal seven minutes from the end. He was also chosen as footballer of the year in 1980 and 1982, an incomparable feat that he was to repeat in 1984 and 1985.

Though O'Shea looks back in disappointment that a last-minute goal for Offaly in the 1982 final prevented Kerry from getting a record five-in-a-row senior titles, he concedes that the good times by far outweighed the sad times. On a personal level he was also saddened to lose the 1983 Munster final to a last-minute Cork goal. In addition, he had been captain that year and had scored two opportunist goals. Still, O'Shea and Kerry had the ultimate consolation when they won another three All-Ireland titles from 1984 to 1986. O'Shea was the proud holder of seven All-Ireland medals. What would 95 per cent of inter-county footballers give just to have one!

O'Shea reckons his own best performance was against Galway in the 1984 All-Ireland semi-final when he scored five points. 1984 was a very special year for Jack, for he captained Kerry to a National League triumph over Galway and was selected at midfield on the *Sunday Independent*/Irish Nationwide football team of the century. Jack continued to play for the Kingdom until 1992. When Clare defeated Kerry that day in 1992 to win their first provincial football title in 75 years, O'Shea decided to retire. 'It was a spur of the moment decision. I regretted it for a while but I know now it was the right decision', added the man who won six All Stars in a row (1980-1985). From 1976 to 1992, Jack O'Shea had strode the playing fields of Ireland, playing senior inter-county football to an unprecedented level of consistency. Always displaying poise and aplomb and a sportsman to his fingertips, his resignation (the last of the 1978–1981 team to do so) finally ended a glorious era for Kerry football.

As a mark of the respect and esteem in which he was held regarding both his footballing and leadership abilities, O'Shea was selected as captain of the Irish team for the 1984 and 1986 Compromise Rules series with Australia. He also toured with the Irish team under the captaincy of Meath's Robbie O'Malley in 1990.

'All three of the series were wonderful experiences. After we had learned all the pitfalls on the 1984 tour, our manager, Kevin Heffernan, had us all well prepared for the 1986 tour. Similarly, Eugene McGee did tremendous preparatory work with us in 1990.

Amongst the players there was great heart, wonderful spirit and camaraderie built up between the team members. We lived like professional sportsmen, training twice daily. We socialised together and, most importantly, we had a common purpose to go out and represent our country to the best of our ability.

Players from the so-called weaker counties were very hard trainers and were as much part of the whole scene as players from the alleged stronger counties. Michael Fagan (Westmeath) and Noel Roche (Clare) were great examples of this. It was also nice to see at first hand players I had not much contact with such as Val Daly (Galway) and Greg Blaney (Down). Everyone took the series very seriously. Unlike the All Stars trips, those games had a competitive edge to them,' added Jack.

When the Irish side toured Australia in 1990, Jack O'Shea was the oldest player and Down's James McCartan was the youngest. Manager Eugene McGee, being conscious of all squad members getting to know each other, accommodated Jack and James in the same room. They got on so well together that McGee did not insist on separating them, as he did with the others, when the team moved to different cities. Jocosely, the other members of the panel referred to them as father and son. One day the RTE Gaelic games reporter Mick Dunne came in asking about the trip. James answered the door.

'What's it like to be rooming with a living legend, James?'

Quick as a flash the wee man from County Down replied, 'You'd better ask Jack that!'

After Jack ended his playing career in 1992, he was appointed manager of the Mayo senior team. Though he lived very far from Mayo and had no knowledge of Mayo club football, Jack, liking a fresh challenge, decided to accept the position. In his first season in charge, Mayo, in a very mediocre game, beat Roscommon by a point in a very low-scoring Connacht final. In the All-Ireland semi-final, they came up against an experienced Cork side, the nucleus of which had played in four All-Ireland finals, winning two of them in the previous six years. Though Mayo played reasonably well for most of the first half, a Cork goal scored just before half time by John O'Driscoll was an omen of worse to come. In the second half, the Mayo challenge totally dissipated and in the end they suffered a humiliating 20 points defeat. In the following year's Connacht championship, O'Shea and Mayo reached another decider. They played Leitrim, now managed by Mayo native, John O'Mahony. Possessing a greater number of quality players than normal and brilliantly organised by O'Mahony, Leitrim held off a late Mayo rally to win their first provincial title in 67 years.

Mayo had been unfortunate in that they were without star forward Kevin O'Neill who got injured just prior to the game. In the eyes of some fickle supporters, Mayo's defeat was seen as a failure on the part of O'Shea. The sad thing in all of these circumstances is that so few people, in any sport, anywhere, seem to realise that in any final there can be only one winner. Inevitably, there has also to be a loser. 'After this defeat I felt I was not getting the support that I required. I knew we had brought in many new players who needed two or three more years to develop properly. Subsequently, Mayo reached two All-Irelands in successive years in 1996 and 1997. The fact that most of the players who played in those finals were playing in 1994 vindicates my view. Anyhow, though I enjoyed the Mayo experience, I decided to resign,' added Jack.

The Kerry man who has been training his club, Leixlip, for the last three years would like at some future date to return to inter-county management. Ideally, he would like to build a team starting off with young players and then develop them. 'It is difficult to take over an established team. Initially, it takes at least a year before you actually know players, their strengths, their weaknesses, their personalities,' said Jack when I met him in his Leixlip home.

Like many others, O'Shea feels that teams do not play enough competitive inter-county football. He is strongly in favour of running the National Football League in the one calendar year from February to May. To avoid clashes with club fixtures, he would play half of those league games either mid-week or on Saturdays. 'Then I would have a round-robin series for the championship with each county guaranteed at least three games. With the present high profile of Gaelic games, this system would keep everyone happy, especially the treasurers of the provincial councils! This should be done in hurling as well. Take a county like Limerick who were knocked out of the Munster hurling championship in May 1999, and do not have another competitive game until the National Hurling League resumes in February 2000. That is definitely unfair.'

When it comes to the method of selecting All Stars in both hurling and football, the plumbing and heating contractor has some solid ideas. 'I think at present the All Stars are selected on the basis of their performances in the All-Ireland semi-finals and final. A player can play very moderately in every round of the championship, get a good supply of quality ball and score 1-6 in the final. Inevitably that man will be selected. The present system does not necessarily give a true image of a player's performance over the whole year. The fairest way, I feel, is that a player is awarded a number of points for each game he plays in the National League or championship. Bonus points should be awarded for the concluding stages of the National League, provincial finals, All-Ireland semi-finals and final,' concluded the six-time All Star.

O'Shea thinks that he was exceptionally lucky to play under a manager of Mick O'Dwyer's calibre, as well as two very positive and helpful county chairmen in Frank King and Ger McKenna. 'Mick O'Dwyer was a player's man who ensured that players were treated decently and fairly at all times. He was a very good man manager who understood the uniqueness of each player's personality, and then got the maximum out of them and for the team on the field of play. No problem was too big to confront or to overcome with Mick. At all times, he made everybody feel welcome, especially the younger players. Having been a player himself he knew what made them tick and each year he thought of a different motivational factor to stimulate them. Trips abroad were always the ultimate incentives. I know this was easier to do in Kerry because if you applied yourself properly in my time, you had a better chance than most of winning an All-Ireland medal. Mick made our training sessions very competitive, yet most enjoyable. Some of the toughest games I ever played in were after those training sessions, especially if a team for a big game was due to be picked.'

Even though the vast majority of the Kerry team always trained under Mick O'Dwyer in Killarney, players based near the capital such as Mick Spillane, Charlie Nelligan and Jack O'Shea trained under Micheál Ó Muircheartaigh in Dublin. Two weeks before a big game, they would join the rest of the squad in Kerry and train four or five nights a week.

Tired of all the long-distance travelling to play club football with his native St Mary's in Cahirciveen, Jack O'Shea joined Leixlip, where he lived, in 1984. In 1986, Leixlip reached the Kildare county final which was fixed for the Sunday prior to that year's All-Ireland final between Tyrone and Kerry. Diplomatic efforts failed to have the game postponed. Thus Jack O'Shea was presented with a huge dilemma. O'Dwyer had always instructed all his players never to play in a week before a big match. Jack, on the other hand, realised what a county final meant to Leixlip and felt guilty that he could not help them in their greatest hour. Jack did not line out at the start but mid-way through the second half, when Leixlip were five points down, he entered the fray. Though he played well, Leixlip were eventually beaten by just two points. To say that Mick O'Dwyer was furious with Jack O'Shea would be the understatement of the year.

On the Wednesday night after the county final and four days before Jack O'Shea's last All-Ireland final he came down with a 'flu virus. Confined to bed from Wednesday to Saturday, O'Shea, still with a temperature of 103°F, made his way to the Kerry team's hotel in Malahide at 8 p.m. When he awoke on Sunday morning he still felt very weak. In consultation with Mick O'Dwyer it was decided, only ten minutes before the game, that he would play. 'It had been one of the most difficult weeks in my whole career. When I look back on it, I could have missed both games. I deeply regret that I did not play for the whole of the county final. After all, I was extremely fit at the time.'

Jack loves all sports, especially athletics, where he numbers John Treacy and Brendan Foster as two of his favourite runners. He is particularly proud that when running for his secondary school, Cahirciveen CBS, he finished fourth behind John Treacy in the Munster Colleges' cross-country championships of 1973. He enjoys reading about people who rise to the top in any sport, and how they trained and worked to get there. Having read autobiographies of so many successful sports stars he has been singularly impressed by the huge sacrifices most of them have made. As for Jack himself, he became a Pioneer in 1977 after he made a conscious decision to stop taking alcohol when he joined the Kerry senior panel. 'I wanted to be a top class Gaelic footballer and I realised that to be one, I had to make that sacrifice. I have never had any regrets about my decision.'

O'Shea, who believes that all county managers should be semi-professional with a common salary fixed by Croke Park, would love to see a 'third official' at all championship games. 'For example, if there had been such an official at the Tipperary/Kerry Munster championship match of 1999, the disputed goal would not have been allowed. The referee should have an ear-piece link with the third official. As well as having such technology for our games, I also believe that the GAA should have a more modern, all-embracing approach to post-match celebrations. After each championship match, there should be a post-match reception for both teams, together with their wives or girlfriends. I think the year 2000 would be a good time to start this. I also am of the definite opinion that medals should be presented to both winners and losers at provincial finals and All-Ireland finals in both hurling and football.

As a young boy, Jack O'Shea used to go beagle-hunting in the Kerry mountains each Sunday afternoon. In doing so, he was following in the hallowed footsteps of such famed Kerry footballers as Mick O'Connell, Mick O'Dwyer, Bill Dillon and Bill Casey. Now, each Christmas, Jack loves to return to his native heath and retrace those mountain footsteps of the 1960s. He has no doubt that climbing that rough terrain, up to heights of 3,000 feet, played a large part in developing his upper body strength and stamina for which he was so renowned.

Jack and his Kerry-born wife Mary, have four children, Linda, Ciarán, Aidan and Orla. The whole family is very sports oriented with Ciarán and Aidan already showing exceptional skill on the Gaelic football fields. Aidan has already featured in the underage Compromise Rules series in 1998. Whatever the future holds, in a football sense for Jack, he will be happy like everyone else, if all of the family enjoy good health and experience happiness in whatever they do.

When it comes to picking his all-time Munster and Ireland teams, O'Shea stressed that his selections were based mostly on players that he played with or against. He did not consider it fair to select any Kerrymen on his Ireland selection.

MUNSTER

Charlie Nelligan
(Kerry)

| Brian Murphy *(Cork)* | John O'Keeffe *(Kerry)* | Paudie Lynch *(Kerry)* |

| Páidi O Sé *(Kerry)* | Tim Kennelly *(Kerry)* | Niall Cahalane *(Cork)* |

Dave McCarthy *(Cork)* — Seán Walsh *(Kerry)*

| Jimmy Barry Murphy *(Cork)* | Maurice Fitzgerald *(Kerry)* | Pat Spillane *(Kerry)* |

| Mike Sheehy *(Kerry)* | Eoin Liston *(Kerry)* | John Egan *(Kerry)* |

IRELAND

Billy Morgan
(Cork)

| Robbie O'Malley *(Meath)* | Mick Lyons *(Meath)* | Niall Cahalane *(Cork)* |

| Tommy Drumm *(Dublin)* | Kevin Moran *(Dublin)* | Martin O'Connell *(Meath)* |

Brian Mullins *(Dublin)* — Peter McGinnitty *(Fermanagh)*

| Val Daly *(Galway)* | Greg Blaney *(Down)* | Larry Tompkins *(Cork)* |

| Matt Connor *(Offaly)* | Colm O'Rourke *(Meath)* | Bernard Flynn *(Meath)* |

When Mícheál Ó Muircheartaigh undertook to look after Jack O'Shea, he took his responsibility very seriously. Initially, he was to ensure that O'Shea would train assiduously, under his command, during the 1975 minor championship campaign. As Jack became an U-21 and senior county player, Mícheál was still in charge of his training schedule. But Mícheál's contribution to Jack's development was far beyond the call of a mere football coach. Confidant, helper, advisor and friend were just some of the roles that the chairman of Bord na Gaeilge fulfilled in relation to Jack O'Shea.

'Of all the good people that I have met over the years and there were many who helped me enormously, Mícheál stands head and shoulders above them all. He developed me greatly as a player but always made me keep my feet firmly on the ground. More importantly, his advice on any social or personal matter was always worth listening to and acting upon. For the past 25 years we have contacted each other practically every week and exchanged views on the topics of the day. A great friendship has stood the test of time,' concluded the unassuming Jack.

When Mícheál and Jack first met, one was a household name and the other an aspirant to fame. Thanks to Mícheál and many others' sustained assistance, Jack has accomplished his full potential as one of the great Gaelic footballers of the second millennium. Possessing a steely inner strength of character and a voracious appetite for Gaelic football it can realistically be said that he has become a legend in his own lifetime.

Liam Griffin

ON THE NIGHT BEFORE the 1996 All-Ireland senior hurling final, Wexford manager, Liam Griffin, got into his car and drove the three miles from his home in Rosslare to a well known place of religious pilgrimage called Our Lady's Island. He wanted to get away from all the hassle, of people looking for precious tickets, of supporters ringing him up to wish his team well and from the press looking for last-minute quotes for the Sunday papers. Liam wanted to focus on the most important day in 19 years for the wearers of the purple and gold. For over two hours, Liam reflected on the great tomorrow. With his mind at ease he arose and strode to his car. He now had no doubt that within the next 48 hours the Liam McCarthy Cup would be winding its way on a glorious homecoming to the Model County for its first major port of celebration in Gorey.

Liam Griffin was born in his mother's native home near Courtown, Co. Wexford in 1946. Shortly afterwards, the family moved to Rosslare where Liam spent the summer Sundays of his formative years huddled around the kitchen table with his Garda father and neighbours listening intently to Micheál Ó Hehir's commentaries on the blossoming Wexford team of the 1950s. At first, he was reticent to show any interest but when Wexford won three-in-a-row Leinster titles (1954-1956) and the 1955 and 1956 All-Irelands, Liam was well and truly infatuated with the sliotar and camán. The hurling deeds of some of those 1950s Wexford hurlers like the Rackard brothers, Nick O'Donnell, Paudge Kehoe, Ned Wheeler and Jim English finally turned into eager enthusiasm.

Liam went as a boarder to De La Salle College Waterford the day after winning 1955 Wexford captain, Nick O'Donnell, had again led his side to victory in the 1960 All-Ireland final. With many of the college's students coming from Gaelic football strongholds in Cork and Kerry, Liam developed a very active interest in both codes. Showing an exceptional aptitude for both, together with blistering pace, the young Rosslare man won many honours during his time there. The talented half forward amassed two Munster Colleges junior football championships and two Munster senior football championships, as well as captaining his college's senior hurling team to the final of the Harty Cup where they were beaten by Limerick CBS in 1965. Incidentally, that Limerick side was captained by Eamon Grimes, who eight years later, in 1973, would captain Limerick to All-Ireland senior hurling success. Paudie and Eamon O'Donoghue of Kerry, Jerry Lucey of Cork and Brendan Murtagh of Cavan, (now prominently associated with the Kingspan Group) were some of the budding football stars of the future that studied along with Liam in Waterford. His proudest, personal accomplishment was his tally of 2-11 against St Flannan's of Ennis in the semi-final of that 1965 Harty Cup campaign.

His consistent Colleges displays came to the attention of both the Wexford minor football and minor hurling selectors. For three years (1962-1964) he represented the underage footballers, whereas he served just one year – 1964 – with the hurlers. 1965 was to prove an especially lucky year for Griffin as he won provincial medals with both the Wexford U-21 and intermediate county sides. That U-21 team then went on to capture the All-Ireland title when they defeated Tipperary. Liam, a sub on that team, had won his first and only All-Ireland medal.

By now, Liam had enrolled in a Hotel Management course in Shannon, Co. Clare and for the next few years played his hurling and football with Clare side, Newmarket-on-Fergus. Initially, he only played intermittently because he had to study both in Switzerland and America as part of his course's curriculum. Nevertheless, in 1967 and 1968, he won two senior county hurling championships, two senior leagues, one U-21 hurling championship and one junior football championship. Never during that time did he play on a losing Newmarket team. Liam's talents were also recognised at county level when he was selected on the Clare senior hurling side in 1967 and 1968. Beating Kilkenny twice in the league and losing a league semi-final after a second replay are his favourite reminiscences. His last game for Clare was the 1968 championship encounter with Waterford when the Rosslare trainee hotel manager notched 1-2 from the corner forward position. Pat Cronin, Liam Danaher, Vincent Loftus, James Callinane and Jackie O'Gorman were, in his mind, Clare's most influential hurlers during his stay with them.

Now qualified in hotel management, Liam joined the Trusthouse Forte Hotel group in England before returning to Dublin with the Intercontinental Hotels group. He made his inter-county debut in Wexford's league side in 1970 but lost interest, as he was not always available owing to work commitments. A tragic event eventually changed the course of his life. His father, who had bought the Old Pier Hotel in Rosslare in 1960, was killed in a car accident in 1970 and his mother was finding it difficult to run the business on her own. So, in 1974, Liam returned to Rosslare, took over the business and revamped it into the ultra-modern Hotel Rosslare.

In 1975, he resumed playing football with the local St Mary's Club in Rosslare and was their player-manager from the centre half forward position when they annexed that year's county junior championship. After this coaching success, Liam was asked to coach the Wexford District team in the Wexford county senior football championship. Again, he brought success as they won the 1977 county title with Liam playing a central role both on and off the field. Sadly, he was also to experience the uglier side of sport when he was viciously assaulted in a club game in 1977. This cowardly act necessitated the removal of a kidney. Liam's 'second' club career, or so he thought, was over.

After his club success, Liam was invited to manage the county senior football team for the following year's league and championship campaigns. They performed reasonably well in the league but Liam then suddenly resigned. There was a five-man selection committee which Liam felt was too unwieldy, especially when instant crucial decisions had to be made on the field of play. When he discovered that some of his fellow selectors wanted Joe Lennon of Down All-Ireland fame to help with coaching for the championship, he decided to retire. He resolved that if he were ever offered a managership again, he would first of all make sure that he had total control of picking his own management team.

Still undaunted, Liam returned to hurling, his first love, attending courses and seminars to perfect his knowledge of skills, tactics and personnel management. Watching the growing influence of soccer in Rosslare in the 1980s and the alarming drop in the number of people playing hurling, he decided to introduce a comprehensive underage hurling coaching structure in Rosslare. 'I believed that proper coaching would be the catalyst to get all the young people involved. Two young brothers, Rod and Dave Guiney, who were later to win All-Ireland medals, were on that first coaching course in 1983,' Liam told me, when I met him in the Ferrycarrig Hotel outside Wexford town. As a result of Liam's promptings a great interest in hurling developed in the Rosslare area and in 1984, with 38-year-old Liam Griffin at centre forward, Rosslare won the junior 'B' county hurling championship. Despite his operation, Liam had made a remarkable comeback to the playing fields and his infectious enthusiasm rubbed off on all the players around him. After the local hurling success, there was a row at that year's Rosslare GAA convention because some club members felt that Liam had promoted hurling at the expense of football within the parish. Liam faced the criticism head on: 'If I get the full commitment of everyone concerned I will train both codes in 1985.' This he did so commendably that Rosslare won the 1985 county intermediate football championship. At the age of 41, he again helped the footballers as a player in 1987, but then decided to concentrate solely on the coaching of hurling. As a result of Liam's work, St Mary's consistently won many hurling competitions at different underage levels.

Having seen what he could do at underage level with his club, Liam yearned for the opportunity to train the Wexford county minor hurling team. Late in 1993, he allowed his name to go forward for the vacant managership of that team but was unsuccessful on that occasion. 'Anyhow, I felt that because I had once trained the Wexford senior football team, there were some people in the county who did not want me to train the hurling team.'

In the 1994 Leinster senior hurling championship, Wexford were beaten in the provincial final by Offaly 1-18 to 0-14. After much debate a small sub-committee of the County Board was nominated to seek a replacement for manager, Christy Keogh, who had retired after the Leinster final. They decided to interview Liam Griffin for the vacancy. Though he had no experience of coaching senior hurling, the sub-committee was thoroughly impressed with his in-depth knowledge of the game, his views on skill drills, team discipline and tactical awareness. Before he left the interview, Griffin told his interviewers: 'If I were you I wouldn't appoint me. I am a loose cannon. However, if you want me to help you find someone who will bring glory back to Wexford hurling, then I'll do my best.'

In the event, the committee unanimously decided to appoint Griffin. With the support of his wife, Mary and family, Michael, Niall, Liam Anthony (a very promising hurler) and Rory, Liam accepted the onerous position. The man who was not considered good enough to manage the county minor side a short time previously was now asked to reincarnate the wonderful days of Wexford hurling of the 1950s and 1960s.

Having learned from his bad experience with the county football team, Griffin insisted on appointing his own two selectors – former county hurlers, Rory Kinsella of Gorey and Séamus Barron from Rathnure. During that opening 1994–1995 National League campaign, though Wexford beat Cork in the Oireachtas Final, they did not fare too well in the league itself. They scored unconvincing wins over Kerry, Carlow and Down but in the last game before Christmas they were unlucky to be beaten by Waterford through a last-minute score. After Christmas however, their form slumped and they suffered embarrassing defeats to Dublin and Meath. This latter defeat made some of the more blinkered, die-hard supporters of Wexford call for Griffin's resignation. In fact, on his way to the dressing room after the Meath game, some so-called supporters taunted him. One of them even spat on him. Unbowed, he was determined that no one would stop him from doing his best to change the fortunes of Wexford hurling. Though Wexford were subsequently defeated in the last league game against Offaly, they still retained their division two status.

In the first round of the Leinster championship, Wexford comprehensively defeated a weak Westmeath side. As they prepared to face Offaly in the next round, Griffin and his management team were dealt a bad psychological blow when one of Wexford's leading club sides, Oulart-the-Ballagh, disobeyed a management directive not to play their county players in a county league tie a week before the Offaly game. As a result, Griffin was forced to remove the captaincy from star county player, Liam Dunne who had played in that game. This decision created a bad atmosphere in the county and this was further exacerbated when Wexford lost heavily to the Midlanders. 'However, the great thing about all of this was that Rory, Séamus and myself were in a much stronger position when we returned in September to prepare the side for the forthcoming league. All of the players now knew that we were deadly serious about improving the lot of Wexford county hurling.'

In the 1995–1996 league, Wexford narrowly defeated Laois, Westmeath, Dublin and Antrim to be top of the division at Christmas. After the Christmas recess, Wexford, in a rather tempestuous encounter, suffered a heavy defeat to a much physically stronger Limerick side. Griffin was particularly annoyed at the over-physical play of one Limerick player and promised his team that never again would they tolerate such abuse. With a marvellous display of first class hurling, Wexford totally destroyed Meath in the next game to avenge their surprise defeat at the hands of the same opposition in the previous year's league. This win guaranteed not only league promotion for the Slaneysiders but also a place in the quarter-final against Offaly. In a second half of outstanding hurling, the Model County, with Ger Cush, Rory McCarthy, Larry Murphy, Tom Dempsey and captain, Martin Storey, particularly prominent, ran out easy winners 1-14 to 2-3 against the Faithful County. However, their new-found confidence was shattered when they suffered a demoralising eight-point defeat to Galway in the league semi-final.

Griffin and his co-selectors were very optimistic for their championship chances after they carried out a detailed analysis of their league performance against Galway. This revealed that the Wexford forwards had actually gained more possession than their western counterparts but that their attempts at scoring were rather poor. What was required, they felt, was much more emphasis on fast, ground hurling. Regardless of how things were going in any particular game, Griffin told his team to stick rigidly to this type of hurling.

After all that he had endured, Griffin now knew that the whole team was in a proper frame of mind to maximise their potential. Thus it was a distinctly confident and determined Wexford side that took the field for the first round of the Leinster championship against Kilkenny. To ensure that Wexford's future mental preparation would remain totally focused, Liam enlisted the help of a young Dublin sports psychologist. This game, against a team of hurling artists like Kilkenny, would be the acid test to judge whether Wexford would be realistic challengers for the Liam McCarthy Cup. Sticking firmly to their game plan Wexford played superbly to lead Kilkenny by 0-9 to 0-4 at half time. Though Kilkenny fought back gallantly to reduce the gap to one point after only seven minutes of the second half, Wexford, inspired by outstanding right half back, Rod Guiney, lifted the siege. When 35-year-old Billy Byrne was introduced as a substitute he notched a vital goal to clinch the game for the Wexford men on a 1-14 to 0-14 scoreline. Another hurdle had been crossed and another bogey laid to rest as Liam prepared his side for a semi-final clash with Dublin. In a dull, uninspiring match Wexford struggled for long periods before overcoming the Metropolitans by six points. In the Leinster final, Wexford faced Offaly who had given a fabulous performance in annihilating Laois in their Leinster semi-final. Wexford started rather nervously allowing Offaly to ease ahead 1-2 to 0-1. The sides then exchanged three further points to leave the score 1-5 to 0-4. Then came the score which best exemplified the new type of first-time, low, ground hurling as preached by Griffin. Left half forward Larry Murphy received a long first-time pass. As he raced through the Offaly defence, he was pulled down and goalkeeper Damien Fitzhenry duly crashed the resultant penalty to the net. This was the catalyst to spark a concerted team display of fast, incisive hurling which was reflected on the half-time scoreboard – Wexford 1-10, Offaly 1-9. The second half produced a brilliant display of guts and determination as each side in turn showed tremendous fetching, exquisite stickwork and magical scores. However, as the game entered its final minutes the positive mind of their manager and the frustrating memories of past defeats entered the minds of the Wexford players. No way would they now yield to the negative inclinations of old. Their hurling was spellbinding in its speed and devastating in its execution. Murphy, Tom Dempsey and Martin Storey supplied the necessary finishing touches to the stalwart outfield play of midfielders, Adrian Fenton and Larry O'Gorman. In the end, Wexford won by an unbelievable eight points. The whole county rejoiced as the heroes in purple and gold trooped happily off Croke Park. Nineteen years after they had won their last Leinster senior hurling title, the loquacious, spirit and tactics-driven Liam Griffin had truly established himself as a hurling Messiah in the making.

Wexford then met their league conquerors, Galway, in the All-Ireland semi-final. Galway had 14 of their league side whereas Wexford had made numerous personnel and positional switches. The game began at a frenetic pace and after 22 minutes, Galway were narrowly ahead 1-4 to 0-6. Then after wing half John O'Connor had to leave the field after colliding with the elbow of Galway's Joe Rabbitte, Wexford got a huge psychological boost. Playing with only 14 men, Wexford's right half-forward Rory McCarthy expertly controlled the sliotar on his hurley and in the same movement sent the ball rocketing to the Galway net. The unfortunate John O'Connor was now replaced by his brother, the legendary 36-year-old George who had made his senior debut for Wexford 17 years earlier in 1979. With McCarthy showing exceptional skills, the Westerners' defence was being sorely tested as Wexford edged further ahead. A Galway goal, however, just before the interval, reduced the deficit as the teams left the field at half time with the scoreline reading: Wexford 1-9, Galway 2-5.

In the second half, the whole Wexford defence, ably marshalled by half backs Liam Dunne and Ger Cush, with goalkeeper Damien Fitzhenry lending valuable support, sternly resisted the stout challenge of the Tribesmen. It was yet again in the last quarter that Wexford dug deepest. Tom Dempsey and Martin Storey scored tremendous points to leave Wexford ahead 1-12 to 2-7. Nine minutes to go and Wexford were holding on resolutely to a two-point lead. It was time for Liam Griffin to play his final ace. The seemingly ageless Billy Byrne then replaced full forward Gerry Laffan. Almost immediately, poacher-supreme Byrne latched onto the ball which broke kindly for him in the goalmouth and he steered it across the line for an opportunist goal. Though Galway scored a third goal just before the final whistle, Byrne's green flag effectively ended the contest. Wexford were now in their first All-Ireland senior final since 1977.

For the final against Limerick, Griffin adopted the mantra 'No intimidation,' an obvious reference to alleged misdemeanours Wexford had endured in the past from different games. Owing to a serious injury sustained in the semi-final, left corner back Seán Flood was declared unfit to play in the final. As a result, the selectors switched John O'Connor to left corner back, Larry O'Gorman from midfield to left half back and introduced veteran George O'Connor to the starting 15 at centre field. 'No intimidation' was a catch cry to keep the players totally focused on the game. No side issues would deflect them from winning the game and, if at all possible, no frees would be conceded. Realising that the Limerick side would probably only do half of the pre-match parade, Wexford players were told to march proudly around the whole stadium with heads high, savouring the occasion while remaining singularly focused. On All-Ireland final day, Limerick duly dropped out of the parade half way around the pitch and the boys of Wexford kept proudly marching on. Psychologically, Wexford had won the first battle.

Though Larry Murphy opened the scoring for Wexford, Limerick seized command and scored the next five points to lead 0-5 to 0-1 after 15 minutes play. Then Larry O'Gorman and John O'Connor, from a 70-metre free, pointed to reduce the margin. In the 19th minute, Gerry Laffan sent the ball towards the Limerick goalmouth where Larry Murphy batted it down to the inrushing Tom Dempsey who hit it to the Limerick net to leave the Slaneysiders 1-3 to 0-5 ahead. For the remainder of the half, the excitement was intense as both teams in rotation, scored five points each. Eight different players shared the scores in that amazing sequence of fluctuating fortunes. Just before half-time, Wexford received a body blow when their left corner forward, Eamonn Scallon, was sent off for allegedly pulling across a Limerick player with his hurley. The unfortunate Scallon was unlucky, as some other players from both sides were guilty of more serious offences in a brief fracas that occurred a short time previously in the Limerick goalmouth. It was a very pensive Liam Griffin who left the field at half time with his side leading by the minimum of margins, 1-8 to 0-10, and reduced to 14 men.

At half time, Liam and his fellow mentors agreed to keep to their original game-plan which consisted of a five-man forward line with the sixth forward acting as a third midfielder. Therefore, essentially the formation of the side (minus the third midfielder) would remain the same for the second half. That second period proved to be an absorbing, enthralling contest with Wexford playing like a team inspired. By the 16th minute Laffan twice, Dempsey and O'Connor had pointed with a TJ Ryan point being Limerick's only reply to leave the Slaneysiders 1-12 to 0-11 in front. O'Gorman and Limerick's powerful centre half back, Ciarán Carey, exchanged points before a 12-minute scoreless period when a magnificent Wexford defence kept Limerick's scoring opportunities down to a minimum. Limerick pointed twice in the last few minutes to narrow the deficit to two points. Shortly after that the referee, Pat Horan, much to the delight of the Wexford supporters, blew the full-time whistle. The Model County, for the first time since 1968, had won the Liam McCarthy Cup. The glorious crusade for Wexford hurling which Liam Griffin had initiated just two years earlier had now, on 1 September 1996, ended in ultimate glory.

All of the Wexford side had performed heroically, especially in those last breathtaking ten minutes. Colm Kehoe, at right full back, though small in stature was truly magnificent as were fellow defenders Liam Dunne, Ger Cush and John O'Connor. Midfielders, Adrian Fenton and George O'Connor forged a perfect link between defence and attack with their tireless running and splendid striking. The physical presence, craft and experience of George, who actually won a county senior football championship medal alongside his manager, Liam Griffin, 19 years earlier in 1977 supplemented the guile and skill of Adrian Fenton and Larry O'Gorman in Wexford's quest for midfield mastery. In a fast-moving and hard-working forward line captain Martin Storey at centre half forward, Tom Dempsey in the right corner and Gerry Laffan at full forward were best in an attack that constantly posed major problems for a hard-pressed defence. Only the magnificence of Limerick goalkeeper, Joe Quaid prevented a much heavier defeat.

Having played the last county game of his life, George O'Connor knelt in prayerful thanksgiving on Croke Park's hallowed turf as Liam Griffin and his fellow selectors rushed to embrace the men who had fulfilled their dream. When Martin Storey raised the Liam McCarthy Cup, thousands of delirious Wexford supporters turned the whole arena into a captivating sea of purple and gold. Liam Griffin joyously recalls how all of them had planned so meticulously for Wexford's greatest hour after so many years of disappointment. 'One morning, about two weeks before the final, I awoke at 6.30 a.m. and made out a huge checklist of issues pertaining to players, the referee, accidents, injuries, press relations, county board, tickets, Mass on the day of the match, hotel reservations etc. I then called Rory and Séamus to meet them immediately in the Ferrycarrig Hotel where we discussed all the eventualities, including the possible sending-off of any of the 30 players on the field on All-Ireland day. After that two and a half hours of discussion, we decided on our overall strategy including how to cope with an extra player, or a player less, in the match itself. We then presented the fruits of our discussion to a players' meeting. I will give you two examples of our tentative plans for dealing with a situation, very real as it turned out, where we had a man less. Our goalkeeper, Damien Fitzhenry, would be instructed to puck out the ball away from the centre of the field. Also in that scenario we would invariably put one of our players on their 'free' man so that he would become confused whether or not he was the extra player. However, when I recall that wonderful day, one astounding statistic pleases me more than everything else. Our defence conceded only one free in the first half, and in the second the team did not commit one foul. That has to be a world record in any code.'

On the previous Christmas Eve in 1995 Liam's wife, Mary, was diagnosed with multiple sclerosis. At once, he wanted to relinquish his managerial role but Mary, knowing how he loved hurling, refused to allow him to do so. As in all good negotiations, a favourable compromise was reached. Liam would resign as Wexford manager as soon as they had played their last game in the 1996 championship. After the All-Ireland, he deferred an official announcement to this effect until the end of the month, so that the celebrations of the players would not be affected in any way. He had confided his intentions only to his fellow selectors Rory Kinsella and Séamus Barron who had also recovered from serious illness. On 30 September 1996, his hurling mission accomplished, Liam Griffin bowed out with the dignity and self assurance of a man who knew what one's real priorities in life should be. Granted, he would continue to coach the underage players in Rosslare but more importantly, in his estimation, he would have more time to spend with Mary.

Liam, who recently sold the Hotel Rosslare to concentrate his efforts in consolidating the other two hotels in which he has a controlling interest, the Ferrycarrig Hotel and the Hotel Kilkenny, rates Wexford's Billy Rackard as the greatest hurler he has ever seen. 'Sonny Walshe of Waterford was my most difficult opponent. Noel Skehan of Kilkenny was a fabulous goalkeeper. Jimmy Brohan (Cork), Pat and Ger Henderson (Kilkenny), Tony Wall (Tipperary) and Liam Dunne (Wexford), would all rate as marvellous defenders. Ned Wheeler and Jim Morrissey of Wexford, Liam O'Brien and Frank Cummins of Kilkenny, Adrian Fenton (Wexford) and Phil Grimes and Séamus Power of Waterford were outstanding midfielders; Paudge Kehoe, Nicky Rackard, Martin Storey and Tom Dempsey of Wexford; Seán Clohessy, Eddie Keher and Pat Delaney of Kilkenny; Frankie Walshe and Tom Cheasty of Waterford and Eamon Cregan of Limerick were all top class forwards.'

In order to develop hurling properly Liam would make the following alterations to the current championship system:

1. I would put Galway, Roscommon and Derry in the Munster championship and Antrim and Down into the Leinster championship. Roscommon and Derry should automatically get a home draw if they drew any of the Munster counties with the exception of Kerry. Antrim and Down should get a home draw if they were picked against Kilkenny, Wexford or Offaly.

2. If any or all of these counties were eliminated in their respective new provincial championship then they should be allowed into a proper 'B' championship which would cater for the rest of the counties. The concluding stages of the 'B'

championship should be held as a curtain raiser to the present All-Ireland and senior hurling championship semi-finals and finals.'

One of the greatest disappointments in Liam's opinion was the failure of a magnificent Dublin side to overcome Tipperary in the 1961 All-Ireland. He believes that if they had won, the popularity of hurling in the capital would have increased a hundredfold. As a tribute to that side, led so capably by Noel Drumgoole, Liam picked a Leinster side excluding all counties except Kilkenny and Dublin which he feels would hold its own against any provincial team.

KILKENNY/DUBLIN

Noel Skehan
(Kilkenny)

| Des Ferguson | Noel Drumgoole | 'Fan' Larkin |
| *(Dublin)* | (Dublin) | *(Kilkenny)* |

| Séamus Cleere | Pat Henderson | Martin Coogan |
| *(Kilkenny)* | *(Kilkenny)* | *(Kilkenny)* |

| Des Foley | Frank Cummins |
| *(Dublin)* | (Kilkenny) |

| Achill Boothman | Seán Clohessy | Eddie Keher |
| *(Dublin)* | *(Kilkenny)* | *(Kilkenny)* |

| Tom Walsh | Billy Dwyer | Mick Bermingham |
| *(Kilkenny)* | *(Kilkenny)* | *(Dublin)* |

Liam also selected an all-time Wexford team from the golden era of Wexford hurling – 1954 to 1968. He describes them as a combination of 'great stickmen,' 'leaders,' and 'brave bleeders,' who, more than anything else inspired him to ensure that the Wexford men of 1996 carried on that proud tradition.

WEXFORD (1954-1968)

Pat Nolan

| Bobby Rackard | Nick O'Donnell | Tom Neville |

| Jim English | Billy Rackard | Jim Morrissey |

| Ned Wheeler | Phil Wilson |

| Jimmy O'Brien | Paudge Kehoe | Paul Lynch |

| Oliver 'Hopper' McGrath | Nicky Rackard | Tim Flood |

Liam also selected an Ireland team to play the Centenary side picked by the *Sunday Independent*/Irish Nationwide in 1984.

IRELAND

Noel Skehan
(Kilkenny)

Jimmy Brohan *(Cork)*	Brian Lohan *(Clare)*	'Fan' Larkin *(Kilkenny)*
Brian Whelehan *(Offaly)*	Billy Rackard *(Wexford)*	Martin Coogan *(Kilkenny)*

Ned Wheeler *(Wexford)*   Frank Cummins *(Kilkenny)*

Martin Storey *(Wexford)*	Tom Cheasty *(Waterford)*	Jamesie O'Connor *(Clare)*
Jimmy Smyth *(Clare)*	DJ Carey *(Kilkenny)*	Eamon Cregan *(Limerick)*

On the evening of Friday 6 September 1996 Liam Griffin, accompanied by his spiritual guide, his mother Jenny, returned to Our Lady's Island. The previous Monday, the Wexford team that he had fashioned and inspired had returned as All-Ireland Champions, in glorious triumph, to their native county. The reception accorded the team in Gorey, Enniscorthy, Wexford town and all the places between was unprecedented in its volume of rapturous support. In total, an estimated 70,000 excited and exuberant fans, in the midst of enormous welcoming bonfires, greeted the all-conquering heroes. As the melodious strains of the 'Boys of Wexford' wafted away in the cool calm air in the county town, Liam Griffin stood up to address the people of Wexford for the first and last time. 'If you have pride in your own county, pride in the place that you come from, you become a special breed of people. This was always a special place and because of yesterday, it becomes a new place and a special place again. But it's up to you to keep that going for the future. Yesterday was only a beginning – not an end.'

As Liam knelt in joyful thanksgiving on that island of prayer he gratefully remembered the fruits of his visit just six days earlier. In turn, the hurlers of Wexford will always remember Liam Griffin. He had restored sporting pride to his native county in its hour of greatest need.

Peter Canavan

TYRONE'S PETER CANAVAN WAS born in the parish of Errigal, which incorporates the town of Ballygawley, in 1971, the second youngest of eleven children. Peter's father managed the local St Ciarán's GFC for a short while, before a split in club loyalties occurred in the parish. One quarter of the parish's total population lived in an area colloquially known as Glencull. In the early 1980s, Glencull, where the Canavans lived, decided to break away from St Ciarán's and form their own club. They applied to Tyrone County Board for separate affiliation but this request was turned down, as indeed it was for the following nine years. All during that period, Glencull could only play challenge matches. Consequently, Peter Canavan never played any underage football with a club. His only competitive football at this level was confined to his school, St Ciarán's High School in Ballygawley, where Peter experienced much success.

He won Tyrone U-14 and Ulster Vocational titles, as well as a Tyrone U-16 title. Both in 1988 and 1989, Canavan, who was rapidly developing into a brilliant footballer of unerring accuracy and perception, was on the Tyrone county senior vocational teams which won All-Ireland championships in those years. In the latter year, he had the honour of captaining the team when they defeated Mayo. Peter acknowledges the tremendous work done by his school coaches, Robbie Hasson of Derry and Mickey Harte of Ballygawley, both of whom represented their native counties in All-Ireland minor finals in 1969 and 1972 respectively.

Despite the absence of competitive club football, Peter and his neighbours spent all their leisure time playing in the nearby Glencull pitch. Unhindered by the necessity to win, Canavan maintains that this, in some ways, was a blessing in disguise, as he could concentrate fully on practising all the skills of Gaelic football. Peter does not hesitate to mention from where he gleaned the skills in the first place.

'In 1984, I followed Tyrone's Ulster senior championship campaign when they defeated Derry and Down before facing Armagh in the Ulster final. That decider was to provide me with a tailor-made hero. Eleven years earlier, in 1973, the marvellously talented 18-year-old, Frank McGuigan had captained Tyrone to a convincing Ulster final victory over Down. Shortly afterwards, he emigrated to America but had returned to live permanently in Ireland before the 1984 championship. I will always remember the immaculate display of catching, sidestepping and pinpoint accuracy with either foot that Frank displayed that day. He gained possession eleven times in all and, unbelievably, he scored on each occasion – all from play. He scored two off his right foot, eight from his left and one with the fist. It was the most wonderful display of individual skill that I have ever seen. When I went home, I decided that I was going to try my best to emulate the vast array of skills that McGuigan possessed. He was my constant inspiration as I practised alone or with others during all those formative years on the playing field at Glencull,' stated Peter when I met him in his home which nestles snugly in the foothills between the small towns of Sixmilecross and Ballygawley.

Meanwhile, an urgent dilemma faced Tyrone minor manager, Francie Martin, from Carrickmore. He wanted the talented wing or corner forward in the Tyrone minor team but he could not play him as he was not an officially registered player. However, Martin soon found a unique and novel solution to the problem of accommodating Tyrone's most gifted underage player. Francie duly enrolled Peter as a member of the nearby Killyclogher hurling club. So Canavan, who never actually played hurling for his new club, was able to field for the Tyrone minor football side which won the 1988 Ulster minor title when they defeated Cavan 2-7 to 0-3 in the final. Thus, in very unusual circumstances, the county career of 17-year-old Peter Canavan was launched. Though Tyrone lost that year's All-Ireland minor semi-final to Kerry, an excited Canavan was already looking forward to greater things to come. 1989 was to prove special in the developing career of Peter as he played for the county at minor, U-21 and senior levels. His senior debut in a National League game against Mayo in the autumn he remembers with great affection. 'There was great hype because Tyrone had only been beaten by three points, a few months earlier, in the All-Ireland semi-final against Mayo. So there was a huge crowd and a great atmosphere. I loved the buzz and the honour of playing alongside such established stars as John Lynch and Damien O'Hagan.'

In 1990, Peter again featured on the Tyrone U-21 side. This was a very talented young team which won the Ulster final when they defeated Down and then went on to beat Meath in the All-Ireland semi-final. However, though Canavan scored 2-3 Tyrone disappointed in the final losing to Kerry by eight points. 'That day, Eamon Breen, Liam Flaherty and Maurice Fitzgerald were particularly prominent for the Kingdom.' A year later, Tyrone again reached the All-Ireland U-21 final when Canavan, who captained the side from left half forward notched a fantastic 2-5 as Tyrone inflicted the heaviest defeat ever on a Kerry team at any level. Played at Newbridge, the final scoreline of 4-16 to 1-5 reflected Tyrone's supremacy throughout the match. In 1992, the O Neill county played in their third successive All-Ireland U-21 final when they defeated Galway in Longford, with back-to-back captain Canavan notching seven points out of Tyrone's total of 1-7.

From those successful U-21 sides, so capably managed by Danny Ball, a nucleus of future senior stars emerged. The Lawn twins, Chris and Stephen, Fay Devlin, Ciarán McBride, Séamus McCallan, Jody Gormley, Ciarán Loughran and of course

Canavan himself were just some of the more prominent heroes who featured in Tyrone senior championship sides as the 1990s unfolded. From the time Peter made his senior championship debut in 1990 until 1994, however, Tyrone experienced a series of dismal first-round defeats in the Ulster championship. The one occasion when they were decidedly unlucky was in the 1992 National League final against near neighbours Derry. With only a few minutes left, Tyrone were leading by three points when a defensive mix-up allowed an Anthony Tohill '45' to go all the way to the net for a lucky equaliser. Derry, who had been outplayed for most of the game, then scored two points to snatch victory from the jaws of defeat. Ironically, that win seemed to be the catalyst which propelled Derry to a first All-Ireland success one year later in 1993. Tyrone, on the other hand, seemed to lose their way for the next two years.

In 1994, Peter Canavan and Tyrone, now under the astute management of joint managers Art McRory and Eugene McKenna, made massive strides to redress the balance between potential and performance. Playing clever and skilful football, Canavan, now a roving full forward, scored 1-17 in total in the Ulster championship as Tyrone defeated Armagh and Donegal in turn, only to lose the provincial decider against Down. When Down won that year's All-Ireland, the optimism in the Tyrone camp increased enormously. Art McRory reinforced this newfound confidence with the succinct words 'You have to lose an Ulster final before you can win one.'

Tyrone easily overcame Fermanagh in the first round of the 1995 Ulster Championship to set up a mouth watering semi-final clash with traditional rivals Derry who had just won the National League for a second time in the 1990s. When Tyrone had two players sent off in the first half, victory for the O'Neill county seemed rather remote. Very often, however, in such adverse circumstances, a team digs deeper and produces a winning formula. Owing to the numerical disadvantage, Tyrone were forced to play possession football for the second half. This they did to devastating effect. When Derry then had a player sent off, Tyrone were further encouraged and they went on to record a famous one-point victory over the Oak Leaf County.

This victory boosted the team's confidence enormously and after the management team of Art McRory and Eugene McKenna had intensified the Tyrone training programme it was an exceptionally fit and hungry side that met Cavan in the Ulster final. Playing superb, fast, incisive football Tyrone easily overcame the Breffni challenge 2-13 to 0-10. At last Peter Canavan, now popularly dubbed Peter the Great, had won his first Ulster senior championship medal. Canavan, in the three provincial games, had emphasised his spectacular scoring ability with an aggregate total of 20 points.

Like their predecessors of 1956 and 1986, the 1995 Ulster champions met Galway in the All-Ireland semi-final. The Westerners were dominating the game until an opportunist goal by the ever-alert Canavan recovered the O'Neill county's composure.

The magnificent Tyrone footballing artist went on to record 1-7 as Tyrone defeated the tribesmen 1-13 to 0-13. At last he had been given the opportunity to parade his considerable talents on a national stage. His wide range of skills, especially his close ball control and devastating sidestep, were proving to be a constant headache for all defences and an absolute joy for all Tyrone and neutral supporters to savour.

As All-Ireland final day against Dublin approached, the major question on all GAA followers' lips was, would Tyrone extend the magical winning sequence of four All-Irelands for Ulster, from 1991 to 1994. Down in 1991, Donegal in 1992, Derry in 1993 and Down again in 1994 had, by their terrific successes, revived the declining fortunes of the past. Understandably, Tyrone supporters, while admiring the achievements of their fellow Ulstermen felt slightly cheated. After all, Tyrone had won provincial titles in 1956 and 1957, before any of the aforementioned teams, only to lose narrowly to eventual winners Galway and Louth respectively in the All-Ireland semi-finals. In addition, Tyrone had led a great Kerry team by seven points at one stage in the 1986 All-Ireland only to subsequently succumb to a heavy defeat by the Kingdom. 'When the final whistle went after the All-Ireland semi-final, I did not immediately realise the significance of our achievement. My immediate thoughts were of my wife Finola's father who had died the previous week. Likewise, my brother in law, Ronan McGarrity who was also on the team, suffered from mixed emotions.'

Joint managers, Art McRory and Eugene McKenna prepared Tyrone meticulously for the final. Art had been through it all before when he managed the 1986 finalists. Eugene McKenna had been the star player of that team. So together they made a perfect combination as they approached another final with diligence and care.

'The support was immense as we made our way onto the pitch on All-Ireland final day. The deafening noise and the contrasting colours of the Tyrone and Dublin supporters created a fantastic buzz as we nervously waited for the match to begin. That nervous tension evaporated totally when the referee Paddy Russell threw in the ball. Nonetheless I would just love to bottle that whole ambience from the moment you arrive on the pitch until the ball is thrown in.'

In the opening minutes of the game, Tyrone's midfielder Fergal Logan dominated proceedings and provided the Tyrone attack with a plentiful supply of ball. The roving Peter Canavan immediately began to wreak havoc with his darting runs in the Dublin rearguard. As a result, frees were conceded and the ever-reliable Canavan pointed three times to leave the Ulster men well in command after only five minutes play. By the tenth minute, however, Dublin, through Keith Barr, Charlie Redmond and Paul Clarke had levelled the game with well taken frees. As that first half progressed, Dublin midfielder Paul Bealin was having an ever-increasing influence in the midfield exchanges and Dublin soon edged ahead albeit by only one point. In the 26th minute, Bealin kicked a long ball to the left of the Tyrone goalmouth. Speedy corner forward Jason Sherlock nipped in between Tyrone defender Ronan McGarrity and goalkeeper Finbarr McConnell to steer the ball into the path of Charlie Redmond who had the simple task of tapping the ball to the net. Just before the interval, after a dashing run, Dublin's magnificent half back Paul Curran sent the ball over the bar to leave the half time score Dublin 1-8, Tyrone 0-6.

With seven minutes of the second half gone, the classy Canavan had coolly reduced the deficit to two points with three excellent white flags. Now, with the score 1-8 to 0-9, everyone waited for Tyrone to complete the sensational comeback and emulate the feats of Down, Derry and Donegal. Then, out of the blue, a bizarre incident occurred. Fergal Logan fouled Dublin's ace free-taker Charlie Redmond who foolishly retaliated. The referee appeared to send Redmond to the line but when play resumed, Charlie was still on the field. However, a linesman soon drew the referee's attention and he had no hesitation in ordering Redmond to the line.

Now, with Dublin down to 14 men, Tyrone's hopes of success were again renewed. Nevertheless, it was Dublin's Dessie Farrell who was the first to respond positively when he pointed to restore a three-point advantage to the Metropolitans 1-9 to 0-9. Twenty minutes to go and it was real back-to-the-wall stuff as Dublin defended heroically against a rather disjointed Tyrone attacking force. Three minutes from the end of normal time, Tyrone's captain Ciarán Corr was fouled and Canavan pointed to narrow the gap to two points. Then, almost immediately, a splendid fifty-yard point from Paul Clarke renewed Dublin's three-point lead. Within the next two minutes Peter Canavan scored two frees, one for a foul on himself and the other for a foul on Tyrone substitute Mattie McGleenan. There was now just one point between the sides as the huge Tyrone following urged on their team for one final, mighty effort.

As desperation spread throughout the Dublin defence, their goalkeeper and captain John O'Leary untypically sent a hasty clearance right into the path of the flying Canavan. Unfortunately for Peter, he slipped as he was about to gain possession but somehow managed to fist the ball to overlapping left half back Seán McLoughlin. Seán then calmly sent the ball over the bar for an apparent equaliser. Tyrone supporters and many neutrals roared their approval. Dramatically, however, the referee's whistle had been blown prior to McLoughlin's shot. A dejected Peter Canavan knew at once that all the excitement and euphoria was in vain. 'Once I had passed the ball to Seán I heard the referee's whistle. He had disallowed the score because he had adjudged me to have touched the ball on the ground. As for my view on the legality of the foul I just do not know as my only concern was to focus properly and get the ball to Seán.'

Shortly afterwards, the full-time whistle went and Dublin had won their first All-Ireland since 1983. Yet again, it was very much a case of so-near-and-yet-so-far for the disconsolate Tyrone men. Though they had only scored two points in the second half, 14-man Dublin had held on to win the narrowest of victories 1-10 to 0-12. Out of Tyrone's total tally the brilliant Canavan had scored an amazing 0-11. In the end, however, Tyrone's inability to find Canavan often enough and accurately enough had proved their undoing. When Peter reflects on what might have been he is clear thinking in his assessment and clinical in his conclusion.

'First of all it was a terrible blow when one of our most dangerous forwards, Adrian Cush, who had been a prominent member of our forward line for the previous five years had to cry off injured before the game. Secondly, for some unknown reason, we did not play as a unit. At times we won enough ball to set up meaningful attacks but our ability to pass the ball properly as well as our general support play left a lot to be desired.'

Not since Derry had won successive Ulster titles in 1975 and 1976 had an Ulster team repeated this feat. So, having suffered the heartbreak of 1995, there was an additional pressure on Tyrone as they started the defence of their provincial crown in 1996. Tyrone, nevertheless, played splendidly in that 1996 Ulster campaign beating Fermanagh by 12 points in the first round before overcoming arch rivals Derry rather easily by five points in the semi-final. Though Tyrone just scraped through by three points in the Ulster final against Down, they nevertheless put to rest the myth of no team being able to successfully retain the Ulster title.

The All-Ireland semi-final saw Tyrone meet Leinster champions, Meath. Tyrone began very well, going into a three-point lead after only three minutes play. But thereafter the Tyrone challenge seemed to become unstuck as a great Graham Geraghty goal for Meath enabled them to go in at half-time level with the Ulster men. Meath scored the first two points of the second half and even though Tyrone's young star Gerard Cavlan, who had a terrific game, replied, the Tyrone side then seemed to uncharacteristically lose their way. A fantastic last quarter by the Royal county allowed them to record an easy victory, 2-15 to 0-12.

However, in the eyes of many Tyrone supporters and indeed some neutral observers, Meath's victory was tainted with at least a modicum of over-physical play. The fact that three of Tyrone's most dangerous forwards, right half forward Brian Dooher, left corner forward Ciarán McBride and full forward Peter Canavan were injured during the course of the game seemed to substantiate this theory. Despite having a huge bandage to protect a head injury, the big-hearted Dooner continued to play but the unfortunate McBride was forced to retire. Injured after only 15 minutes, it was obvious that Peter Canavan was severely hampered in his movements for the rest of the game. Peter himself ruefully recalls that day. 'There is no doubt that Meath played a very hard physical game but it would be totally wrong to infer that any Meath player deliberately went out to injure any Tyrone player. However, there were some very tough challenges and three of us got very badly injured. In the past, we have all received hard knocks in championship football but we were always able to bounce up from them and continue to play our normal game. For whatever reason, on this occasion we were not able to do so. Brian, though he played on, was not able to have any effective role and Ciarán, who was playing great football, had to retire. In that game, I suffered badly torn ankle ligaments from which it took me almost two years to recover fully. It must also be remembered that all of these injuries occurred in the first half when we were playing very well and had every chance of winning the game. I have no doubt in my mind that our injuries had a major bearing on the eventual outcome of the game. It was only after our team had been badly depleted that Meath gradually took control of the game. Definitely, they played very well in the last 15 minutes to run out easy winners.'

After that disappointing end to Tyrone's 1996 championship, the management team of Art McRory and Eugene McKenna stepped down to be replaced by Danny Ball, Tyrone's highly successful U-21 coach in both 1991 and 1992. However, Danny was not to experience the best of luck, as, in his first championship in 1997 after beating Down following a replay in the first round, Tyrone flopped badly against Derry in the Ulster semi-final. In 1998, at Omagh, Tyrone bowed out after a first-round defeat against Down. 1999 appeared promising for the O'Neill county when they easily disposed of Fermanagh to set up another championship clash with Down for the fourth successive year. Playing well, Tyrone seemed in command with 20 minutes gone in the first half against the Mourne men. Then, inexplicably, Tyrone seemed to suddenly lose their impetus and in the second half they played second best to a rather mediocre Down side. After three years in charge, the unfortunate Danny Ball decided to retire as manager. In September 1999, the former joint managers Art McRory and Eugene McKenna (who incidentally holds the distinction of winning All Star awards in three different positions) were invited to take up the managerial reins. There is no doubt that no stone will be left unturned by these two very able men to ensure that Tyrone's inherent potential will be maximised.

When former Armagh manager Fr Seán Hegarty, who had played for the Orchard county in the 1961 All-Ireland minor semi-final, came as a curate to the parish of Errigal he had another football mission to accomplish – the solution of the ongoing club dispute in his new parish between St Ciarán's GFC and Glencull GFC. Using his diplomatic skills and football know-how, the diminutive priest acted as a mediator between the representatives of both clubs. The amicable result was that a new club under the name of Errigal Ciarán was formed in 1990. The parish was now totally united and no longer would the title 'Killyclogher' appear after Peter Canavan's name in official match programmes. A great team spirit was gradually built up and Peter, along with his inter-county brother Pascal and his other brothers, Barry and Stephen, played a central role as the new club annexed three county championship titles in 1993, 1994 and 1997. When they defeated Down champions Downpatrick in the 1993 Ulster club final, they became the first Tyrone club to do so. The folly of divided parish loyalties had dissipated as a unity of purpose had made Errigal Ciarán the top club in the province.

Some months later, in the spring of 1994, Errigal Ciarán played famed Cork club Nemo Rangers in the All-Ireland club semi-final in Newbridge. It was only after extra time that the Cork champions won the game. The loyalty and dedication of Peter Canavan was then shown in its full glory. Immediately after that club defeat, he travelled home to a function in his native Ballygawley. The following Sunday morning, his brother-in-law drove him the long, tiring journey to Ennis where Ulster were playing Munster in the Railway Cup final. The match was delicately poised when Peter Canavan, despite his exertions of the previous day, was introduced as a sub. In a fantastic six-man movement involving John Joe Doherty (Donegal), Ross Carr (Down), Ger Houlihan (Armagh), James McCartan (Down), and Anthony Tohill (Derry) the clinical Canavan sent the ball to the net for the winning goal. As a result, Ulster had become the first province to win five successive Railway Cup titles and no man deserved that fifth title more than Canavan who had made such a personal sacrifice to represent his province.

Peter, who was also a star performer and vice captain in the Compromise Rules series versus Australia in both 1998 and 1999, enjoyed that experience immensely. Playing with other top players from other counties and representing his country made him a proud man. 'The atmosphere was great and the management team complemented each other very well. John O'Keeffe was an excellent physical trainer, Mickey Moran was superb at adapting GAA skills for the Compromise Rules game and Colm O'Rourke was a fabulous man manager. The fact that all three of them were great footballers themselves made the players very comfortable with their instructions.'

Canavan, like so many others, would like a radical change in the GAA championship system. 'I would run the provincial championships as they are within a much tighter time scale. Then I would hold two rounds of an open draw for the All-Ireland championship. After that I would allow the provincial champions into the draw. This would necessitate some extra games as there would be now 12 teams left in the championship. I think that this system would be much more exciting as each county would be sure of at least two competitive games.'

Peter, who rates Derry's Kieran McKeever as his most difficult opponent, would love to have Kerry's Séamus Moynihan, Derry's Anthony Tohill and Kerry's Maurice Fitzgerald on any team he played with. 'They are three of the most skilful, fair and gifted footballers in the country.' Peter, who likes all sports, nominates hurling as his number one outside football. 'I really like all the top exponents of hurling but two Clare men have made a special impression on me. Ollie Baker exerts a great dominating influence in the centre of the field and Jamesie O'Connor is an exceptionally skilful forward.'

Canavan would love to see a situation evolve where all county players are treated decently and fairly regarding travelling expenses, football gear and loss of earnings through missing work. 'We in Tyrone have no complaints on that score but I know of one incident where players, as often happens, swapped jerseys after an inter-county championship game. At the next team meeting of one of the 'offending' counties, the county board's treasurer announced that the price of the swapped jerseys would be deducted from the travelling expenses of the 'guilty' players. That should never be allowed to happen.'

Peter Canavan attended St Mary's College of Education in Belfast from 1990 to 1994. The previous year, the college under the joint managership of Jim McKeever and Peter Finn, had won the Sigerson Cup for the first time. In Peter's time, the teacher training college, with a very small population, reached the 1993 Sigerson final only to be defeated by a Queens University side which included a host of stars such as Kieran McGeeney and Paul McGrane of Armagh, Paul Brewster of Fermanagh, Anthony Tohill and James McCartan.

Peter has been hugely influenced by all the coaches he has played under at club, county, college and provincial levels. Danny Ball with club and county, Jim McKeever at college, Brian McEniff with Ulster and Art McRory and Eugene McKenna with Tyrone have all developed him not only as a player but as a coach himself. Peter, who won three All Star awards in successive years (1994, 1995 and 1996) has himself experienced coaching success at Holy Trinity College in Cookstown where he is a PE teacher. As well as many county successes, he steered his school to the All-Ireland U-18 Vocational Title in 1998.

Peter, who is married to Finola has two young daughters Áine and Claire. When nominating his all-time Ulster and Ireland selections, Peter picked the following players. He did not consider any Tyrone players for his Ulster team or any Ulster players for his Ireland selection.

IRELAND

John O'Leary
(Dublin)

Stephen O'Brien
(Cork)

Darren Fay
(Meath)

Kenneth Mortimer
(Mayo)

Paul Curran
(Dublin)

Glenn Ryan
(Kildare)

Séamus Moynihan
(Kerry)

John McDermott
(Meath)

Niall Buckley
(Kildare)

Michael Donnellan
(Galway)

Jarlath Fallon
(Galway)

Trevor Giles
(Meath)

Tommy Dowd
(Meath)

Pádraig Joyce
(Galway)

Maurice Fitzgerald
(Kerry)

Subs: Seán Óg de Paor (Galway), Dessie Farrell (Dublin), Peter Brady (Offaly)

ULSTER

Michael McVeigh
(Down)

Kieran McKeever
(Derry)

Declan Loughman
(Monaghan)

Tony Scullion
(Derry)

Gary Coleman
(Derry)

Henry Downey
(Derry)

Kieran McGeeney
(Armagh)

Anthony Tohill
(Derry)

Dermot McCabe
(Cavan)

James McCartan
(Down)

Greg Blaney
(Down)

Martin McHugh
(Donegal)

Joe Brolly
(Derry)

Tony Boyle
(Donegal)

Mickey Linden
(Down)

Peter Canavan is following in the proud tradition of brilliant Tyrone forwards who have exuded class, skill and determination in their pursuit of All-Ireland glory. Iggy Jones, Eugene McKenna, Jackie Taggart, Frankie Donnelly and his own role model Frank McGuigan were the more conspicuous in a long list of Tyrone attackers who epitomised that high standard of footballing excellence. Unlike them, Peter has more than a sporting chance to fulfil his dream of winning the Sam Maguire Cup for the O'Neill County. With Art McRory and Eugene McKenna back in command, that dream could be fast approaching reality. No one would deserve that prized gold medal more than the exquisite talent that is Peter Canavan. All Tyrone await with ever-growing expectation.

Micheál Kearins

IN 1964 MICHEÁL KEARINS, at the age of 20, made his Railway Cup debut for Connacht against Leinster in Ballinasloe. Before the game began Paddy McCormack, popularly known as the Iron man from Rhode, made his presence felt in a rather unusual manner. McCormack, who was scheduled to mark Kearins in that provincial semi-final had played a star role for Offaly in the 1961 All-Ireland final against Down and despite his comparative youthfulness was a seasoned campaigner. Just before the throw-in, he made, with the heel of his boot, a ten-yard long track in the ground half way between, and parallel to, the 14-yard and 21-yard lines.

'You're young Kearins from Sligo, I believe. I presume you want to go back to Sligo this evening,' the Rhode man jokingly said to the debutante.

'Hopefully,' an astonished Kearins replied.

'Well, if you don't pass that line of mine you have a fair chance of getting back!'

Seventy minutes later, safe and sound, Micheál had not only passed the mark several times but had also scored four points from play.

Born in Dromard, Co. Sligo in 1943, Micheál, growing up in his native parish, had two major GAA influences. His father had been a prominent club footballer who had also represented the county. Local priest Fr McHugh, an avid GAA fan, was instrumental in getting all the boys of the parish interested in Gaelic football. It was however, when Micheál went to St Muredachs College in Ballina that Kearins' football career really began to flourish. Coming under the guiding light of college football coach Fr Horan, a former Sligo Rovers soccer player, Kearins rapidly developed into a footballer of immense promise. Fr Horan, realising the extraordinary natural ability that Micheál possessed, wanted to eliminate any flaws in his young protégé. Seeing that Kearins relied solely on his right foot, as most players do, the far-seeing priest reckoned that the Dromard youth would be practically unbeatable if he became equally proficient with his left foot.

'Fr Horan literally spent hours and hours making me turn to the left foot and then kick with the weaker foot. Even though I was only three years in St Muredach's I had perfected the art of kicking with both feet long before I left. This was a huge advantage to me when I became an inter-county player. Many great county players can only kick with one foot but compensate by kicking the ball very high to avoid being blocked. Jack O'Shea and Pat Spillane were the best one-footed players I ever saw because they were very adept at kicking the ball high,' Micheál told me when I met him in his native Dromard.

Kearins first made the Sligo minor team in 1960 but they were beaten by a talented Galway 15 who went on to win that year's All-Ireland minor title. In 1961, with Kearins again eligible, Sligo reached the Connacht minor final only to suffer a heavy defeat by Mayo. 1961, nevertheless, was a hugely significant year for Kearins as he represented the Yeats county in all three grades, minor, junior and senior. After giving very impressive performances with the minors and juniors, Kearins made his senior inter-county competitive debut when he played in a National Football League match against Cavan in Ballymote in the autumn of 1961. Playing at left corner forward he was marking Ulster Railway Cup star, Gabriel Kelly. The following year, Kearins made his senior championship initial appearance when Sligo played current provincial champions Roscommon. In a terrific game, played at Charlestown, Kearins gave a marvellous display. With time almost up, Sligo were leading by two points as their supporters encircled the ground to greet a surprise success. A last-minute goal, however, by Roscommon stopped them in their tracks. Kearins, though naturally disappointed, looked to the future with great hope. It was three more years, nevertheless, before Sligo really achieved anything. That year, 1965, a resurgent Sligo, with centre half back Cathal Cawley, midfielders Brendan McAuley and Bill Shannon, Micheál Kearins at left half forward and corner forward Joe Hannon all playing key roles, Sligo reached their first Connacht final since 1956. Inspired by the electrifying pace and the devastating forward play of the mercurial Kearins, Sligo played magnificently in the final against All-Ireland champions Galway. With Bill Shannon lording the midfield exchanges, Sligo led at half time, 2-3 to 1-2 and were still level with their more illustrious opponents as the game entered its concluding stages. However, two points by the ever-accurate Cyril Dunne and one by his fellow half forward Mattie McDonagh saved the All-Ireland champions from a sensational defeat and the Tribesmen went on to record a 1-12 to 2-6 victory.

Giving such a tremendous performance against a side who were rated among the all-time great teams of Gaelic football was a huge incentive to Sligo. But, as so often happens, Sligo had flattered only to deceive and it was a further six years before they again reached a senior provincial final. Some encouraging league performances as well as a decidedly unlucky defeat to Galway in the 1970 Connacht championship instilled a newfound confidence in Sligo as they faced Galway at Castlebar. In a game of fluctuating fortunes Galway led at half time 1-8 to 1-5. The excitement in the second half was intense as two well drilled sides fought tenaciously for the Nestor Cup. The introduction of two substitutes, Jim Colleary for Sligo and Willie Joyce for Galway increased the tempo. Both gave aerial displays of exquisite quality. With one minute to go the Tribesmen were leading by a point when Sligo were awarded a close in free. Amidst nail-biting tension, Micheál Kearins pointed to snatch a deserved equaliser. When the full-time whistle went, with the sides still level, both teams were relieved. Galway were deemed the luckier as Sligo had allowed a three-point advantage to slip away from them as the game entered its final quarter. Nevertheless, the game will always be remembered for a magnificent display of unerring accuracy by Kearins. It is true there were many other terrific performances but Kearins deservedly received the most kudos as he pointed from all angles and all distances. Thirteen points in all he scored; three from play, one from a '50', a fantastic kick from a line ball and eight frees. It was a truly remarkable feat under the most intense pressure.

Everyone looked forward with eager anticipation to the replay. With John Brennan and Cathal Cawley now playing excellently in the heart of the Sligo defence and Barnes Murphy winning a lot of midfield possession to supply Kearins, David Pugh and Gerry Mitchell, it was a spirited Sligo outfit that awaited the replay. A terribly wet day spoiled the occasion as neither side could produce football of any telling quality. The weather conditions definitely did not suit the silken skills of Kearins. Thus, without Kearins at his most effective, Sligo were deprived of any real penetration in their forward line. Still they fought gallantly and only lost by the narrowest of margins 1-17 to 3-10. After ten years in his native county colours, Micheál Kearins was starting to think it would be a case of Sligo always being in the corner of the vanquished.

Any doubts he may have harboured about the value of training without competition success were soon dispelled in that winter of 1971. It became a winter of content when Micheál was selected at left half forward on that inaugural All Stars football team. To be selected along with a group of top-class players, 13 of whom had won either All-Ireland senior or provincial medals or both (Andy McCallion of Antrim was the other exception, Ray Cummins of Cork had won his All-Ireland medal in the 1970 All-Ireland hurling final against Wexford) was a tremendous personal honour.

'I was unbelievably happy when I was informed of my selection. Unfortunately due to family and work commitments, I could not go on the All Stars trip to America. However, I was delighted to be allowed nominate my replacement, Jim Colleary, who was playing brilliantly for the county team at centre half forward, as my choice. As I had been playing very well the following year, 1972, I also expected to be selected either at left half forward or left corner forward. Instead those awards were given to Tony McTague, the Offaly All-Ireland winning captain of 1972 and Paddy Moriarty of Armagh. Still it was a great privilege to receive it once. It is something I will always treasure.'

The following year Kearins turned in another virtuoso performance when he notched 14 points against Mayo in the Connacht championship. Yet again he experienced the ignominy of defeat. Similar stories of dismal defeats continued. As 1975 arrived there was no apparent reason for any undue optimism. Seventy minutes of scintillating attacking football against old adversaries Galway, was to change all that. In the semi-final of the Connacht championship, Sligo totally overwhelmed the Tribesmen on a 1-13 to 0-6 scoreline to secure their first championship victory over Galway in 28 years. After this surprise victory over the Connacht champions, all Sligo supporters were convinced that their long awaited dream of a provincial senior title was about to be realised.

In the Connacht final against Mayo in their own Markievicz Park, the gods appeared to be on the side of the men in black and white. Playing at a home venue situated in the shadow of beautiful Ben Bulben, on a sunny Sunday in July was a romantic's paradise.

However, the game itself did not match its splendid setting. Sligo, it is true, totally dominated the possession stakes but they were not able to transform their outfield superiority into scores. Still, with 15 minutes to go they led by six points. Mayo, however, sensing that Sligo were unable to deliver a killer blow that would finish the contest, raised their own game and gradually whittled down the six-point lead. Indeed, but for some terrible misses, Mayo would have won the match. As it turned out, the sides finished level – Sligo 2-10, Mayo 1-13. For Sligo in general and Micheál Kearins in particular it had been a most frustrating afternoon. Unusually for him, he found it extremely difficult to get into the game, only occasionally showing glimpses of his true form. Sligo knew that they had been exceptionally lucky to survive, especially in those dying minutes when their full back John Brennan almost single-handedly defied the advances of the Mayo forwards.

Three weeks later, the replay took place in Castlebar. In a tough and physical encounter Mayo gained the upper hand in the first half and led by 0-9 to 0-7 at half time. The second half saw Sligo midfielder John Stenson give an immaculate display of high catching. With captain and team manager Barnes Murphy now also dictating the pace of the game from the centre half back position the supply of quality ball to the Sligo forward line increased substantially. Just before the final whistle Sligo edged in front and when it sounded Sligo had won on a 2-10 to 0-15 scoreline. Sligo had stars throughout the field with John Brennan, Barnes Murphy, Mattie Hoey and Dessie Kerins being particularly effective. However the real matchwinner was the man from Dromard Micheál Kearins. Twice in the first half he scored brilliant points under the most difficult of circumstances. In the second half he was upended in the square by a Mayo defender and he expertly tucked away the resultant penalty to put Sligo into the lead. But it was another aspect of his versatility that finally applied the coup de grace to this game. Gaining possession some 20 yards out from the Mayo goal and spotting the inrushing Dessie Kerins free in the right corner forward position he nonchalantly flicked the ball inside and Dessie sent it to the net. This was the clinching score in a narrow but deserved victory.

When captain Barnes Murphy raised aloft the Nestor Cup, McHale Park became a sea of black and white as ecstatic Sligo followers sought their heroes. Led by the inimitable Kearins and Murphy the whole team raced around the inner perimeter of the ground in a glorious lap of honour. For the first time since 1928, Sligo had won a Connacht senior championship. The millstone of past miseries, hard-luck stories and disappointing displays had been suddenly lifted from the necks of players and supporters alike. The success-starved Sligo supporters raised the decibel levels to new heights, as choruses of exultation engulfed the ground. After 14 successive championship campaigns, Micheál Kearins had at last savoured provincial victory. The constant training after all those years had finally reaped him his due reward. A civic reception was accorded the team the following Saturday in Sligo's town hall. Fittingly, eight surviving members of the first Sligo team to win the Connacht championship in 1928 also attended.

In the All-Ireland semi-final, Sligo were unceremoniously brought back to earth again when they were demolished by Kerry 3-13 to 0-5. Sligo were really unfortunate to come up against a Kerry team about to enter the history books as one of the greatest sides in the history of Gaelic football. The burgeoning wiles and skills of John O'Keeffe, Páidí Ó Sé, Paudie Lynch, John Egan, Mike Sheehy and Pat Spillane allowed Kerry cruise to the easiest of wins. A missed penalty by Micheál Kearins after only ten minutes of play (Kerry goalkeeper Paudie O'Mahony finger tipped the ball around the post for a fruitless '50') sadly symbolised Sligo's day of despair. Though disheartened by their inept performance, Sligo and Kearins knew that the Connacht final had been their All-Ireland. Greater sides, they consoled themselves, than Sligo would feel the wrath of that Kerry team in the years to come.

For three more years, Micheál Kearins played for Sligo. When he retired after Sligo's elimination by Galway in the Connacht semi-final of 1978, an outstanding 17-year career had finally ended but another was due to begin. Before he retired, Micheál had refereed at club level in Sligo and had enjoyed the experience immensely. His availability now attracted both the Connacht and Central Councils of the GAA and in the next 11 years, Micheál was to referee countless National League and provincial championship games as well as four Connacht finals, one National League final, one Under 21 All-Ireland final and one All-Ireland semi-final. His dearly-held wish to officiate at an All-Ireland senior final did not materialise. He believes a set of unfortunate occurrences were responsible for this.

'I was appointed to referee the All-Ireland semi-final in 1989 between Cork and Dublin. I was hoping that everything would go well as I reckoned that I had a good chance of refereeing that year's All-Ireland. In the game, a confrontation took place between a group of players and Keith Barr whom I had warned earlier, ran 40 yards to get involved. I had no option but to send the Dublin defender to the line. When it was suggested to me after the game by two GAA officials that I should have balanced the number of players that I sent off, I knew the die was cast against me. Still that should not have affected my chances of refereeing the final. When the referee selection committee decided to appoint Paddy Collins of Westmeath I was totally disillusioned and hurt. I was not annoyed with Paddy whom I consider, along with Jimmy Hatton (Wicklow) and John Moloney (Tipperary), to have been the three most outstanding referees in my lifetime. I was very disappointed especially when some people from my own county vetoed my selection for the final of 1989. When I discovered that, I decided to retire from refereeing.'

When I asked him for his opinion of present refereeing standards, Micheál was equally forthcoming. 'There are not too many Dickie Murphys around at the moment. Dickie is an excellent hurling referee but the overall standard is very poor and inconsistent. Too many referees seem to think that when they have a whistle in their mouth that they are lord and master of everything on the field. Referees need to be able to communicate with players as opposed to adopting a dictatorial attitude. John Moloney had a great way with players and Paddy Collins always looked very comfortable when refereeing.'

Like most competent referees, Micheál Kearins only hit the headlines when he sent off a very prominent inter-county player, Colm O'Rourke, in a league game against Armagh in November 1984. Kearins' decision incurred the wrath of some Meath supporters who felt that their idol had been hard done by. Micheál explains the incident as he saw it.

'Colm grabbed the ball firmly into his chest. He then got a very heavy but fair, in my opinion, shoulder tackle. This made the ball spin out of O'Rourke's hands. An Armagh player then gained possession and soloed downfield with the ball. Instead of trying to retrieve the ball, Colm ran after me, verbally abusing me. I told him "if there's one more word out of you, I'll send you off." O'Rourke continued to chase me as I followed the play and kept up his verbal abuse, so I did send him off. This was just after the start of the second half and some Meath fans continued to voice their disapproval of my decision for the rest of the game. Five minutes before the end of the game, Armagh defender Jim McKerr also verbally abused me. In order to be consistent, I also sent him off. When the match ended there was a lot of hassle before I eventually left the ground.'

In the 1988 All-Ireland final, Micheál and Colm were again at loggerheads. The Meath player hotly disputed a line-ball decision which Micheál, acting as a linesman, had given to Cork. 'I knew after I watched a video replay of the incident on television later that evening that I was wrong and that Colm was correct in that the line ball should have been awarded to Meath,' Micheál candidly acknowledged.

When it comes to good footballers, Kearins is fulsome in his praise of the Skyrne clubman. 'Colm O'Rourke was the chief playmaker in that Meath side that won two All-Irelands in 1987 and 1988 and appeared in two others in 1990 and 1991. He was simply too good for all his opponents and made valuable space for his fellow forwards, Brian Stafford and Bernard Flynn to score.

I have carefully watched all the TV analysts like Enda Colleran, Pat Spillane and Colm O'Rourke over the years on 'The Sunday Game'. O'Rourke is by far the best man to analyse what has happened. No one has a greater understanding of the game than he has. There have been some good journalists too. I loved to read Mick Dunne when he worked with the *Irish Press*. Liam Horan of the *Irish Independent* is also a very accurate reader of the game. However, the journalist I like best is Eugene McGee. He is a very good judge of the game and he tells it as it is.'

Micheál, who would love to see the first round of the provincial championship played over two legs with the team with the highest points aggregate going through to the second round, feels that the present rules should be left as they are. In his view, the GAA should abolish all rules dealing with the exclusion of people being allowed to join the association or with other codes being forbidden to play on GAA grounds.

For the first ten years of his inter-county life, Micheál Kearins trained regularly and assiduously at least four days a week, in addition to his inter-county and club training. Each morning of those four days he would get up at 6 a.m. and then run the one mile from his home to the sea and back again before running another two miles in the fields behind his home. In the evenings, after his work commitments in his thriving cattle business had been fulfilled, he would come home and run two miles on the road, then take a rest and finish with an intensive hour and a half of exercises. This ritual was designed to maximise his stamina, speed and alertness.

Oddly enough, he did little or no place-kicking practice except for a five-minute session before each game. In the latter years of his inter-county career, increased work commitments and waning interest curtailed his extra personal training programme. Nevertheless, he still continued to train constantly with both club and county.

In the 1950s and early 1960s, Micheál's Dromard had no senior team so he played with nearby Ballisodare with whom he won senior championships in 1963 and 1964. Having won the county junior championship in 1964, Dromard were promoted to senior (there was no intermediate grade in Sligo) and Micheál was on board when Dromard won their first senior championship in 1968. Micheál, who was the manager of that team also had three of his brothers James, Peadar and Noel playing as well, James being on the historic 1975 provincial championship winning side. That 1968 success was the forerunner of four other senior championships for Micheál in 1970, 1971, 1973 and 1974. Though on the losing side, he was awarded 'Man of the Match' in the 1982 county final. After his beloved Dromard lost the 1984 county decider, the now 40-year-old Micheál Kearins finally retired from club football. Twenty-five years of club action had come to an end. Such longevity of service and loyalty to one sport has always been very rare.

Kearins, who nominates Donegal's Brian McEniff, Galway's John Donnellan and Liam O'Neill as his most difficult opponents, rates Seán Purcell as the greatest all-round player that he ever saw. He also admired Mick O'Connell for his fetching and passing ability while Kerry's John Egan impressed him with the inventiveness of his forward play. Another former star whom he respects greatly for his total dedication to the cause of Kerry football is his close friend Páidí Ó Sé.

For 13 consecutive years (1963-1975), Micheál Kearins starred in the Railway Cup series. Playing in such exalted company as the magnificent Galway players from their three-in-a-row team, Pakie McGarty of Leitrim, John Morley and Joe Corcoran of Mayo and Dermot Earley of Roscommon made Kearins appreciate the relevance of the interprovincial series for all players especially those from the 'weaker' counties. His two Railway Cup medals, obtained in 1967 and 1969 are among his most treasured mementoes.

Kearins is nationally recognised as one of the greatest scoregetters in the history of Gaelic football, chalking up many outstanding individual match totals. In 1968 he created a national record by scoring 2-135 (141 points) from 24 games. In 1972, he totalled 4-130 (142 points) from 19 games. He topped the All-Ireland charts on three separate campaigns in 1967–1968, 1970–1971 and 1973–1974. He amassed the staggering total of 36 goals and 1158 points (1266 points) in 215 games at inter-county and provincial level – a phenomenal feat by any standards.

Micheál, whose son Karl played for Sligo in the mid-1990s, is a follower of all sports, especially soccer. Johnny Giles, David O'Leary, George Best, Liam Brady and Frank Stapleton were particular favourites. On the music scene he loved the showbands of the 1960s. He was a great fan of Paddy Cole, Brendan Bowyer and Joe Dolan. Politically, he had great admiration for former EU Commissioner and ex-Tánaiste Ray McSharry. 'He did tremendous work for Sligo. A highly intelligent man, Ray deserves great credit because he really was self-educated.'

Micheál, whose wife Frances hails from Dublin, has two sons and two daughters. Karl and Adrian are gardaí whereas Valerie is a solicitor and Evanna has just qualified in Media and Communication Studies.

When making his Ireland and Connacht selections Micheál picked the following:

IRELAND (1960-1980)

Johnny Geraghty
(Galway)

Donie O'Sullivan *(Kerry)*	Noel Tierney *(Galway)*	Tom O'Hare *(Down)*
Brian McEniff *(Donegal)*	Gerry O'Malley *(Roscommon)*	Martin Newell *(Galway)*

Mick O'Connell *(Kerry)*   Jim McKeever *(Derry)*

Matt Connor *(Offaly)*	Seán Purcell *(Galway)*	Pat Spillane *(Kerry)*
Mike Sheehy *(Kerry)*	Seán O'Neill (Down)	Paddy Doherty *(Down)*

CONNACHT (1960-1980)

Johnny Geraghty
(Galway)

John Carey
(Mayo)

Noel Tierney
(Galway)

Bosco McDermott
(Galway)

Liam O'Neill
(Galway)

Gerry O'Malley
(Roscommon)

Martin Newell
(Galway)

Dermot Earley
(Roscommon)

Mick Garrett
(Galway)

Pakie McGarty
(Leitrim)

Seán Purcell
(Galway)

Séamus Leyden
(Galway)

Joe Corcoran
(Mayo)

Willie McGee
(Mayo)

John Keenan
(Galway)

A token of the immense esteem in which Kearins was held took place at a banquet held in his honour on 24 April 1981. Organised by former Sligo star and then PRO' of the County Board, the late Joe Masterson, 400 specially invited guests turned up for a 'This is your Life' tribute to Micheál. The legendary Mick O'Connell of Kerry, the great Seán Purcell of Galway and John Donnellan and Séamus Leyden of Galway's famous three-in-a-row team were just some of the most famous GAA personalities present. It was a superb night of nostalgia and celebration for the man who three years later would be selected on the *Sunday Independent*/Irish Nationwide Centenary team for footballers who never won an All-Ireland medal.

Micheál Kearins was a true Gaelic football artist whose deeds of wizardry were admired throughout the land.

In 1964 Paddy McCormack asked him not to breach a certain man-made line. After his 1981 tribute and the 1984 Centenary award, Micheál Kearins has crossed the Rubicon into the Hall of Fame reserved for 'the greats' of Gaelic Games. Nothing or no one will ever take that supreme accolade from him.

Colm O'Rourke

IN 1974 A TALL, skinny, 16-year-old youth pleaded to be included in his club's senior championship side. Despite his plaintive pleas for inclusion, one person kept saying 'no' to his ambitions. The 'no' came not from the club's management team but from the boy's mother who feared for the safety of her very talented son. When all hope seemed lost the boy played his final card. It was an ace. 'If anyone tries to intimidate me you can be sure that my four brothers on the team will look after me.' Hearing these words of reassurance Mrs O'Rourke gave in. So, in that championship game against Walterstown, Colm O'Rourke made his senior club debut. When he came on as a sub for his brother, Ciarán, Colm was on top of the world. He had made the big time. Little did he then realise that was only a small beginning compared to what the new Skryne clubman would achieve during the next two decades.

Born in Aughavas, Co. Leitrim, the second youngest in a family of twelve, the family moved to a larger farm in Skryne Co. Meath in 1966. All of the eight boys played for Skryne and the oldest son, Fergus, actually played county football for Leitrim during the 1960s. When Meath defeated Cork to win their first All-Ireland senior football title for 13 years in 1967, Colm, though from Aughavas, had become a fully-fledged Meath supporter. Stars on that team such as Jack Quinn, Red Collier, Pat Reynolds, Noel Curran and Captain Peter Darby were his new heroes.

The young O'Rourke quickly progressed through the underage ranks at club level and was selected on the Meath minor team of 1975. In the autumn of the same year and just a few days after his 18th birthday O'Rourke made his senior inter-county debut in a National League game against Mayo. Unlike his mother's fear of a mere 18 months earlier, Colm's ability to look after himself in the meantime had assuaged any doubts she may have had. His promotion to the senior inter-county team underlined that fact.

In 1976, O'Rourke made his championship debut against Wicklow and progressed to the Leinster final only to suffer a two-point defeat to Dublin. To compound his disappointment, the new UCD Arts student missed a penalty. Nevertheless, that despondency paled into insignificance when compared with the horrific injury O'Rourke received five months later in December 1976. In a club tournament game, against old rivals Walterstown, Colm twisted his knee so badly that medical experts doubted whether he should ever play football again. Having suffered a torn cartilage and, more seriously, severed medial and cruciate ligaments, the general prognosis did not bode well for a top-class playing career. A strenuous daily exercise procedure, allied to excellent specialist consultative advice from Dr Joe McGrath, a top orthopaedic surgeon in Navan, ensured that O'Rourke gradually regained full fitness. By February 1978, just 14 months after the injury, O'Rourke deemed his rehabilitation sufficient to allow him play in a Sigerson cup match with UCD. Sheer willpower and an unyielding determination to overcome adversity had made possible his return to the football field.

For the next four years, Meath football was essentially in a state of disarray. It was only when former hurling star Seán Boylan was appointed football manager in September 1982 that things began to change for the better. Seán brought a new sense of purpose and man management skills to Meath football. Regular and varied training techniques not only made the team fit but also established a necessary bonding between the whole panel of players.

The first breakthrough for Boylan's Meath occurred in 1984 when they won the Centenary Cup. This was an open draw competition inaugurated to commemorate the founding of the GAA in Thurles a hundred years earlier. Beating Monaghan in the final was O'Rourke's first major achievement with Meath. Despite this win, Boylan and his fellow selectors realised that Meath needed many new players so they trawled the county for new talent. By the spring of 1986, Liam Harnan, Terry Ferguson, Robbie O'Malley, PJ Gillic, Bernard Flynn, David Beggy and Brian Stafford had joined the ranks. In addition, former goalkeeper Mickey McQuillan had reclaimed the goalkeeper's spot. These young lions plus the four men who had served the county for most of the previous ten years, Joe Cassells, Gerry McEntee, Mick Lyons and Colm O'Rourke were to form the core of the new side. When Martin O'Connell was switched to left half back from full forward and Liam Hayes became McEntee's regular midfield partner a winning combination was in place at last.

The first signs of greatness emerged when Meath defeated Dublin in the 1986 Leinster final. Dublin's stranglehold on the Leinster title was broken and Meath had won their first senior provincial since they defeated Offaly 16 years previously in 1970. However, Meath celebrated their Leinster success too well and Kerry easily accounted for them in the subsequent All-Ireland semi-final. When the team reassessed their 1986 campaign they realised that they had the potential, with proper preparation, to win an All-Ireland title.

In 1987, they again defeated Dublin in the Leinster final and went on to brush aside the challenge of Derry in the All-Ireland semi-final. Now the Royal County were pitted against Cork in the All-Ireland final. After a slow start, when they went five points down, things looked bleak especially when Cork's Jimmy Kerrigan bore down on goal. However, a brilliant block by full back Mick Lyons on Kerrigan's goalbound shot saved the day and inspired Meath to raise their game. Meath then proceeded to dictate the exchanges, adding points at will. When Colm O'Rourke scored a decisive goal and David Beggy added a spectacular point, the pendulum had swung decidedly in Meath's favour and they went on to claim a six-point victory. For the first time in 20 years the men from Meath had claimed the coveted Sam Maguire Cup. It was a tremendous achievement for all concerned especially manager Seán Boylan who had been unwavering in his belief that this day would come. For Colm O'Rourke and his four wise colleagues, Cassells, Lyons, Hayes and McEntee the victory was especially sweet. 'I was glad that all of us had been there to share this moment of elation. After all we had soldiered together in the bad old days. Now it was nice to sample success at the very highest level,' O'Rourke told me in his sports shop in Navan Shopping Centre.

In 1988, Meath again reached the All-Ireland final with Cork once more their opponents. In terms of possession, Cork controlled the game but wasted many chances and Meath held on for a draw. The pundits were, at this stage, suggesting that Meath would now win the replay as they had an innate capacity to improve and to raise their game when the occasion demanded it. This thesis was based on the premise of Meath's National Football League victory over Dublin after a replay, just four months previously. In a rather tempestuous game in which Meath's Kevin Foley was sent off, Meath gave a brilliant performance to emerge victorious with a convincing score of 2-13 to 0-11. The drawn All-Ireland was tough and dour with more emphasis on the physical exchanges than on the ball. Similarly, in the replay several players on both sides tried to exact retribution for what had happened in the drawn game. However, after referee Tommy Sugrue of Kerry sent off Gerry McEntee for allegedly striking Niall Cahalane the game settled down and Meath, thanks to the accuracy of Beggy, Flynn and O'Rourke, carved out a one-point victory. Most neutral observers would claim that Cork had caught Meath off guard with their more physical approach in the drawn encounter whereas Meath upped the ante in the replay. Whatever the merits or demerits of that supposition and despite the fact that there was a certain ill will now between the sides, one must conclude that Meath were worthy champions. Cork, for their part, were to compensate for their back-to-back disappointments by going to win the next two All-Irelands in 1989 and 1990. So, retrospectively, one could say that both sides eventually got their due reward.

Colm O'Rourke could hardly believe that he was now the proud holder of two All-Ireland medals. Before his eventual retirement he was destined to play in two more finals in 1990 and 1991. O'Rourke would have liked to win the 1990 All-Ireland especially as he was now the team captain but Cork deservedly ran out winners on a 0-16 to 0-9 scoreline.

When GAA historians recall the contribution of Meath's Seán Boylan, there will be a special section devoted to the four-game marathon in the 1991 Leinster championship. Initially, in three of the matches Dublin dominated, only to be pulled back by the never-say-die spirit of the Royal County. In the first game, O'Rourke was switched from his customary corner forward position to centre half forward. This enabled Meath to peg back a five-point deficit with PJ Gillic literally obtaining a lucky bounce of the ball to equalise in the dying moments of the game. Though Meath led at half time in the second game, they had had the advantage of a strong wind and only had a three-point advantage. In the second half, Dublin drew level, took control but this was not reflected on the scoreboard. Nevertheless, only a magnificent save by Meath goalkeeper Michael McQuillan prevented Dublin from winning at the end of normal time. With the heat now intense and the pace of the game much slower, both sides again finished level after extra time.

In the third encounter, Dublin were leading by five points with ten minutes to go. A brilliant goal by the classy Bernard Flynn and two converted frees, courtesy of impeccable shooting by free taker Brian Stafford, again brought the sides level just before the end of normal time. In extra time the sides, incredibly, scored 1-4 each to send the series to another meeting.

When the two teams ran onto the field for the fourth meeting, Croke Park literally exploded in a welter of excitement. Seldom, if ever, has there been such a cauldron of noise, tension and expectation in any stadium as 30 of the world's greatest amateur sportsmen prepared for the throw in. A packed headquarters, an estimated live television audience of one million people and thousands more listening on radio set the scene for the most exciting saga in Irish sport. Though Meath took the lead in the beginning of the match, it was again Dublin who dictated the pace and with two minutes left to play they were leading by three points. At last, or so it appeared, Dublin were about to progress to the next round. Then, as the stewards began circling the field to prepare for the end of the match defender, Kevin Foley, realising that time was nearly up, threw caution to the wind and decided to join the attack. There was nothing to lose and plenty to gain. Within seconds of Foley's move forward, the most famous passing movement in the GAA's history unfolded before the eyes of all those privileged to witness it. Involving seven players, two of them (O'Rourke and Foley) twice, the ball eventually reached defender turned attacker, Kevin Foley, on the edge of the square. Promptly, he dispatched the ball to the net for one of the greatest goals of all time. With fleetness of foot and dexterity of hand, this brilliantly conceived goal was scored in the most dramatic of circumstances. The teams were now level. Winning the ball from the ensuing kick out, Liam Hayes passed it to PJ Gillic who transferred it to David Beggy who sent it over the bar for the lead. When referee Tommy Howard, another hero of the series, blew the full time whistle one minute later, 340 minutes of Gaelic football at its very best had ended. Colm O'Rourke and Meath were both relieved and elated. Understandably, the Dublin players were totally devastated.

Meath had to play four further games before they won that year's Leinster title, drawing with Wicklow before winning the replay, then disposing of Offaly in the semi-final and overcoming Laois in the final. In the All-Ireland semi-final, a now tired and ageing Meath side were lucky to eke out a one-point win. Nevertheless, Meath were in their fourth All-Ireland final in five years. Whatever the result in that year's final against Ulster champions Down, their place in posterity as one of the great GAA sides was assured.

As it turned out, this was to be the most disappointing occasion in Colm O'Rourke's footballing life. In the week prior to the game O'Rourke contracted viral pneumonia and on the Saturday before the game he was pronounced unfit to take part. While listed as a substitute he did not experience the full trauma of his bad luck until the following announcement was made over the PA system. 'Fógra, tá athrú amháin ar fhoireann na Mí. Ní imreoidh uimhir a trí déag Colm Ó Ruairc.' Colm's air of despondency was not helped as a rampant Down side dominated the proceedings. They were eleven points ahead when O'Rourke, who had come on some minutes earlier in the second half, took the game by the scruff of the neck. The inspiration he imbued in his team mates, allied to his magnificence in winning quality possession, will be forever etched in the memory of those who observed this most marvellous comeback. Even though Down held on for a famous victory by a two-point margin, Colm O'Rourke's central role in that grandstand finish has earned him a permanent place in Gaelic football's hall of fame. 'It had been a long season with ten intense championship games. If we had won, it would have really been the icing on the cake for a lot of us,' O'Rourke sadly recalls.

O'Rourke played for his beloved Meath for a further four years. When the 1995 championship season came along he made a conscious decision to retire. He was approaching his 38th birthday and was finding it difficult to maintain his enthusiasm and the necessary level of fitness for top class football. In addition, he was no longer guaranteed his place. He came on as a substitute in the first round against Offaly and scored 1-2. This display ensured that he regained his place and he started all the remaining games in the Leinster championship against Longford, Wicklow and the Leinster final against Dublin. He gave an immaculate and inspirational display in the final only to end up on the wrong side of a ten points defeat by Meath's arch rivals. The final scoreline really humiliated O'Rourke. 'As far as I was concerned the whole team was going nowhere. I had had a good innings and was pleased with my performance. So that was my last competitive game at either county or club level. I was proved wrong, however, when Meath went on to win the next year's All-Ireland. I would have liked to have played in that campaign but time had moved on. It was important that Meath should progress with the players that had been playing all year rather than have someone like me joining their ranks,' added O'Rourke rather philosophically. Thus the end of the career of one of the greatest footballers of our time had come to its inevitable end. For 20 years (1975 to 1995) he had graced the playing fields of Ireland. He had spearheaded the revival of the footballing fortunes of his adopted Royal County. In that time, he had played 109 National League matches and had scored 18 goals and 167 points in the competition. During the same period, he had taken part in 62 championship games, amassing a total of 16 goals and 153 points. It was a colossal achievement for any striker but when one considers that O'Rourke was essentially a playmaker, the immensity of his contribution becomes even more pronounced.

Colm O'Rourke is a man of many talents. After the All-Ireland final of 1988, David Walsh asked him to write an article for the *Sunday Tribune*. For the following eight years he wrote a weekly column on GAA affairs before transferring to the *Sunday Independent* in 1996. The vast majority of GAA supporters generally agree with O'Rourke's appraisal of games and players. His views on topical GAA matters are awaited with interest and they stimulate debate on such issues as refereeing standards, competitive structures and the level of skill in Gaelic football. On the other hand, those who write to him tend to vehemently disagree with his opinions and accuse him of being biased against their native county particularly if he has been critical of their performance in a given match. Still, most GAA aficionados feel that O'Rourke has been both fair and consistent in his analysis of games. For example, he has always been trenchant in his condemnation of the overuse of the handpass. He has also constantly maintained that a long accurate kick pass is much more effective in terms of creative forward play. He points to how Galway in 1998 got the balance right between short, hand passing as a support system and long kick passing as the most incisive way of opening gaps in a defence. In O'Rourke's opinion, Gaelic football fulfils it true potential when this is done.

When it comes to accurately forecasting results of matches O'Rourke is proud of his success rate. 'A great advantage that I have over other journalists is that, through my involvement with "The Sunday Game", I get tapes of many games around the country. As well as that, I believe that one of the reasons for establishing my credibility is the fact that I go to a variety of games throughout the whole National League and championship competitions. This gives an extra insight into the actual worth of every team. As a consequence I have learned to watch games from a totally objective viewpoint. I maintain that this was one of the reasons why I was able to predict, from a fairly early stage, that Cork would win the 1999 League.'

As well as being involved in the print media, Colm has been an active participant in 'The Sunday Game' sports programme on RTE. This began in 1991 when the producer of the programme, Bill Lalor, changed the format to include a current player. O'Rourke has been a regular analyst ever since. Recognised for his ability to read a game quickly and succinctly, O'Rourke's views, whether they are for instant reaction in a live game or for post-match analysis, are eagerly awaited.

O'Rourke, who teaches Business Studies and Geography in St Patrick's Classical School in Navan, is also a key member of the GAA's football development committee. Its chief function is to make recommendations as to the future of Gaelic football with specific reference to its rules, disciplinary procedures and competition structures. To Colm, the last issue is the most important one facing the GAA. He feels that the needs, demands and expectations of players, team managements and supporters alike are not being fulfilled at present. From a personal viewpoint O'Rourke would abolish both the current National Football League and the current senior All-Ireland football championship for an experimental period of two years.

'Senior inter-county footballers, after all the effort they put into training should be guaranteed at least ten real, competitive games per season. I would combine the league and championship into one competition. There would be three divisions of the league with eleven teams (including London) in each section. The leagues would be seeded on the basis of the performance of teams in the previous year's league and championship. Each division of the league would have a winner in its own right and then the excitement would really begin. The top four teams in Division One, the top two in Division Two and the top two in Division Three would then be the only entrants for the All-Ireland senior football championship quarter finals. A televised open draw for the quarter finals would be the perfect forum to promote this.

The remaining 25 teams would then be put into a proper 'B' championship with a lucrative reward such as a holiday to Florida. The final could be played as a curtain raiser to the All-Ireland minor and senior football finals on the last Sunday in September.'

O'Rourke, married to Patricia, with two children, Shane and Elaine, is of the firm opinion that with a much tighter, pre-planned championship league format between March and October the GAA would benefit immensely, not least financially. More importantly, the quality of football would improve dramatically. Each county could set itself a more realistic target and players and supporters would have more matches at the proper time of the year. Colm maintains these types of proposals are usually dismissed by counties on the grounds that internal club games would be disrupted. On the contrary, O'Rourke holds the view that a clearly defined county season from 1 March to 1 October would enable each County committee to plan accordingly.

The man who is now involved in underage coaching with Simonstown GFC on the outskirts of Navan believes that there is a great need to recruit more young referees into the GAA. 'Young aspiring referees are being put off by the bad publicity that surrounds some referees. Even though this negative publicity may not be warranted the perception is there and as a result it makes recruitment all the more difficult. What is required is that 40 skilled men with an aptitude for refereeing are recruited and trained. They should take charge of all National League and championship games. Their progress should be reviewed on a match by match basis and the Referees Advisory body should review the whole position each year. Finally, they should be given very generous expenses. This would make what is a very onerous task much more attractive, especially for the younger referees,' added Colm who acknowledges Tipperary's John Moloney as his all-time favourite referee.

When it comes to reflecting on the great players that he has met in his travels O'Rourke dwells mostly on the players from the teams that he has either watched or played against during his career. Understandably, he did not consider any Meath player when making his choices.

'John O'Leary (Dublin) was the best goalkeeper that I have seen. He had tremendous agility, an innate ability to read the game, possessed a good kick out and was an expert shot stopper. Mick Kennedy, Robbie Kelleher, Keith Barr and Tommy Drumm of Dublin and Paudie Lynch of Kerry (both at midfield and half back) were the best defenders that I encountered. However, I would have to say that by far the best footballer that I played against was John O'Keeffe (Kerry). He really was an outstanding player. Brian Mullins (Dublin) and Jack O'Shea (Kerry) were my favourite midfielders. Peter Canavan (Tyrone), Mickey Linden (Down), Mike Sheehy (Kerry), Matt Connor (Offaly) and John Egan (Kerry) were all exceptionally talented forwards. Eoin Liston (Kerry) was a very intelligent target man in the full forward position and Pat Spillane was simply a fantastic footballer,' added the man who says that the Kerry team of the 1970s and 1980s was the best team that he ever saw.

O'Rourke relishes the idea of Physical Education becoming a subject for second-level examinations both in Northern Ireland and in the Republic. He believes that Gaelic games, given its special and unique place in Irish society should be an integral part of that programme. 'There is nothing wrong with our national games getting precedence in our own country. That is not to detract in any way from any other sporting activity that merits inclusion. This would boost the games in our GAA schools as well as providing County Boards, Provincial Councils and Croke Park with an ideal opportunity of promoting Gaelic games in non-GAA schools.'

The three-time All Star insists that the GAA should undergo a huge promotional and development programme in urban areas, particularly in the cities of Dublin, Belfast and Cork. Regarding the existence of the 'foreign' games ban on GAA pitches and the ban on members of the Royal Ulster Constabulary (RUC) from playing Gaelic games, Colm maintains that such bans have no place in any sporting organisation. 'It is the rules and procedures of an organisation that guarantee the proper standards and conduct of its members. When that exists, as it does in the GAA, then there is no need for other rules. The GAA is big enough and strong enough to implement its own rules without having additional bans to do the work for them,' concluded O'Rourke.

The man who devotes much of his spare time to coaching with St Patrick's in Navan watches and loves all sports. O'Rourke, who loves travelling abroad for holidays has also visited many of the world's greatest sport stadia including the Nou Camp in Barcelona where he saw Manchester United complete the dream treble of the English League, FA Cup and the European Championship. Outside of Gaelic games, horse racing is his favourite pastime and he loves nothing better than to go to a race meeting in Fairyhouse, the Curragh or Navan. O'Rourke, who has ownership shares in a few horses attributes his attraction for flat racing to his friendship with champion trainer Jim Bolger.

In October 1998, the GAA and the Australian Football league authorities revived the Compromise Rules Series which last took place in 1990. Twenty-three thousand people turned up to see the first test match in Croke Park only to see the Aussies snatch a last-minute victory on a score of 62 pts to 61 pts. Despite a sterling performance by the Irish, the management team of Colm O'Rourke and his assistants Mickey Moran (Derry) and John O'Keeffe (Kerry) were not happy with some of the more physical aspects of the Aussie game. Having witnessed at first hand some of the fights that marred the 1986 and 1990 series, O'Rourke was determined that if the series was to have a meaningful future all dangerous tackling and brawls must be eliminated. So, after the first test both management teams and referees met and discussed what needed to be done to secure a viable future for the series.

The second and deciding test on the following Sunday was a showpiece for all that is good within both codes. Thirty-five thousand people attended and thousands more watched on television as each side proceeded to enthral us all with a scintillating display of great fetching and brilliant scores. Played at a breathtaking pace, the chants of 'Ireland, Ireland,' as the Irish spectators indulged in Mexican waving made for compulsive entertainment. When Ireland won the second test by an eleven-point margin, they had secured the series on an aggregate total of 128 to 118. As well as a national victory, the occasion was especially sweet for Irish manager, Colm O'Rourke.

In October 1999, Ireland, again under the leadership of Colm O'Rourke, travelled to Australia to play a two-test series. The games were tremendously successful as 60,000 spectators turned up for the first test in Melbourne and 46,000 attended the second test in Adelaide. Both countries were exceptionally pleased, not only with the superb, competitive displays of athleticism but also by the huge media interest. There is no doubt that the Rules Series provides a meaningful international outlet for Gaelic football and Australian Rules.

'Colm O'Rourke has been good for Gaelic football and Gaelic football has reciprocated. In 1986, O'Rourke toured Australia as a player with the Compromise Rules Test team. He vividly recalls how enjoyable it was. 'It was a marvellous opportunity to train for a month under one of the all time great GAA coaches, Kevin Heffernan. Seeing the MCG stadium in Melbourne where Ronnie Delaney won his Olympic gold medal in 1956, visiting the Grand Opera House in Sydney and the most beautiful city I have ever seen – Perth – in Western Australia as well as Freemantle with all its wonderful watersports made me appreciate the beauty of the world that we live in.'

One day in January 1992, Colm O'Rourke nearly bade farewell to this valley of tears. Along with fellow Meath players Liam Harnan and Kevin Foley, Colm was swimming in the balmy waters off the coast of Fort Lauderdale in Florida. Suddenly, a mighty undercurrent drove the three men relentlessly seawards and out of their depth. They were on a 16-day holiday courtesy of the Meath team sponsor, Kepak, and the Leinster Council of the GAA who rewarded them for the exploits in the 1991 Leinster championship with a huge financial contribution. After all the skill, power and utter determination that they had displayed through all their footballing lives they found themselves helpless against the force of nature. Forunately, a vigilant lifeguard high upon his perch some 50 metres away noticed the imminent danger and dispatched three colleagues to where Colm, Liam and Kevin were literally 'on their last legs'. Safely and gratefully, they were escorted back to the shore. After all those years of playing on the fields of Ireland, Colm and Meath had won their greatest victory in the waters off Florida. Meath had again been rescued when all seemed lost.

When Colm O'Rourke looks back on all these experiences from 1975 to 1995 he is very happy. In the past, Gaelic football made him what he was. Today he has helped considerably to make it what it is.

Michael 'Babs' Keating

ON TUESDAY 7 JULY 1998, just after 5 p.m., the telephone rang in RTE's newsroom. Popular newsreader, Colm Murray, took the call. Just two days had elapsed since Kilkenny defeated Offaly in the Leinster senior hurling final. The current midlanders' manager was sensationally poised to draw the curtain on his managerial career. That man, Michael 'Babs' Keating, was desperately anxious to publicly announce his decision.

'Colm, would you take a personal statement for the Sports Department?' enquired the frustrated and annoyed Tipperary native.

'I wish to announce my immediate resignation as Offaly senior hurling manager,' concluded the somewhat controversial supremo.

Those 12 succinct words were to signal the end of an inter-county hurling career that began in 1960. Then, at the tender age of 16, Michael first donned the blue and gold of Tipperary when he played for their minor hurling team. In the interim he had played football and hurling at county and interprovincial level. In addition he had collected three senior All-Ireland hurling medals as a player and two more as a manager with the Premier county.

When he put down the phone, Babs was both a relieved and relaxed man. During the previous few weeks, a series of events had gradually made him totally disenchanted with Offaly hurling. Why should he punish himself any further? After all, he had been an integral part of the competitive thrust for success both as a player and a manager with Tipperary. The internecine problems of managing another county team were superfluous to his needs. These were the main thoughts that permeated the inner sanctum of his mind as he reflected on how everything had looked so different, such a short time previously.

The events of that July evening were the sad culmination of all that had occurred since Michael Keating took up the position of Offaly manager in the previous October. After an initial meeting with County Secretary Christy Todd and a further meeting with the Chairman, Brendan Ward, Keating decided to accept the position of Offaly team manager.

'From a selfish point of view it appealed to me because Offaly had the talent, if properly organised, to win an All-Ireland. As the new league did not begin until the following February, there was plenty of time to plan our tactics for the following year's championship. Wisely, the County board told me not to worry about the league.'

Eight members of the Offaly hurling panel were on the Birr club side which had ambitions to win the All-Ireland club championship. Their successful campaign meant that these players were not available until after St Patrick's Day. 'In my job with Esso, I was very familiar with the county's geography and it was much closer to my home in Dublin as opposed to Tipperary. So there would be much less travelling involved than when I was managing my home county,' stated 'Babs' when I met him in his Castleknock home.

In preparing the team for the championship, Keating enlisted the expert guidance of old friend Colonel John Murray to train the side and two selectors, Paudge Mulhaire and Pat McLoughney, were also appointed. When the 1998 campaign opened on 24 May, Offaly easily accounted for Meath. However, three weeks later, they were decidedly lucky to overcome Wexford in the provincial semi-final by the minimum of margins – 1-15 to 0-17. Still, a win was a win and Babs, along with his co-selectors, relished the clash with old rivals, Kilkenny in the Leinster final. Nevertheless, as the final approached, it became clear that two key members of the Offaly defence, Hubert Rigney and Kevin Kinahan, would be missing through injury. This, according to Babs, made their task against Kilkenny extremely difficult. So despite Offaly giving a somewhat lacklustre display, Babs was not too disappointed at suffering a five-point defeat to the Noresiders in the Leinster final. After all, he reckoned they were still in the championship (thanks to the back-door system, which allowed defeated provincial finalists into the All-Ireland quarter finals). They had the potential to improve considerably and would, hopefully, have the injured duo back for the next game.

'If everything appeared so rosy, what led you to resign in the immediate aftermath of the Leinster final?' I asked.

According to Keating, there was a combination of reasons. In order to deal with this whole contentious issue in its totality, Keating made the following points to me.

1. There was a history of indiscipline in Offaly hurling. The two previous managers encountered this inherent problem. Despite managing Offaly to an All-Ireland title in 1994, Eamon Cregan left two years later. Likewise, when former Tipperary player, John McIntyre, came in to replace Cregan he had the same problem to deal with. As a consequence, he was not reappointed.

2. When the County board asked Keating to become manager they stressed how important it was to ensure that the players were fairly and firmly disciplined. It was because of his track record in this regard that they wanted him as manager.

3. Along with his management team, Keating set the same training programme and the same targets as he had done all his management life. Everything was geared to having the team at peak fitness in the middle of May. A profile on

each player and a computer printout of each player's progress was updated on a weekly basis. In other words, a very professional approach was adopted.

4. A week after Tipperary had been defeated by Waterford in the 1998 Munster senior hurling championship, his old friend and former colleague, Donie Nealon, remarked to him that Tipperary had played like a 'flock of sheep in a heap.' This was the phrase that was to haunt 'Babs' and ultimately lead to his resignation from Offaly.

5. So, when journalist Vincent Hogan asked him for his views of the Leinster final he remarked that Offaly had played like a 'flock of blooming sheep in a heap.' According to Keating, it was just a flippant comment. He understood that the players took exception to the use of the word sheep. He did not mean it negatively and it was not said to be hurtful.

6. When Vincent Hogan used his passing comment as a banner headline in the *Irish Independent* on the Monday following the game, Keating was annoyed. On reflection, this article was the catalyst that was to initiate a chain reaction against him in Offaly. Furthermore, he was incensed that Hogan should write such an article. After all, Keating had given the Tipperary-born journalist free access to his winning Tipperary team during the All-Ireland final of 1991.

7. In the weeks prior to the Leinster final, his experience told him that certain things were not right in the Offaly camp. He could not pinpoint them exactly but he sensed disapproving vibes. The players definitely showed great commitment but two distinctively negative signals surfaced – one from the County chairman and one from his fellow selectors.

8. Since his time as manager of Tipperary, a young eleven-year-old boy, Pádraig Roche, son of former jockey Christy Roche, always travelled with Babs to matches. On the Tuesday night prior to the Leinster final, the chairman informed Keating not to bring Padraig to the Leinster final. He thought that this was insensitive, to say the least, particularly as it was done publicly in front of five or six people.

9. On that Tuesday night also, his two fellow selectors did not follow the normal consensus approach when selecting the team. They basically had decided between themselves what the team would be. This especially galled Keating because he had asked them to glance over the players during the pre-training warm up.

10. On the Thursday night before the game, one of his fellow selectors lambasted the players. In Keating's opinion, it was the most viciously worded address that he had ever heard in any dressing room. But what really infuriated him was the fact that no one subsequently seemed remotely upset about this speech. According to Keating, his 'sheep' comments were exceptionally mild by

comparison. Keating himself did not say anything on that occasion as he was unwell and under medical supervision.

11. After the final on the Sunday, Keating gave a short address to the players and was very kind and generous in his comments to them. He stressed that they would continue with the same training programme for the All-Ireland quarter-final. Then, suddenly, star player Brian Whelehan, turned on some of his colleagues. He thanked 'Babs' for what he had said but added, 'if we had not so many fellows drinking last night we might have played better!' Keating thanked Whelehan for his contribution but told him that he should have been made aware of this before the game. If he had done so, and had been informed of the names of the offending players, Keating would not have allowed those players to play in the game.

12. On the Monday night after the game, the County board officials and the management team met. They discussed all the aspects of the previous day's game and agreed on what they intended to do for the future of Offaly hurling. At the outset of the meeting, Keating apologised to the County board and his fellow selectors regarding the 'sheep' comment. He explained the background to them with specific reference to Donie Nealon and explained that he did not mean them in the way they were presented by Vincent Hogan. He also said that he intended to apologise directly to the players at the next training session. However, the main business of that evening's discussion centred on Brian Whelehan's dressing room outburst.

13. On the following day (Tuesday) the County chairman, Brendan Ward, contacted Keating seeking another meeting with him that night. When Babs asked him why was there a need for another meeting he said: 'Things are not right in Offaly.' Keating agreed with him but his mind and thoughts were now crystallised. He would leave the Faithful County. He had said all he had wanted to say the previous evening. Keating had thought there was unanimity on the way forward and that his promised apology to the players would be the end of the saga. As thoughts of further meetings, hassle, misunderstandings, protracted issues flashed across his mind. Babs instantly decided enough was enough, so he said to chairman Ward:

'Brendan, do you know what you'll do now. Turn on the RTE news at six o'clock and you will hear enough from me.' He put down the telephone and mentally left all thoughts of Offaly hurling behind him.

'How did you feel when Galway's Michael Bond took over the team after that and then subsequently steered them to All-Ireland success?' I ventured.

'I was happy for the players and for Michael to see Offaly win. I was even happier for myself as I had backed them at 12 to 1. So my wife, Nancy, and myself got a free Christmas holiday in Dubai as a result,' concluded Babs.

For Michael Keating, the Offaly experience had followed two years of frustration as manager of Laois a short time previously. In early September 1995 he was asked to become manager of Laois senior hurling team. Impressed with the commitment of chairman Tom Hassett and secretary Michael Carroll, Babs decided to devote himself wholeheartedly to improving the status of Laois hurling. Along with selectors Seán Cuddy, Michael Peters, and trainer John Murray, they prepared the Laois team diligently. Their hard work was rewarded when they achieved their prime target of getting Laois promoted to Division One of the National Hurling League in the spring of 1996. The progress was further enhanced when Laois reached the semi-final of the league. Babs had restored pride to the O'Moore County.

Michael Keating had been singularly responsible for his company, Esso, sponsoring Laois for the two years he was in charge. However, his generosity was not reciprocated. When Babs took up the position, he had been promised a 'good deal' by a person outside the County board. This promise had never been fulfilled, even though the officers of the Laois County board had always acted very honourably towards him. That salient fact, along with the growing realisation that the Laois players were not sustaining their commitment made Keating decide to resign. This he did when they were knocked out of the 1997 Leinster championship. Laois won't win anything until they have more commitment. They are not prepared to learn. They do not wish to be compared to anyone. Underage hurling in the county is a disaster,' stated the brusque Keating.

This whole episode of his experiences of managing both Offaly and Laois were a far cry from Keating's achievements, both as a player and as a manager with his native Tipperary. Born in Grange, on a small farm in south Tipperary in what was essentially a football part of the county, Babs took to the small ball game with great enthusiasm. This was principally due to the influence of his father who regaled him with stories of great Tipperary hurling sides of the past. In addition he recalled how his own uncle, Tom Ryan, had played football in Croke Park on Bloody Sunday. So Babs became a lover of both codes, though in the beginning, hurling was to take precedence. Annual pilgrimages to Cork, Limerick and Thurles reinforced the love of hurling in the young Keating.

He credits one of the Christian Brothers, Br Collins, at the high school in Clonmel for making a hurler out of him. In three successive years – 1960 to 1962, Babs played for Tipperary in an All-Ireland minor hurling final only to be on the losing side on each occasion. One outstanding feat of Babs at this time was that he played on the minor and senior county football teams on the same day in the 1962 Munster championships.

When he made his senior hurling debut for the county in a challenge game against Galway in 1963, Babs had realised his first major dream. In the following year, 1964, Keating played in his first All-Ireland hurling final against Kilkenny. Giving a superlative performance at left half forward he was selected as the *Irish Independent's* Sportstar of the Week. A new hurling icon was born. His native Grange welcomed home, with open arms, its first All-Ireland senior hurling medal holder. Of all the magnificent moments that were to occur in his life, this was the most satisfying of all. To see his father, Dan, who had done so much to revive hurling in this part of Tipperary, smile so happily made the young Keating a very fulfilled individual.

Owing to an injury and a consequential loss of form, Keating was only a sub on the Tipperary side that won the following year's All-Ireland title against Wexford. Keating was to play in two further All-Irelands in 1967 and 1968, which Tipperary lost to Kilkenny and Wexford respectively, before he made his final winning appearance in Tipperary's victory of 1971. In this, the first eighty-minute All-Ireland, Tipperary won by three points. This victory was especially sweet for Keating and their great centre half back, Mick Roche, as they were the only remaining playing members of the 1964 team. What made that year even more significant for Keating was the fact that he was selected as Texaco Hurler of the Year as well as being picked as centre half forward on the first All Stars hurling team.

Four years later, in 1975, Keating retired from the game that he had graced for so long. When he won a Railway Cup Football medal in 1972 he had joined that elite group of individuals who had won Railway Cup medals in both codes. That, allied to the 1971 All-Ireland success, paved the way for Keating's eventual retirement. He had achieved much more than most. It was time to move on.

During the following ten years Keating had, briefly, been a Tipperary hurling selector as well as being their football manager in 1980. However, an inkling of what the future held in store for him was the fact that he managed a Joe McDonagh-led Galway to the 1979 senior All-Ireland hurling final. He was disappointed that he was not asked to remain on and this was further exacerbated the following year when Galway won their first senior title since 1923. Nevertheless, the call that he always yearned for came in September 1986 when he was asked to manage Tipperary. Until 1994, Michael Keating and Tipperary hurling were destined to become inseparable.

Through the foresight of County chairman and TD, Michael Lowry, Keating was allowed to appoint his two selectors. This appealed very much to Babs and he chose former playing colleague and Munster GAA secretary Donie Nealon and work colleague and former fellow player Theo English. At this stage, Tipperary hurling was perceived to be in a 'state of chassis.' No All-Ireland, and worse no Munster title, had been attained for 15 years. At the first team meeting, Keating told the players that they had the talent to win the coveted Liam McCarthy cup. What was required was a belief in themselves that they could do it. To achieve their ultimate goal, total commitment and dedication was essential on the part of players and management. In order for players to be treated properly, Keating was instrumental in setting up the Tipperary Supporters Club – the first of its kind in Ireland. The finance that accrued from this ensured that players' expenses were paid promptly, proper accommodation was provided and good playing gear was always obtained. Thus, a new, mutual respect developed between players and management.

In his first season in charge, Keating led Tipperary from Division Two to Division One of the National Hurling League in the spring of 1987. Defeating Kerry in the first round of the Munster championship, Tipperary went on to defeat Clare, at the second attempt, quite comfortably in the Munster semi-final. In a pulsating encounter, Tipperary and Cork drew in the Munster final. The replay in Killarney has been labelled as one of the greatest games of all time. Cork led by a five-point margin at the interval. Thanks to the individual brilliance of ace forward, Nicholas English, a resurgent Tipperary pegged back the deficit. When the final whistle sounded the sides were level. A spontaneous standing ovation then acknowledged the magnificence of the spectacle that a packed Fitzgerald Stadium had just witnessed. In extra time, substitute Michael Doyle (son of the legendary John) scored two wonderful goals to seal victory for the Premier county on a scoreline of 4-22 to 1-22. When Tipperary captain Richard Stakelum began singing 'Slievenamon' on receiving the Munster Cup, all Tipperary supporters were ecstatic in their excitement. A 16-year famine of Munster titles had ended. However, a subsequent six-point defeat to Galway in the All-Ireland semi-final tempered, somewhat, the initial euphoria.

When they again defeated the Rebel county in the 1988 Munster final, hopes were high that Tipperary would make the long-awaited breakthrough at national level. Beating Antrim in the All-Ireland semi-final brought them within sight of the finishing line. However, a thoroughly competent team display by Galway again prevented that happening. Notwithstanding this, Babs was happy. Each year his side had progressed one step further in the championship.

In 1989, Tipperary cruised to their third successive Munster title, defeating Waterford 0-26 to 2-8. When they conquered Galway by a three-point margin in the All-Ireland semi-final, the whole county held its breath. This was because they were playing a so-called weaker county – Antrim – in the final. The Glensmen had unexpectedly accounted for Offaly in the other semi-final. In a magnificent cameo of hurling artistry, Nicholas English amassed a total of 2-12 in an easy 18-point defeat of a deflated Antrim side. Babs' promise of three years previously, when he first met the players, had been delivered. The famine was over. Nevertheless, an oft-quoted phrase of Keating's 'a pat on the back is only six inches from a kick in the backside' soon came to pass. The euphoria of Tipp's first All-Ireland in 18 years soon evaporated. When Cork defeated Tipperary in the Munster final of 1990 the cynics had a field day. As Tipperary had not defeated a 'traditional' county such as Kilkenny or Wexford in the 1989 final, that victory was now infamously referred to as a 'Woolworth's title.' This hurt Babs and made him more determined as the Munster championship of 1991 commenced.

However, Babs and Tipperary silenced their cynical critics by the way in which they claimed the 1991 All-Ireland Championship. It was time to get tough and this Keating did by decrying all dissent as 'not being worthy of real hurling men.' In a rallying cry after losing to Offaly in the semi-final of the 1991 National Hurling League, Keating effectively told his players to 'buckle down and shut up or leave the squad.' The players responded brilliantly as they crushed Limerick in the Munster semi-final.

The Munster final was against their deadly rivals, Cork. In a game of power and pace, of exhilarating momentum, the tide ebbed and flowed as, first Cork and then Tipperary assumed control. Nevertheless, it took a last-minute, angled point from Pat Fox to snatch an equaliser for the men in blue and gold. In the replay, Tipp's cause looked in vain when half way through the second half they found themselves nine points in arrears. In a magnificent fightback, led by substitutes Aidan Ryan and Joe Hayes, Tipperary eventually overcame Cork to win by four points. It was a truly remarkable achievement that underlined the indomitable spirit Keating had ignited within each player. Now he would show the fickle supporters who doubted the real merits of his team. To emphasise this, a fading Galway side were overwhelmed 3-13 to 1-9 in the All-Ireland semi-final. Now, Tipperary would be facing a 'real' hurling county – Kilkenny – in the final. In a poor quality game, Tipperary, after a slow start, triumphed 1-16 to 0-15. The residual apathy towards the 1989 success and the bitterness towards Babs because of his controversial removal of Theo English as a selector dissipated with the final whistle. For the second time, as a manager, Keating had steered Tipperary to the Liam McCarthy Cup. No one could argue with that. In his opinion, Keating had nothing further to prove.

Babs Keating stayed on as manager for three more years during which another Munster title was annexed. Despite winning the National Hurling League against Galway in 1994 Tipperary were sensationally knocked out of the Munster championship a few weeks later, against Clare. After eight years in charge, Keating decided to resign. Losing his dominant influence, internal County board politics and mounting injuries all contrived to make up Babs' mind. The Clare result had merely compounded his decision. Anyhow he felt that he had restored Tipperary's status as a hurling county worthy of the name.

When it comes to airing his views on the present state of hurling, Keating is, as always, forthcoming. 'The ball should be larger and heavier. Scores are too easily obtained from long distances and midfield play is practically eliminated. For spectators, especially those not familiar with the game, the ball is going too fast for them to follow it.'

Keating would also abolish the so-called square ball in both football and hurling. 'It is impossible, very often, for a referee to adjudicate whether or not this rule is being infringed, especially when the ball is high in the air. This leads to conflicting decisions. For example, in similar circumstances, in the 1992 All-Ireland football semi-final between Dublin and Clare, Dublin were awarded a goal and Clare denied one.'

Referring to his proud record of only having one player sent off in his Tipperary managerial career, Keating maintains that the GAA should put more pressure on managers to instil discipline in their teams. 'Before every game the referee should visit each dressing room and say, "Listen, I'm here to do an honest job. If anyone indulges in any blackguardism let him face the consequences." In my final team talk before any major game I devoted ten minutes to a discussion on discipline. It was made clear that the game alone should be focused on. Anyone sent off was doing a disservice to his team.'

Welcoming the decision of the 1999 GAA Congress to have central bodies for the appointment of referees and the implementation of disciplinary procedures, Keating nevertheless, had this to say on refereeing standards. 'While I do not condone, in any way, the cowardly attack on leading referee Mick Curley at the Cavan v Wexford game in 1999, I think he was responsible for not awarding a blatant penalty in a football league game a few weeks previously between Derry and Monaghan. Mick is one of our top referees. If he makes such a mistake, something is missing. This is one area where the GAA has to show considerable improvement. Players train too hard for too long to be on the wrong end of a bad refereeing or indeed umpiring decision.'

Keating also highlights his view that both the current hurling and football National Leagues are being treated by the GAA as inferior competitions. He is of the opinion that these should be given a new lease of life by organising a two-week holiday to Florida or the Bahamas for that year's league winners in both codes. The All-Ireland senior hurling championship should also be revamped according to Keating. 'This should take place on two separate levels. Galway should be included in the Munster championship and Antrim in the Leinster championship. The provincial finalists in those two provinces would then be paired against each other in the All-Ireland hurling semi-finals. All the remaining counties including the weaker teams from Munster and Leinster should be put into a separate championship of their own. This should be played concurrently with the All-Ireland senior championship. The winners of this competition should be rewarded with a luxurious two-week sun holiday. This would help those counties to develop at their own level and to achieve realistic targets.'

To emphasise how lowly the hurling league is rated in the GAA's pecking order Keating points to one undisputed fact. After leading their respective counties to National League success many managers, in recent years, were dispensed with within a few short weeks of their success. He cites the following as examples of this: Fr

Michael O'Brien (Cork), Tom Ryan (Limerick), Mattie Murphy (Galway), Ollie Walsh (Kilkenny) and himself.

Having discussed a whole plethora of GAA issues, both current and past, Keating is adamant about what the GAA's role in Irish life is. 'I could not imagine a situation without the GAA. I hate to see it criticised mainly because of what it has done for me and thousands like me in rural Ireland. However, the future of the GAA is in urban Ireland. Hundreds of coaches and development officers should be sponsored by the GAA and sent in to all urban areas particularly the cities of Dublin, Belfast, Cork, Derry, Limerick and Galway. As well, it is the responsibility of each Provincial Council and each County board to develop Gaelic Games within the schools which do not play Gaelic Games and which are under their jurisdiction,' added the loquacious Michael.

Now as he looks back upon the glories and disappointments of the past, Babs (so called because there were two other older Michael Keatings in his primary school classroom) savours the present. True, he has many fantastic memories both as a player and as a manager. Those All-Ireland victories, naturally, take pride of place. He is privileged to have played alongside some of the greatest hurlers Tipperary have ever produced – men such as John Doyle, Theo English, Donie Nealon and Liam Devaney. And yet, two other players stand above all others in Keating's affections. 'Mick Roche was the best all-round hurler that I ever saw and top class forward Jimmy Doyle was the most accurate striker of a ball that I had the good fortune to witness.'

That phone call to RTE in July 1998 may have terminated one aspect of Babs life but it certainly reawakened him to the much wider picture of society. 'Now I intend to spend the rest of my life resting and relaxing with my wife Nancy, son Michael, and daughter Orla who is married to champion jockey Johnny Murtagh. My family, our health and our enjoyment of life especially golf and racing means most to me now,' concluded Michael when I met him on his 55th birthday in April 1999.

Michael Keating may have trod the managerial touchlines for the last time but his talents, successes and even his controversies have left a positive indelible imprint. This has not only impressed our minds but indeed impacted upon the great game of hurling. Four decades of Gaelic games commitment has seen to that.

Martin McHugh

AT THE AGE OF four, Martin McHugh's next door neighbour, Hugh Shovlin, brought Máirtín Beag, as he was known in his native area, into the fields around Kilcar in West Donegal. There, for the next eight years, Hugh and Martin played football day and night. By the time he had left his local primary school Martin had perfected all the skills of Gaelic football. The ability to side-step an opponent, at will, was his greatest forte. When he went to Carrick Vocational School his talents were spotted by school coach Barry Campbell who made Martin the lynchpin of his forward line for the school team at each of the different age levels. That school team duly won the county title in each of those age groupings enabling Martin to amass the remarkable total of eight county vocational medals. In his final year Martin was selected on the county senior vocational team where midfielder Packie Bonner was later to achieve fame as a Glasgow Celtic and Republic of Ireland World Cup star. From the two clubs that supplied the majority of players to Carrick school, four past pupils, Martin, his brother James, Noel Hegarty and John Joe Doherty subsequently won All-Ireland senior football medals with Donegal in 1992. Martin attributes that record to the wonderful work that Barry Campbell put in.

In 1979, Martin McHugh was not considered good enough to make the Donegal minor side. One year later, Martin's career took off after a virtuoso performance in the 1980 county championship final for Kilcar against Ardara. Both from play and frees he accumulated a total of ten points in a 1-13 to 0-9 scoreline. Watching the game was county manager Brian McEniff who immediately promoted the teenager on to the Donegal senior panel. In October of that year McHugh made his debut in a National League game against Tipperary. His three points on that day obliterated any lack of self-confidence and for the following 14 years all Donegal supporters broke into frenzied excitement whenever the wee man from Kilcar had the ball.

In 1981, McHugh starred for the Donegal U-21 side which suffered a narrow two-point defeat to Monaghan in the Ulster final. Playing alongside McHugh were future soccer stars Denis Bonner and Charlie McGeever. The following year, with McHugh playing at right half forward, Donegal gave a glimpse of greater things to come when they not only annexed the Ulster U-21 title but the All-Ireland as well.

In the All-Ireland final, the magnificent McHugh scored five of Donegal's eight points in a three-point victory over Roscommon. Included in that Donegal team were five players who would star on All-Ireland final day a decade later. Along with McHugh,

Anthony Molloy, Donal Reid, Matt Gallagher and Joyce McMullen were the men who were destined to inscribe their names indelibly in the history of Donegal football.

The following year, with McHugh in sparkling form, Donegal notched their third senior provincial championship when they defeated Cavan in the decider. Though they lost by a mere point to Galway in the All-Ireland semi-final, McHugh was not too despondent as Donegal were now playing much better as a team than heretofore. When Donegal won another All-Ireland U-21 title in 1987 he was impressed with the talented members of that side which included John Joe Doherty, John Cunningham, Barry McGowan, Manus Boyle, Tommy Ryan and Barry Cunningham. Now he knew that those players, when added to the quality players that they already possessed should contribute to a winning championship side.

Two years later, McEniff, using basically the nucleus of those two All-Ireland U-21 sides, steered Donegal to another Ulster final, losing out after a replay with Tyrone. When Donegal annexed the Ulster title the following year, 1990, McEniff, McHugh and company were delighted. Another rung on the upward ladder to All-Ireland glory had been climbed. Having been promoted to Division One of the League, they were expected to do well in the All-Ireland series but as in the past they seemed to lose their way on the big occasion and flopped to an eight-point defeat to Meath. They reached their third successive Ulster final in 1991 against Down. Again, probably due to a certain amount of complacency and the fact that they were missing key players such as midfielder Anthony Molloy and stout defender Martin Shovlin, Donegal succumbed to a heavy defeat by Down. McHugh however, still saw light at the end of the dark tunnel. Down had played brilliantly and his optimism was justified when Down went on to win that year's All-Ireland.

A determined McEniff promised that 1992 would finally be the year that Donegal would achieve the Holy Grail. When Donegal had another good league run and led Dublin by four points with four minutes to go in the League quarter-final, McEniff's prophecy seemed to be coming true. Incredibly, Donegal's defence lost their composure and within the space of two minutes, Dublin scored two goals. Soon afterwards the final whistle sounded. 'Would Donegal ever win any senior national title?' was the most common query as they began the 1992 Ulster championship campaign.

In the first round of that year's provincial championship against Cavan, Martin McHugh sent a tremendous 50-yard kick over the bar to edge Donegal in front as the game neared its end. Then, as the referee looked at his watch, Cavan's Damien O'Reilly volleyed the ball over the bar for a sensational equaliser. Having comprehensively beaten the Breffnimen in the replay, Donegal then easily accounted for Fermanagh in the Ulster semi-final. This was their fourth successive Ulster decider. Though their opponents, Derry, had come through the much tougher half of the draw and had overcome All-Ireland champions Down in a very impressive semi-final performance, Donegal were ready. It was now or never.

The first half of the final was a see-saw affair. With the wind in their favour Donegal did not dominate and when new star full forward Tony Boyle was injured, Donegal's case for success looked rather bleak. When corner back John Cunningham was sent off before half time, Donegal's chances looked even more remote.

'At half time that day, we all made a conscious decision that we must play the game of our lives. If we didn't win that match, the future for a lot of us was not good. Too many of us were reaching the veteran stage. It would have almost been physically and mentally impossible to start another championship campaign if we did not win against Derry,' stated McHugh when I met him in the Abbey Hotel in Donegal town.

In that second half, Donegal played the best football imaginable in such adverse circumstances. Like a top-class conductor with a leading orchestra McHugh directed that fine second-half performance. Always available for broken ball in the vital midfield sector, he ran, kicked and passed like a true master craftsman. One fabulous point, which he kicked over his right shoulder, is still talked about as one of the game's remarkable highlights. His astute brain and exquisite football dictated Donegal's necessary possession game and frustrated any Derry moves. When the full-time whistle sounded, Donegal had won by two points.

It was the All-Ireland semi-final against Mayo that McHugh really feared. After their brilliant display against Derry, Donegal were rated hot favourites to reach their first senior All-Ireland final. Even though, in terms of possession, Donegal began well against Mayo, a definite nervousness appeared rampant throughout the team. Wide after wide ensued and by half time the Ulstermen trailed the Westerners 0-8 to 0-6.

As the second half progressed, there was no visible improvement in Donegal's scoring rate. Then manager McEniff made two positional switches, which helped sway the balance. Manus Boyle, renowned as a man for the big occasion but not for his work rate, came into the forward line. Barry Cunningham, who had just returned from America, was brought in at centrefield. Cunningham steadied the team with some fine fetching and Manus Boyle with three pointed frees instilled a new-found confidence in the whole team. At last Donegal converted their possession into scores and went on to record a 0-13 to 0-9 victory.

'Now I knew we would win the All-Ireland. We had proved ourselves when we were up against it in the Ulster final and we had rediscovered our confidence in the latter stages of the Mayo match. The jinx of never winning an All-Ireland semi-final was gone. I will never forget, before the end of the Mayo game, when we were leading 0-12 to 0-9 and were awarded a penalty. When Brian McEniff nodded for Declan Bonner to put the ball over the bar and he did so, I knew we had won. It was both a relief and a joy to hear that full-time whistle,' added Martin who trained twice a day every day of his fourteen-year career – an hour in the morning and another hour in the evening.

McEniff left no stone unturned as he prepared his side physically, tactically and mentally for the greatest day in the history of Gaelic football in Donegal. He reckoned, correctly, that the major strength of their Dublin opponents stemmed from their half back line. Their attacking flair, with centre half back Keith Barr being especially prominent, was the platform on which their attacks were launched. If Donegal were to succeed, McEniff stressed that the forward movements of the Dublin half back line would have to be curtailed. Central to the implementation of this strategy was centre half forward Martin McHugh. In his primary role McHugh was the playmaker of the Donegal team. In addition, he would now have to fulfil a very important secondary role. He would have to prevent his opposite number, Keith Barr, from attacking.

When the game began, Dublin took early control and went two points ahead. After Dublin's Charlie Redmond missed a penalty in the ninth minute, Donegal got a huge psychological lift. With the whole team now rapidly gaining in confidence and putting their pre-match plan into action they took the game to their more vaunted opposition. The whole forward line, expertly managed by Martin McHugh, continually pressed the Dublin defence. Manus Boyle (3), Declan Bonner (2), Martin McHugh (3), James McHugh (1) and Tony Boyle (1) all scored to enable Donegal lead at the interval 0-10 to 0-7.

At half time, Brian McEniff just told them to keep playing as they were. If they did so, he said that there would be a marvellous homecoming to Donegal the following evening. For the first 25 minutes of the second half, Man of the Match Manus Boyle scored four points (three from frees) and Declan Bonner added another free to Dublin's two points to leave the score at 0-15 to 0-9. With just ten minutes to go, Dublin suddenly realised the urgency of their plight. In a glorious three-minute spell they had reduced the deficit to a meagre three points. Then, Manus Boyle and Charlie Redmond exchanged points to leave the score 0-16 to 0-13, as the game entered the last five minutes. A minute later, the ever-reliable Manus Boyle raised the white flag again. It was his ninth and Donegal's 17th point of the game. Just before the end, Paul Clarke pointed for Dublin before Declan Bonner sent over the insurance point, a brilliantly angled effort. Seconds later the full-time whistle went and Donegal had won, not only their first senior All-Ireland title, but the hearts of a nation by their imaginative, creative style of play.

Martin McHugh was overjoyed. He had implemented Brian McEniff's plan to perfection, chasing and harassing Barr on the rare occasions that he did gain possession. Before the game, McHugh had psyched himself up so that under no circumstances would he let Barr up the field. The one time that Keith did manage to escape McHugh's attention, An Fear Beag raced back and blocked his kick. He was particularly proud of that block. 'When the game ended and before I could start to enjoy myself, I put my pre-match contingency plan into action. I had planned to get the match ball when Donegal won. So, as the full-time whistle approached and I knew we were going to win I placed myself, judiciously, near the referee. When the whistle sounded, Declan Bonner had fallen heavily to the ground as the ball broke from him. I ran in and dived on the ball, grabbed it and ignored referee Tommy Sugrue as he ran over to claim it. I still have the ball at home with the autographs of all the team on it. It is a precious possession. Nobody can touch it now. I was so confident that Donegal would win that I had planned in advance how I would capture the ball,' recalled McHugh.

On that All-Ireland final night, after the celebrations in the Grand Hotel Malahide, Martin McHugh went to bed relatively early at 1.30 a.m. He wanted to get up early and savour all the festivities that were likely to be held during that week. The next morning the two McHugh boys – Martin and James, who had starred on the field of play the previous day, along with their wives, strolled around the streets of Dublin. Brothers in arms and brothers in blood they had, along with their county colleagues, achieved what was thought well nigh impossible at half-time in the Ulster final against Derry.

Initially, the tragic death of a Donegal youth in Dublin after the game marred the celebrations as had a false rumour, heard on entering the winners' dressing room, that a brother of one of the Donegal players had died. Nevertheless, as time passed, the whole ensuing week was a glorious outpouring of joy and emotion. The journey to Sligo by train, the marvellous reception through the counties of Longford, Leitrim and Sligo, and crossing the county border where the River Drowes welcomed them to their native county were golden memories of a fantastic time.

'Of all the great memories, my fondest is of going into the Diamond in Donegal town on the night following the game. Twenty-five thousand happy, cheering Donegal people waved and shouted. When they sang 'Simply the Best', my whole inner being became emotional. The next morning I went home, got our two-year-old son, Mark, and brought him to join the cavalcade as we journeyed around the county. Mark, who, incredibly, distinctly remembers the homecoming, was then placed in the cup as we headed to my home in Kilcar where it all began for me. As we approached my home parish, the bus stopped outside my parents' farmhouse. Personally, that was my proudest moment as I watched my father and mother shed tears of joy as their two small sons passed their homestead on their way to a tumultuous reception in Kilcar itself. Watching all my neighbours and friends share this splendid moment was an unforgettable experience.'

Martin McHugh played for two further championship seasons for Donegal before a torn medial ligament forced him to retire, prematurely, after the Ulster semi-final against Tyrone in 1994. When Brian McEniff retired shortly afterwards as Donegal manager, Martin was tipped by some to succeed him. In the event, PJ McGowan, who had the experience of managing the U-21 side, was given the position. However, Cavan chairman Brendan Keaney persuaded McHugh to manage both the Cavan senior and U-21 sides.

1. In Year One to have Cavan promoted from Division Three to Division Two of the National Football League and to defeat Antrim in the first round of the 1995 Ulster Championship.

   In the League Cavan were promoted and were only narrowly defeated by eventual National League winners, Derry, in the quarter-final. As well as beating Antrim they also defeated Monaghan only to lose to Tyrone in the Ulster final. Their display, however, was put into better perspective when Tyrone were decidedly unlucky to lose the 1995 All-Ireland against Dublin.

2. In Year Two to concentrate on the U-21 campaign and to gain promotion from Division Two to Division One of the National League.

   Not only were they promoted in the league but their U-21 side won the Ulster title and reached the All-Ireland final as well. In the All-Ireland semi-final, they beat Meath after a replay. Cavan supporters were now in festive mood as they went in their thousands to Semple Stadium in Thurles for the All-Ireland U-21 final against Kerry. On 8 September, 35,000 people watched a thrilling encounter though Cavan were always chasing the game. In the end, Kerry finished the stronger, winning by 1-17 to 2-10. However, the individual displays of captain Peter Reilly, Dermot McCabe, Terry Farrelly, Anthony Forde, Jason Reilly, Larry Reilly and Mickey Graham gave evidence of greater things to come. The whole episode was a personal triumph for McHugh. The second year's target had been reached with interest.

3. Year Three targets were simple
   (a) Retain Division One League status and
   (b) Win an Ulster senior football championship.

In January 1997 McHugh informed chairman Keaney that this would definitely be his last year in charge. While he had a nucleus of good footballers from the successful U-21 side, the backbone of this Cavan team consisted of many players in the twilight of their careers. Players such as Stephen King, Damien O'Reilly, Ronan Carolan and Fintan Cahill had been around a long time. McHugh realised that 1997 would have to be the year for a provincial success.

Surprisingly, Cavan and McHugh's championship plans nearly came unstuck in the first round when it took an injury-time point by substitute Anthony Forde to equalise against supposedly lowly Fermanagh. In another sub-standard performance, Cavan only won the replay by three points. In the Ulster semi-final, a wonderful display of whole-hearted endeavour plus accurate finishing in the last quarter ensured a famous victory for Cavan over Donegal. The players had responded magnificently to

McHugh's game plan even though the match was very much a game of conflicting emotions for Martin. While he was happy for Cavan, he was, nevertheless, disappointed that it was his native county who were on the receiving end.

'The Cavan players won the game themselves. The whole scene was very awkward for me and made me feel ill at ease. I was particularly close to most of the Donegal players, especially Declan Bonner, John Joe Doherty, Noel Hegarty and Tony Boyle. I let the Cavan players celebrate their own victory and I went back to Donegal to console their players. At the end of the day, Donegal is my native county. Cavan was the county that gave me a chance to cut my inter-county managerial teeth as it were. I will always be grateful to them for that,' added McHugh in a voice still filled with contrary feelings of emotion.

In the Ulster final, Cavan faced Derry. There was a great air of expectancy within the county that they would win their first senior provincial crown since 1969. That dream was still very much alive when both sides retired to the dressing rooms at half time on a score of nine points each. In the second half, Derry began to gain the upper hand and with nine minutes to go were leading 0-15 to 0-14. Then, long-serving Damien O'Reilly grabbed the ball in the Derry danger area and, though well shackled, he managed to flick the ball inside to speedy substitute Jason Reilly who sent it to the Derry net. Cavan were now leading 1-14 to 0-15. Despite intense pressure by Derry they could only manage a solitary Joe Brolly point before the final whistle sounded. The Cavan supporters were euphoric in their celebrations of this long-awaited provincial success. The famine of Ulster titles which had existed since 1969 was over. Martin McHugh had achieved his Year Three target and Cavan had restored pride to a historically great footballing county. In the All-Ireland semi-final, Cavan were paired against Kerry. On the day, Kerry were much the better side and in the end had an easy enough 1-17 to 1-10 victory.

As promised at the beginning of the season, Martin McHugh retired immediately after the All-Ireland semi-final. He had given three years of total commitment to Cavan football, attained his pre-ordained targets and restored morale to a football-loving county. McHugh had, proverbially speaking, brought Cavan out of the footballing wilderness into a respectable position on the Gaelic football landscape. 'The long hours of travelling and the considerable amount of time spent away from my young family of Mark (6), Ryan (3) and baby Rachel made life more difficult for my wife Patrice. On the three normal training days I left for work at 8.30 a.m. in the morning, then went to Cavan for training and was not back at home until 2 a.m. In the championship season, I had training on Saturday mornings as well as Friday nights so I stayed in Cavan on the Friday nights which meant that I was not home until Saturday evening. In addition, I usually had to go back to Cavan for a game on the Sunday. All in all, between travelling for my firm, Martin Donnelly of Clare and going to training I clocked up 300,000 miles. I just could not endure any more physical and mental anguish,' added McHugh.

Martin, who also had acted as his club's player/coach for several years, taking them to a county title success in 1989 is at present involved with the Donegal U-16 side. He was known as a very perceptive reader of the game on the field and has brought this prowess to the coaching sphere and to the studios of RTE and BBC where he has served as a Gaelic games analyst.

McHugh, who rates former All-Ireland winning captains DJ Kane (Down) and Henry Downey (Derry) as his most difficult opponents, maintains that the most talented footballer he has ever seen was Offaly's Matt Connor. 'Matt was the greatest, most skilful and naturally talented footballer of all. His close control was unbelievable and he was very strong – a wonderful athlete. I remember seeing him in the Kilmacud seven-a-side tournament kicking a curled point from the right-hand touch line and putting it over the black spot on the crossbar.'

The man whose favourite referees were Patsy Devlin (Tyrone) and Tommy Sugrue (Kerry) and present knight of the whistle Pat McEneaney, has immense respect for the fantastic promotional work that all GAA journalists do for Gaelic games. McHugh, who writes a column in *The Star* has tremendous regard for the professionalism and perfection of RTE's Ger Canning and BBC's Jimmy Smyth. However, his most memorable media experience was in much different circumstances. Just before his Ulster final debut for Donegal against Cavan in 1983, the team had a light lunch in a Clones hotel. McHugh was feeling very confident. Though he had not played in the semi-final, he had scored seven points in the first match against Derry. Then suddenly his boyhood hero, the masterly commentator Micheál Ó Hehir walked in. As meticulous as ever in his pre-match commentary preparation, he wanted to see the Donegal players standing up, one at a time. If they stood up, he said, he would be able to recognise them by their stance when they were on the football field. As McHugh stood up Ó Hehir said. 'I knew you were small, but I did not realise you were that small.' While still appreciating the greatness of Ó Hehir as a commentator, McHugh's hitherto confidence for playing in his first Ulster final disappeared with the casual remark of the GAA's best ever ambassador.

Referring to the future development of Gaelic football McHugh thinks its future success is dependent upon two major changes taking place, both in terms of competition structure and attitude within the GAA. 'Ideally, what Gaelic football requires is a full-round robin system for the All-Ireland championship. However, I feel at present that is not possible but I have no doubt in years to come that it will. My proposals for the future of Gaelic football are as follows:

1. I would run off the National League between February and May and then have the provincial championship

2. After the provincial championships had been decided, I would hold an open draw for the remaining 28 counties. The first round of the open draw would be on a two-leg, home and away basis. The overall winner would be the team with the highest aggregate score.

3. After the first round of the open draw was completed I would add in the four provincial champions and continue the All-Ireland championships on a knock-out basis. Before one could reach the last eight there would have to be extra games for some counties because of the mathematics involved.

The world revolves around money. If we got that competition structure in place and properly organised I have no doubt that considerably more revenue would flow into the coffers of the Association. Players give an unbelievable commitment to the game and that commitment should be rewarded in a tangible way. With so much pressure on people nowadays, the time for voluntary dedication to anything is fast disappearing. I believe that each year the County board in each county should draw up a contract with its inter-county panel of players and agree that each of them will be paid the same amount of money for 'X' number of games they play during that season. Tied in with that contract would be the condition that those players must continue to play with their native clubs or the clubs within the catchment area where they permanently reside. This latter proviso would eliminate the poaching of players by bigger clubs, especially in city areas. A large percentage of the extra revenue accrued from the extra games as well as corporate sponsorship should be used to finance these inter-county player contracts.'

Martin made the following Ulster and Ireland selections (no Donegal players were considered).

ULSTER

Brian McAlinden
(Armagh)

Kieran McKeever
(Derry)

Gerry McCarville
(Monaghan)

Tony Scullion
(Derry)

Eugene Hughes
(Monaghan)

Henry Downey
(Derry)

DJ Kane
(Down)

Anthony Tohill
(Derry)

Eugene McKenna
(Tyrone)

Peter McGinnity
(Fermanagh)

Joe Kernan
(Armagh)

Greg Blaney
(Down)

Mickey Linden
(Down)

Frank McGuigan
(Tyrone)

Peter Canavan
(Tyrone)

IRELAND (1990– Present)

John O'Leary
(Dublin)

Robbie O'Malley
(Meath)

Mick Lyons
(Meath)

Tony Scullion
(Derry)

DJ Kane
(Down)

Henry Downey
(Derry)

Séamus Moynihan
(Kerry)

Anthony Tohill
(Derry)

John McDermott
(Meath)

Trevor Giles
(Meath)

Greg Blaney
(Down)

Larry Tompkins
(Cork)

Mickey Linden
(Down)

Peter Canavan
(Tyrone)

Maurice Fitzgerald
(Kerry)

McHugh, who also believes that inter-county managers should be contracted to County boards, thinks the ban on foreign games in GAA grounds is outdated and hypocritical especially when pop concerts have taken place in Páirc Uí Chaoimh and Croke Park. The Neil Diamond fan, nevertheless, is of the opinion that the ban on members of the RUC joining the GAA should only be lifted when the six County boards within the political jurisdiction of Northern Ireland decide to do so.

McHugh, who likes to occasionally help his father on his sheep farm, vividly recalls his own Donegal boyhood heroes such as Martin Carney, Michael Carr and Finian Ward. Later the wonderful Dublin and Kerry teams of the 1970s and 1980s whetted his appetite. In the present game he rates very highly Meath full back Darren Fay, Kerry defender Séamus Moynihan, Derry midfielder Anthony Tohill and forwards Jarlath Fallon (Galway) and Joe Kavanagh (Cork).

Though not really a soccer fan, Martin would like to meet Alex Ferguson, manager of the 1999 treble-winning Manchester United winning team. 'I would love to learn his training procedures, his coaching techniques and see how he spots talented players at such a young age. It would be great to see what methods he uses to make sure that a young player's potential is fulfilled. Sometime, in the not too distant future, I would like to return to inter-county management. Before I do, I would like to accumulate as much knowledge as possible from right across the sporting spectrum,' concluded Martin.

On the field of play, the pocket dynamo from Kilcar could dramatically change the course of a game with radar-like positional play and unerring accuracy. Now the canny, perceptive manager-in-waiting is refining and updating his skills. In the future, McHugh would surely love to walk the touchline in Ballyshannon or Ballybofey, urging on his fellow countymen. If a vacancy should occur, at some time in the future, Martin McHugh is ever ready and only too willing.

Stephen White

BORN IN THE PARISH of Cooley in Co. Louth, Stephen White's first hero was Eddie Boyle the great full back who starred for the 'Wee' county in the 1930s and 1940s. Eddie, who was later selected in the 1984 Team of the Century for footballers who had never won an All-Ireland medal, won Railway Cup medals with Leinster in 1935, 1939, 1940, 1944 and 1945. Inspired by the talented Boyle, the 16-year-old White gave marvellous performances for Cooley Kickhams when they won the Louth Second Division League title in 1944. In 1945, just after World War Two had ended, White went as a student to the Agricultural  College in Mountbellew, Co. Galway. When he returned home for the Easter holidays of 1946 he was very disappointed not to be given at least a trial with that year's Louth minor team. His disappointment was to turn to elation when Galway GAA officials, Brendan Nestor and John 'Tull' Dunne invited him to join the Galway minor squad. Having obviously impressed the Galway selectors Stephen was chosen at midfield to partner the blossoming talents of future brilliant All-Ireland star, Seán Purcell. In a side that also included Frankie Stockwell – the other half of the famous Purcell/Stockwell 'Terrible Twins' partnership of the 1950s – Galway reached the Connacht final. However, a fine Mayo side which included 'Flying Doctor' Padraic Carney and Peter Solon, who were to win senior All-Ireland medals in the early 1950s, defeated the Tribesmen. White, who had been scheduled to play for the Galway junior side immediately after the minor encounter, had to withdraw from that team as he was injured in the latter stages of the curtain raiser. The Galway senior selectors were so pleased with the dashing style and positional sense of White that they picked him to play for the county team later that year, in a challenge match with Kerry.

When his agricultural course was completed the following year, in 1947, Stephen returned permanently to his native county. A disappointed White was only selected as a sub on Cooley's junior side but, incredibly, a fortnight later he made his senior inter-county debut at left half forward. A determined White intended to justify the county selectors faith in him. An unbroken 16-year inter-county career from 1947 to 1963 was to consolidate White's reputation as one of the county's greatest players. Meanwhile, the somewhat uneasy relationship with some officials of the Cooley club was to reach an all-time low in 1948. 'On one occasion my brother and myself walked three miles for a bus to pick us up for a club game. When the bus arrived, we were told that it was full and there was no room for us. So we had to walk home and miss the game. I was totally disgusted and decided to join Dundalk Young Irelands the following year. I spent 14 happy years with them from 1949 to 1963,' Stephen told me when I met him in his home in Castlebellingham.

The greatest consolation for White was that his promising inter-county career was coinciding with a revival in Louth's inter-county performances. In 1948, with Stephen giving a sterling performance at left half forward, Louth won their first Leinster senior championship since 1912, when they defeated Wexford in the final by five points. In the All-Ireland semi-final they were only beaten by three points by the then All-Ireland champions, Cavan. Stephen was relatively happy with Louth's progress. When Cavan went on to retain their All-Ireland title, that happiness was compounded. In the 1949 Leinster championship, after a three-game saga with neighbouring Meath, Louth were eventually beaten by a point. The fact that the Royal County went on to win their first All-Ireland made White realise that with a little more effort, Louth could win their first All-Ireland since 1912. Having also reached their first ever National Football League final, only to lose by two points to Mayo, made the Louth team of 1949 look forward eagerly to 1950.

When they regained the Leinster championship by beating Meath after a replay, Stephen was excited. For the second time in three years Louth were in an All-Ireland semi-final. Playing brilliantly, they overcame the might of Kerry by two points to reach the All-Ireland final. The young man who a few years earlier was not considered good enough for the county minors, was in his first All-Ireland senior final. However, that Louth side was to be deprived of the services of three of the county's star forwards. All-Ireland sprint champion Fr Kevin Connolly, Fr Hardy and Fr Carr were banned from playing inter-county competitive football. An Irish hierarchy ruling of the time forbade priests from playing such games. The absence of these three forwards was too big a burden and Louth, though they fought gallantly, lost the All-Ireland final to Mayo on a 2-5 to 1-6 scoreline. Despondent but not downhearted, Louth still looked to the future with confidence. Stephen recalled that day with a mixture of joy and sadness.

'Tom Conlon and Jim Tuft in the full back line were fantastic and Jimmy McDonnell gave a wonderful display in the forwards. Mayo had a lot of top-class players like their captain Seán Flanagan, full back Paddy Prendergast and midfielder Padraic Carney and full forward Tom Langan. If we had our three missing men we could easily have won.'

Three years later, in 1953, Stephen won his third Leinster medal when Louth again beat the Slaneysiders in the Leinster final. Munster champions Kerry awaited them in the All-Ireland semi-final. 'For several weeks before the game we went into full-time training or collective training as it was then called. Every morning we trained from 10.00 a.m. to 12.15 p.m., then had our lunch and played a game each afternoon from three to four o'clock. We were very fit when we took the field against the Kingdom. But we tried to score goals instead of taking our points and we were eventually beaten 3-6 to 0-10. Playing under his mother's maiden name, the unlisted Fr Connolly came on as a substitute in the second half. He really gave an electrifying performance. If he had been on earlier and if we had taken our points we could have won the game.'

The three major defeats, in the concluding stages of the All-Ireland championships, in 1948, 1950 and now 1953 were beginning to have a demoralising effect on the Louth team members. Players began to lose interest, selectors were chopped and changed and nothing appeared optimistic as Louth experienced three barren seasons before the 1957 Leinster championship. When the Wee county gave a rather inept display in overcoming Carlow in the first round, the horizon looked as bleak as ever in the eyes of Louth GAA followers. One man, for no apparently logical reason, had other ideas. Stephen White prophetically proclaimed after that lacklustre display that Louth were going to win the 1957 All-Ireland. Two missing stars, he reckoned, should be persuaded to rejoin the team.

These men, Tom Conlon and Jimmy McDonnell had prematurely retired from the inter-county scene. The long-serving, outstanding full back Conlon had become disillusioned and had just drifted away. Stephen's brother-in-law, Jimmy McDonnell, had a serious kidney operation the previous year and had not returned to inter-county football. His loss was immense as he was an extremely talented, tricky and accurate forward who had won three successive Railway Cup medals with Leinster in 1953, 1954 and 1955. White himself, who had played with McDonnell in those three winning teams as well as the successful 1952 side, was only too aware of McDonnell's pure class. Using his considerable persuasive powers of tact and diplomacy, White eventually succeeded in convincing Tom and Jimmy to rejoin the squad. It was an exceptionally enthusiastic White who informed selector Brian Reynolds of their availability. Before long, promising starlet, 18-year-old Frank Lynch, who had decided initially to stay with the Louth junior side would join the senior panel. The missing pieces in White's jigsaw for All-Ireland success were gradually fitting into place. Indeed, captain Dermot O'Brien, would be the only forward from the first-round match against Carlow who would feature in Louth's last championship game of the 1957 season.

In the second round, Louth trailed Wexford by five points at half time. But, with Conlon now manning the full back position in his customary commanding style, a magnificent second half display by the Wee county saw them deservedly emerge victorious 1-12 to 0-9. With Jimmy McDonnell fit again and available for the semi-final clash with the current Leinster champions, Kildare, White was confident. In that game, the class of McDonnell shone like a bright beacon as he wreaked havoc at full forward against the Lilywhite defence. In a virtuoso display of speed, skill and accuracy, Jimmy notched a personal tally of three goals and three points to allow Louth reach their first Leinster decider since 1953.

The Leinster final was to see Louth face Dublin who only two years earlier had played magnificently only to lose narrowly to Kerry in the All-Ireland final.

Spearheaded by excellent footballers such as Cathal O'Leary, Ollie Freaney, Jim Crowley, Padraig Haughey and the redoubtable Kevin Heffernan they would provide very formidable opposition.

To crown the county's and White's increasing expectations, their Ardee captain, Dermot O'Brien, who was a professional accordionist, decided now to cancel all his musical engagements for the remainder of 1957. Instead, he was going to devote his full energy and time to maximising the county's football preparations and aspirations. With the dedication of trainer Jim Quigley and the application of the players, no stone was left unturned so that the Wee county could achieve their full potential. The quest for championship glory was on in earnest. First of all, however, there was the little matter of beating Dublin. This was accomplished in the most impressive of fashions as the whole team gave a marvellous display to defeat the metropolitans 2-9 to 1-7. Stephen White, now at left half back, Dan O'Neill at midfield and the brilliant McDonnell were the more prominent individuals in a team of stars. McDonnell added another 2-2 to his ever growing total. All of this was achieved against a background of three exceptional performances by Dublin's Jim Crowley, Cathal O'Leary and Kevin Heffernan. The extent of Louth's achievement can be more accurately gauged by the fact that the nucleus of this Dublin side were destined to win the All-Ireland, one year later, in 1958.

Simultaneously, Tyrone, who had only been beaten by two points, by eventual winners Galway in the previous year's All-Ireland semi-final had retained their Ulster title when they defeated Derry. The Tyrone side had quality players in the Devlin brothers – Eddie and Jim – youthful midfielder Jody O'Neill, the dashing penetrative Jackie Taggart on the '40' and the deadly accurate Frankie Donnelly at corner forward. Most of all, they had in their ranks, the inimitable Iggy Jones. The diminutive right half forward was a superb footballing artist who had tormented defences throughout the country since he gave an exhilarating performance for St Patrick's College, Armagh when they won the initial All-Ireland colleges final eleven years earlier in 1946. No man was more conscious of the wiles and wizardry of Jones than Louth's free taker Kevin Beahan. Beahan had, some years later, attended the Armagh College and had been fed a daily football diet of the skills and achievements of Jones. This was to prove invaluable to Stephen White who would be marking Jones in their All-Ireland semi-final with the Ulster champions.

For the first 15 minutes of the game, Tyrone played fantastic football to lead 0-5 to 0-2. Then disaster struck the O'Neill county when their ace midfielder Jody O'Neill was injured. Thus Tyrone's previous midfield superiority was curbed. With White closely marking the elusive Jones, Louth started to dominate and sneaked into a one-point lead at half time, 0-6 to 0-5. A Tyrone equaliser in the second minute of the second half seemed to spur on Louth rather than Tyrone. After Kevin Beahan had restored their lead the normally reliable White missed a penalty. When Tyrone again equalised through Frankie Donnelly, two minutes later, the crowd anticipated a first ever All-Ireland appearance for Tyrone. However, it was not to be, as a more determined Louth upped their performance. With Kevin Beahan unerringly accurate from frees, Louth consolidated their position. Two '50s', one 55-yard free and one prodigious 65-yard effort from Beahan ensured the demise of a brave Tyrone. Points from Jim Roe and Jimmy McDonnell were merely the icing on the cake as Louth won comfortably 0-13 to 0-7. Tyrone followers were left pondering what might have happened if three excellent goal chances and several opportunities for points had not been spurned. They consoled themselves that Jackie Taggart had been magnificent on the '40' and that Jody O'Neill was injured.

As far as Stephen White was concerned, that Tyrone conjecture was all in the realm of supposition. What mattered most now was that Louth were in the All-Ireland final. For Jimmy McDonnell and himself, it was an ideal opportunity to avenge the disappointment of their 1950 All-Ireland final result. Those words spoken after the Carlow game were now not an idle promise. It was essential that trainer Jim Quigley and the players would, along with the selectors, assiduously prepare for the greatest day of their lives.

Cork, who had lost the 1956 All-Ireland final to Galway, had beaten the same opposition by the minimum of margins in the 1957 All-Ireland semi-final. The smallest county in Ireland was now to play the largest, for the first time, in the decider. The general consensus was that Cork's vast experience would boost their chances of a first senior football title since 1945. Possessing players of the calibre of Paddy O'Driscoll, Denis Bernard and Paddy Harrington, father of Irish international golfer, Pádraig in defence, midfielders Eric Ryan and Seán Moore, and star forward 'Toots' Kelleher merely added substance to an expected Rebel county success.

Before the final began there was sheer bedlam in the Louth dressing room. Their captain Dermot O'Brien had not appeared. Dermot had taken over the captaincy when regular captain Patsy Coleman had been declared unfit for the Leinster final. When Patsy resumed full fitness they tossed up for the honour and Dermot won. Dermot had gone for an injection to treat an injured shoulder on the morning of the game and was marooned outside the closed gates at the dressing room section behind the Cusack stand. With extreme difficulty he succeeded in gaining admission at the Hogan stand entrance at the opposite side of the ground. Thanks to being recognised by a Roscommon friend, the stewards allowed Dermot entry to the pitch. As he ran across the field towards the dressing rooms the loudspeaker asked for the Louth captain to report to the dressing rooms immediately. Twelve minutes from throw in time a relieved Dermot joined his colleagues, quickly togged out and led his team onto the field. Dermot's and his team's personal trauma was over. The scheduled All-Ireland proceedings were due to commence.

When the game began Cork took total control, gaining possession in every sector of the field. In spite of their outfield dominance, however, their forwards missed many easy scoring opportunities and they only led at the interval 1–4 to 0–5. With their midfielders on top form, Cork began the second half as they had ended the first. When 'Toots' Kelleher added another point, Cork had eased into a three-point advantage. It appeared Louth's All-Ireland ambitions were about to be dashed yet again. Louth then made two vital positional switches. Right half forward Séamus O'Donnell exchanged places with midfielder Kevin Beahan and left half back Stephen White swapped with centre half back Peadar Smith who had replaced the injured Jim McArdle before the game began. Those switches proved masterly as Stephen White gave an impeccable display of fielding, excellent anticipation and darting runs up the centre. A rejuvenated Beahan, on the wing, was causing all kinds of problems for an increasingly pressed Cork defence. Two points from Beahan and one from Jim Roe levelled the game, after nine minutes, at 1–5 to 0–8. Corner forward Seán Cunningham pointed Louth into the lead only for two magical points from the ever dangerous 'Toots' Kelleher to edge Cork into a 1–7 to 0–9 advantage. With six minutes to go, Louth were awarded a sideline kick after Cork defender Paddy O'Driscoll had cleared an abortive Beahan '50' into touch. The astute Beahan deftly floated the resultant sideline ball high into the Cork goalmouth. The alert Seán Cunningham rose highest to fist the ball to the net for a dramatic goal and the lead for the 'Wee' county who were now in front, 1–9 to 1–7. Two minutes later Louth were almost caught napping in a quick-fire Cork attack. A timely goal line interception by tigerish Louth left corner back Jim 'Red' Meehan saved the day. Stephen White takes up the story as Cork attacked again as the full time whistle neared.

'We were again caught exposed at the back. I managed to get the ball. Thoughts of the 1950 final against Mayo, when we conceded a soft goal and lost by just two points entered my head. I did not want history to repeat itself. Being under pressure by the Cork attack I decided to hit the ball as high and as long as I could into the Cusack stand. This would give time for our defenders to get back in numbers. Luckily, just after Cork's sideline ball was taken the full time whistle went,' added Stephen.

Louth had won that elusive All-Ireland. Stephen White, who had been the star player afield, was mobbed by exultant supporters. He was happy for everyone but especially for Tom Conlon and Jimmy McDonnell who had shared so many disappointments with him. It had been a wonderful team triumph with defenders Tom Conlon, Jim Meehan and forwards Kevin Beahan, Jim McDonnell, Jim Roe and goal hero Seán Cunningham especially prominent. In the eyes of the football connoisseur, Stephen White's second half performance had been the difference between defeat and victory. Stephen's prophecy of four months before had come true.

When Dermot O'Brien raised the Sam Maguire Cup, a week of unprecedented celebrations by Louth followers began. Bonfires blazed along the roadside as the winning entourage, led by captain Dermot O'Brien entered Drogheda. An excited throng of 40,000 supporters heralded the heroes. On to Dundalk and another sea of cheering thousands saluted Louth's first All-Ireland success for 45 years. At three o' clock the following morning, the cavalcade arrived at Dermot O'Brien's home town of Ardee. Officially, the celebrations were ended for the night. The Louth team of 1957 had restored honour and pride to a county which had been starved of All-Ireland glory for so long.

Stephen White played for Louth for a further six years before he retired in 1963. Two unsuccessful Leinster final appearances in 1958 and 1960 were Stephen's last big games in the red and white of Louth. The New Ireland Insurance representative had played 16 years for his county, represented his province for over a decade and played for Ireland against the Combined Universities on three occasions. When Stephen was selected at left half back on the 1984 *Sunday Independent*/Irish Nationwide Team of the Century, the final accolade of greatness had been bestowed upon him.

White, who would abolish all kicks from the hand in the modern game believes that forwards are not being fairly treated by referees. 'More fouls are being committed by defenders on forwards than vice versa yet forwards appear to be penalised as often. I also think the National Football League should revert to four divisions of eight teams each, based on geographical areas. This would eliminate promotion and relegation. The top team in each section would then go through to the league semi-final.'

Stephen's biggest regret from his playing career concerns his former playing colleague, Frankie Stockwell. 'Frankie worked in Dundalk in 1949–1950. I played with him, both for my club Young Irelands and the Louth county team. Just before the 1950 championship began, Frankie left for London. If he hadn't done so, I'm convinced that Louth would have won the 1950 All-Ireland. He was a great footballer, a very nice fellow and deserved to win his All-Ireland medal with Galway in 1956. It was funny that Frankie and Seán Purcell, my Galway minor colleagues in 1946, should win a senior All-Ireland medal just the year before I won mine.'

'Seán Purcell was the best player I ever played with or against. I saw him play full back, centre half back, midfield, centre half forward and full forward. He was equally good in all those positions.'

The now retired Stephen who has always been a fanatical Manchester United soccer fan rates their late manager, Matt Busby, as a perfect role model for aspiring managers in any sport. 'One of my saddest memories is hearing of the Munich air disaster in 1958 when seven Manchester United players were killed. I was on my way to a ploughing match and I just could not believe what I was hearing.'

Looking as fit as a fiddle, Stephen is now at ease with himself and his memories. His son, Stefan, is a current Louth senior footballer renowned for his scoring prowess and intuitive ability. Watching his son play for the county that he served for so long and so well keeps Stephen hoping that some day soon, Stefan will win at least a

Leinster provincial medal with the Wee county. Stephen and his wife, Carmel, have three other children, Bernadette, Anne and Pauline.

Stephen selected the following players on his Ireland and Leinster teams.

IRELAND (1947–1963)

Jack Mangan
(Galway)

Jerome O'Shea   Paddy O'Brien   Seán Flanagan
(Kerry)   *(Meath)*   *(Mayo)*

Seán Murphy   John Joe O'Reilly   Seán Quinn
(Kerry)   *(Cavan)*   *(Armagh)*

Mick O'Connell   Jim McKeever
(Kerry)   *(Derry)*

Seán O'Neill   Seán Purcell   Cathal O'Leary
(Down)   *(Galway)*   *(Dublin)*

Frank Stockwell   Jim McDonnell   Kevin Heffernan
(Galway)   *(Louth)*   *(Dublin)*

LEINSTER

Andy Phillips
(Wicklow)

Micheál O'Brien   Paddy O'Brien   Jim Tuft
(Meath)   *(Meath)*   *(Louth)*

Gerry O'Reilly   Paddy Dunne   Andy Murphy
(Wicklow)   *(Laois)*   *(Carlow)*

Seán Brennan   Jim Rogers
(Kildare)   *(Wicklow)*

Paddy Meegan   Ollie Freaney   Cathal O'Leary
(Meath)   *(Dublin)*   *(Dublin)*

Peter McDermott   Jim McDonnell   Kevin Heffernan
(Meath)   *(Louth)*   *(Dublin)*

Over 50 years ago, a young boy stood on a tin box in the townland of Crossalaney in the Cooley Peninsula. The avid sports follower was imitating the magical commentating voice of the late lamented Gaelic games broadcaster, Mícheál Ó Hehir. The deeds of the great Cavan and Kerry teams that played in the famous Polo grounds final of 1947 were being recalled. The boy's neighbour and friend Stephen White looked on in amazement as the perfectly wonderfully fluent speaking voice parodied the great Ó Hehir. The Cavan full forward line of that historic final was Joe

Stafford, Peter Donohoe and TP O'Reilly. The normally meticulous would-be commentator made one deliberate mistake as he recited the names of the Cavan full forward line. 'Top of the right is Joe Stafford, full forward is Peter Donohoe and top of the left is Jimmy Magee.'

Half a century later, that little boy on the tin box has become a household name in many sporting disciplines. Two neighbours and two friends from one parish have put Louth on the map of sporting excellence. During the course of his brilliant career as a broadcaster, Jimmy Magee has admired many outstanding athletes throughout the world. In his mind, the boy from across the fields, Stephen White, is one of those he admires most.

Dermot Earley

BORN IN CASTLEBAR, Co. Mayo in 1948, Dermot Earley did not move to Roscommon until he was seven years old. His father, Peadar, was appointed to a teaching position in Gorthaganny in the parish of Lough Glynn in west Roscommon where the elder Earley founded a GAA club called Michael Glaveys in 1956. With a GAA father and a wildly enthusiastic GAA pal, Haulie McNulty, the young Dermot soon became immersed in Gaelic football, spending the long summer evenings honing his playing skills. Roscommon star and local resident, John Lynch and the legendary great Roscommon centre half back, Gerry O'Malley, were the role models as they enacted out many successful All-Ireland triumphs around the fields of Roscommon.

In 1960 Dermot went boarding to St Nathy's College, Ballaghaderreen simply because it had a fantastic GAA tradition. His progress as a noted and developing skilful player was rapid as he captained St Nathy's to a Connacht juvenile title in 1963 and their junior side to another provincial football title in 1965. Though making his debut with the county minors as a 15-year-old in 1963, it was not until 1965 that Dermot made his Croke Park debut when Roscommon minors were defeated by Derry in the All-Ireland semi-final. A missed penalty in that game left the Gorthaganny youngster totally despondent. A month later, Earley made his first appearance for Roscommon seniors when they met Leitrim in a Gael Linn Cup competition. Those who witnessed the 17-year-old scoring three points from the right half-back position knew that a new star had arrived. Some weeks later the letter he had been anxiously waiting on arrived, informing him that he had been selected to join the Irish army as a cadet. Earley's career, both in a sporting and professional sense, had taken root.

Just one year later Dermot was to scale the heights of success when he played in a Roscommon team that won the 1966 All-Ireland U-21 final. With ten minutes to go their opponents, Kildare, were leading by five points when Earley was switched from centre half forward to midfield. In a marvellous display of high fielding and astute passing Earley created two goal chances which his colleagues Jim Keane and Jimmy Finnegan duly converted. The full time whistle blew and Roscommon had won the title by the narrowest of margins, 2-10 to 1-12. For Dermot Earley it was a perfect ending to a wonderful year. He had also made history by being the first player to play for his county at minor, junior, U-21 and senior levels in the one year. Three years later Dermot and Roscommon reached another All-Ireland U-21 final only to suffer a one-point defeat to Antrim.

The next highlight of Dermot's career was when he won his first senior provincial medal in 1972, defeating Mayo 5-8 to 3-10. Though he scored a goal, Roscommon were well beaten by Kerry in the subsequent All-Ireland semi-final. In 1974, Roscommon reached the National Football League final. They played brilliantly and, with time almost up, they led by three points. However, a last-minute equalising goal by Kerry's John Egan sent the game to a replay that Kerry won easily. It appeared to Earley that finals and Roscommon were synonymous with defeat. After another provincial championship elimination in 1975 Earley left Ireland for an 18-month peace-keeping mission with the Irish army in the Middle East.

In January 1977, Dermot Earley returned to Ireland. Away from the hazards of the Middle East, Earley made intensive preparations for that year's provincial championship. Since Earley's last appearance in a Roscommon jersey, a new Roscommon star had arrived. This man, Tony McManus, was not only an excellent playmaker but a very accurate scorer as well. In Earley's opinion, this was an added reason why Roscommon could do well in 1977. A marvellous Connacht campaign ended with a narrow victory over Galway. The All-Ireland semi-final with Armagh ended on a controversial note when Armagh manager, Gerry O'Neill, ran across the field as Dermot Earley was about to attempt a long-distance free for the winning point. O'Neill shouted something but Earley did not hear and did not blame him for the fact that he sent the ball wide. The game ended in a draw and Armagh went on to win the replay by a point.

These failures on the big occasion were beginning to have a devastating effect on the morale of Earley and his fellow players. History repeated itself when Roscommon were defeated in both the 1978 and 1979 All-Ireland semi-finals by Kerry and Dublin respectively.

However, there had been some compensation when Roscommon won the 1979 National Football League final against Cork. This was the county's first national senior success since Jimmy Murray captained the Westerners to back-to-back All-Ireland senior football titles in 1943 and 1944. For Earley, it was a personal triumph as he scored seven of his side's 15 points in the 0-15 to 1-3 defeat of the Rebel County.

When Roscommon won their fourth consecutive Connacht title in 1980 the whole team, under manager Tom Heneghan and captain Danny Murray, were more determined than ever to reach an All-Ireland final. The fact that, once again, Armagh, their old adversaries of 1953 and 1977 were their opponents, made them double their efforts. An inspirational display by Earley and a magnificent scoring performance by Michael Finneran ensured that Dermot would at last play in an All-Ireland senior final. A six-point winning margin made them look forward eagerly to meet Kerry.

In the final itself, the stylish, jinking John 'Jigger' O'Connor had the ball in the Kerry net after only 25 seconds. Shortly afterwards Séamus Hayden and John O'Gara added points to leave the score 1-2 to 0-0 in Roscommon's favour after only 13 minutes. However, Roscommon could not translate their outfield superiority into more scores and gradually Kerry fought back to equalise with a Mike Sheehy goal in the 20th minute. As the teams left the field at half time, the scores were level at 1-3 each but Roscommon had to face a stiff wind and driving rain in the second half.

In the third quarter, Kerry took the initiative and edged ahead by two points. Meanwhile, Roscommon missed several easy scoring opportunities, notably from frees by the normally reliable Michael Finneran. Still, when O'Connor pointed in the 23rd minute, the sides were level at 1-6 each. Despite magnificent defensive play, with left corner back Gerry Connellan especially prominent and goalkeeper Gay Sheerin making some great saves, Roscommon's ineptitude in attack proved the decisive factor for the remainder of the game. On one occasion, however, there was a ray of hope. Suddenly, Roscommon seemed destined to take the lead, when, with Kerry keeper Charlie Nelligan beaten, wing forward Aidan Dooley shot towards an empty net. But, out of nowhere Kerry star defender Páidí Ó Sé dived across the goal line, caught the ball and the danger was averted. Notwithstanding a fantastic rally in the final stages, led by the inimitable Earley, Roscommon failed to score again and Kerry added three pointed frees to clinch the game on a 1-9 to 1-6 scoreline. In the final analysis, Roscommon's fouls were penalised, whereas Kerry's were not.

After the game, many commented on what they considered to be the undue physicality of the Roscommon players. Kerry manager Mick O'Dwyer went so far as to say that if Roscommon had played football they would have won. However, respected Kerry players such as Jimmy Deenihan and Páidí Ó Sé, while admitting that Roscommon played hard football, said that they did not resort to dirty tactics. Almost 20 years later, Dermot Earley reflects on the whole scenario. 'We were hugely disappointed as to how we responded to this game. At vital times we tended to be negative in our approach. This was not planned or decided by anyone during the game. It just happened. I think the fear of losing overcame the hope of winning. If we had continued, as we did at the beginning, to move the ball at speed, I have no doubt but that we would have won,' stated the man who was only sent off once in his life when he had an altercation with Dublin's Bobby Doyle in a league game in 1976.

When the final whistle sounded in that 1980 final, Kerry had won three All-Irelands in a row and Roscommon had left empty handed. Earley continues his analysis: 'I will never forget how disappointed I was. I also realise that the losers on All-Ireland final day should not be ignored as they are. They should be brought up to the rostrum and receive their losers' medals just as they do in the FA Cup. It is only right that they should receive the acclamation of their supporters. After all they have played a major role in the making of such a wonderful occasion,' concluded the man whose son, Dermot (Jnr) suffered the same fate when his adopted county of Kildare were defeated by Galway in the 1998 All-Ireland final.

At 32 years of age at the time of that unsuccessful attempt to win a coveted All-Ireland medal in 1980, Dermot knew that his gold medal chance was gone. For the next five years he soldiered on hoping against hope that Roscommon might make the long awaited breakthrough. It was not to be. In 1982, Dermot was joined on the Roscommon team by his younger brother, Paul, who was 16 years his junior. Dermot has many happy and proud memories of their times together on the team, though these were interrupted by Dermot going on another peace-keeping mission to the Lebanon from the summer of 1982 to May 1983. Their mutual admiration and friendship was very real. This is best illustrated by a story Dermot tells against himself.

'I remember telling Paul about meeting a man one Saturday night in Roscommon town. I was proud that the man had thought that I was Paul and I told Paul this with great relish. "I know how you felt," Paul retorted rather impishly. "I also was in Roscommon on the following night and a man came up to me and said, tell your father I was asking for him!" '

In 1985, at the age of 37, Dermot Earley, after 23 years of loyal service wearing the primrose and blue colours of his native county, decided to retire. When Mayo defeated Roscommon in that year's Connacht final, Dermot bowed out of the game that he had graced for so song. As the final whistle sounded, the Mayo players, led by midfielder Willie Joe Padden, spontaneously lifted Earley onto their shoulders. Both sets of supporters momentarily forgot the result of the game and applauded Dermot off the field.

Roscommon had given many great men to the GAA. Stalwarts such as 1940s winning captain Jimmy Murray, former All-Ireland player and ex-GAA President Donal Keenan and the fabulous player and captain of the 1962 All-Ireland team, Gerry O'Malley had brought honour and glory to the county. Now, arguably their greatest ever servant, Dermot Earley, has joined that illustrious hall of fame.

Dermot, who was selected as an All Star in 1974 and 1979, (incidentally, his brother Paul was also selected as an All Star in 1985) loves reminiscing about the great players and exciting teams of the past.

'Willie Casey of Mayo was a fantastic corner back with a great drop kick. The best goal that I ever saw was scored by Seán Purcell against Mayo goalkeeper Mick Corkery who incidentally also made many wonderful saves in his time. Purcell and Stockwell were a marvellous combination. I always had great regard for the Galway three-in-a-row team of 1964-1966. I remember going to my first All-Ireland in 1963 when Galway were defeated by Dublin. Three men stood out for me that day, Martin Newell, Noel Tierney and Mattie McDonagh. Little did I realise then that I would be playing my first Connacht championship game against them three years later in 1966,' stated Dermot when I met him in his Newbridge home.

When he retired from playing, Earley reluctantly acted as assistant manager to Seán Young from August 1986 up to Roscommon's exit from the 1987 championship. In that year also, Dermot was appointed as Assistant Military Advisor to the Secretary General of the UN, Javier Perez de Cuellar. For four years, Earley and his family moved to New York. In August 1991, the Earley family returned to Ireland and in September 1992 Dermot took over the position of Roscommon team manager. During his two-year tenure he experienced no success. In 1993 they were beaten by Mayo and in 1994 they were rather unlucky to go down narrowly to a Leitrim team then riding the crest of a wave. Due to all the physical demands of long-distance travelling, hassle and family commitments, Earley stepped down after the 1994 championship defeat. After Mick O'Dwyer had relinquished his position as manager of Kildare in 1994, a call went out to Earley. Living in Kildare eliminated the arduous travelling he had to endure going to Roscommon, so Earley eventually agreed to accept the position. However, Dermot was again left with no managerial honours when Kildare lost in the early rounds of both the 1995 and 1996 championships. The craving for instant success in a football county such as Kildare was just too much so he decided to resign.

'When Mick O'Dwyer brought them to a League final in 1991, Kildare's appetite for success was truly whetted. However, in a transition situation you need time to develop players. For example, some of the players that were starring in the Kildare teams of 1998 were players that I introduced in 1994-1995. Each team needs to introduce at least two or three quality players annually if a team is to develop properly,' said Dermot.

Having played with his native Michael Glaveys up until 1978, Earley then decided to transfer his allegiance to Newbridge Sarsfields. The excessive travelling plus the need for his young family to establish a local identity were the prime reasons for this move. Inspiring them to win a Kildare championship in 1982 and a League/ championship double in 1986 made Earley, now a player coach, very much an accepted part of the structure of the GAA in his adopted county. Urban centres such as Newbridge is where Earley sees the GAA's greatest challenge. Being a senior club selector and his involvement in Saturday morning underage coaching sessions gives Earley an insight into the development of Gaelic games. 'It is much easier to organise Gaelic games in rural areas. There are so many more distractions as well as varied sporting counter attractions in urban areas. It is therefore incumbent upon those of us in the GAA to produce a product which is not only attractive but also well organised. If those factors are present then our potential customers will go away well satisfied. Now, thanks to massive TV exposure, Gaelic games are becoming much more fashionable particularly in the 20-40 age group. In order to maximise this interest I think there should be a huge marketing drive to simultaneously promote hurling and camogie under the one administrative arm rather than the two separate bodies at present. Similarly, ladies football and men's football should be promoted jointly,' asserts Dermot.

It is when suggesting changes in the present league and championship systems at inter-county level that Earley is especially fluent in explanation and innovative in thought.

'We must move away from the idea of arranging fixtures around the perceived financial viability of County Boards, Provincial Councils and Central Council. This outmoded concept has had a stultifying effect on the development of our games. Under the present system the average county team plays up to 25 games per year. Two thirds of these games are made up of meaningless subsidiary competitions, tournament games and friendly matches. My proposals would envisage having three distinct competitions which would be more substantial and still guarantee a minimum of at least ten real, competitive matches per county:

1. Beginning the National Football League each March, I would run off the competition without a break right up to the championship. This would guarantee at least seven proper games per county as they prepared for the championship.
2. I would introduce a round-robin series within each province for the All-Ireland senior football championship. For example, in Leinster I would have four groups of three teams who would play each other, thus guaranteeing at least two championship games per county. After this preliminary round had been completed, the top two teams in each section would be in the Leinster quarter-final. Simultaneously, I would use three groups of three in Ulster and two groups of three in Connacht (including London) and in Munster. I would play all these games in the different provinces on three successive weekends. Thereafter the championship would continue on a knockout basis. However, to add more excitement to the competition I would hold a televised open draw for the next round in each province just after the round-robin series had been completed. The top two teams in each of the two groups in Munster and Connacht would qualify for the provincial semi-finals. In Ulster, the top team in each of the three groups would qualify for the semi-finals. The fourth semi-final qualifier would be selected by picking the remaining team with the highest score difference.

I would also introduce an open draw competition. This could be held on Wednesday or Friday nights and run off within a short time span during the summer months.

The overall benefits of these proposals would be that each county would have many more quality games. Players, managements and supporters would prefer that the energy, which is at present expended on worthless games, would be channelled into a proper, nationally structured system. The use of Friday nights and Saturdays for the National Football League and midweek games for the open draw competition would allow counties to fulfil their club programmes. Indeed, if this new inter-county programme were successful it could serve as a blueprint for competitions within each county. As an incentive, I would suggest that the winners of these three major competitions should play each other in the USA each October. This would bring a new and exciting dimension to our national competitions,' stated the loquacious Earley.

Dermot also feels that the GAA should market Gaelic games in a much more sophisticated manner. 'We have a marvellous product and our players train every bit as hard as Premiership soccer players. The GAA should advertise their games on TV in a way befitting their outstanding quality. Players like Glenn Ryan, Anthony Daly, Peter Canavan, DJ Carey and Jarlath Fallon should be continuously on our screens telling us what Gaelic games means to them. Similarly, our games should be promoted in North America, Australia or wherever Irish communities are either established or developing. Playing the Railway Cup final abroad each year could serve as a catalyst for this. With the new competition structures, as I have outlined, and advanced marketing techniques, the potential for further growth of our games is limitless.'

When discussing the games' present rules Earley is as always clear thinking and logical. 'I would not abolish the handpass. There is essentially no difference between the handpass and the fisted pass because to execute either there has to be a clear striking action. The only difference is that the hand is closed for one and open for the other. The so-called square ball should be eliminated. It is much too difficult to legislate for it when the ball is up in the air. Anyhow, the fact that no one can touch the goalkeeper is protection enough.' Earley, who believes in the abolition of all GAA bans also thinks that for serious fouls such as punching, kicking, spitting, head butting and personal abuse a specified number of games suspension system should be introduced.

In the modern game Earley rates Tyrone's Peter Canavan as the game's outstanding forward. 'He is very skilful, a great thinker and, even though small, a fantastic scorer. Niall Buckley (Kildare), Anthony Tohill (Derry) and John McDermott (Meath) are the game's three best midfielders at the moment,' says the man who rates his friend and former keen rival, Galway's Billy Joyce as his most difficult opponent.

Based mainly on his playing days (1965-1985), Dermot Earley selected his all- time Ireland and Connacht selections. One man whom he did not consider was Kerry's Mick O'Connell. Mick was coming towards the end of his career when Dermot was in his prime. Nevertheless, Earley considers O'Connell as the most skilful player he ever saw. Another Kerryman whom he did select, Pat Spillane, disappointed him with his lack of generosity in his writing towards some of his former colleagues. However, he admits that that should not detract in any way from Pat's fantastic ability on the football field.

IRELAND

Billy Morgan
(Cork)

Enda Colleran
(Galway)

Jack Quinn
(Meath)

Tom O'Hare
(Down)

Paudie O'Shea
(Kerry)

Nicholas Clavin
(Offaly)

Martin Newell
(Galway)

Jack O'Shea
(Kerry)

Jimmy Duggan
(Galway)

Matt Connor
(Offaly)

Ogie Moran
(Kerry)

Pat Spillane
(Kerry)

Mike Sheehy
(Kerry)

Seán O'Neill
(Down)

John Egan
(Kerry)

Subs: Brian Mullins (Dublin), Eoin Liston (Kerry), Johnny Geraghty (Galway)
Tony McManus (Roscommon), Michael Kearins (Sligo), Kevin Moran (Dublin)

CONNACHT

Johnny Geraghty
(Galway)

Enda Colleran
(Galway)

Noel Tierney
(Galway)

Willie Casey
(Mayo)

Ronan Creaven
(Roscommon)

Gerry O'Malley
(Roscommon)

Martin Newell
(Galway)

John Morley
(Mayo)

Jimmy Duggan
(Galway)

Cyril Dunne
(Galway)

Mattie McDonagh
(Galway)

Micheál Kearins
(Sligo)

Pakie McGarty
(Leitrim)

Tony McManus
(Roscommon)

John Keenan
(Galway)

Subs: Harry Keegan (Roscommon), Pat Lindsay (Roscommon), Séamus Hayden (Roscommon), and Cathal Flynn (Leitrim)

N.B. Seán Purcell and Frankie Stockwell were not considered as their 'glory days' were really in the 1950s.

To Dermot Earley, the GAA is a very pervasive and unifying influence across Irish society. 'It is the most supported and supportive organisation in the country. This is especially true in times of need and in particular when a staunch GAA member dies. The whole GAA community immediately assists and honours the family of the bereaved. If I was in Donegal or Kerry or Antrim or Wexford and I required assistance I know that I would get help from the local GAA community simply because I played Gaelic football.'

In his professional life, Dermot Earley has risen to the top echelons of the Irish Army. At present a Lieutenant Colonel, Dermot Earley is stationed at Defence forces headquarters in Dublin with specific responsibility for conciliation and arbitration. In his private life Dermot, the family man (he and his wife Mary, have six children – David, Conor, Dermot, Paula, Anne-Marie and Noelle), though not looking upon himself as a religious person, nevertheless has great trust in God, in the discipline that religion places upon one and enjoys practising his Catholicism. While those twin strands of career and religion are two of the most stabilising influences in Dermot's life, the whole person is very much a GAA enthusiast, a doer, a helper and a philosopher who intends to bring these qualities to the young around him for the rest of his life.

'I want to tog out for as long as I am able to be with kids, imparting knowledge and encouraging them to be better players and better people. What is most important to all of us is how we react to playing the game, to winning and losing, to being skilful and being less able, to dominating and to being under pressure. Your whole character is on display in the GAA field. If you can respond correctly, not in a dominating way but in an appropriate manner you are a better person and that is the greatest tribute of all,' concluded Dermot Earley.

No man has answered so many of those questions more correctly than Lieutenant Colonel Dermot Earley. All of us who have watched and listened to him over the years have undoubtedly gained much from what he has given us. Let us hope that we will hear more of him in the public domain. He still has much to offer.

Seán O'Connell

ONE SUNDAY MORNING IN 1957, two tall handsome students went to Mass in St Agnes' Church in the Anderstowntown district of Belfast. They came home to their 'digs' and ate a hearty breakfast. At one o'clock they had a light lunch before getting a taxi which brought them 50 miles to Ballinascreen where Derry were hosting Armagh. One of the passengers, an Armagh man, wore the number three jersey for the Orchard County, the other occupant, a Derry man, donned the number 14 shirt for the Oak Leaf County. In the game, the two friends marked each other fairly and squarely with no quarter asked or none given. After Derry had won the game convincingly, the two students joined each other for a meal before returning by taxi to Belfast. During the journey, they conversed quite animatedly on a variety of subjects. However, in the time-honoured tradition of both individuals, no reference whatsoever was made concerning the game. That evening, the duo later went to a dance in Belfast's Fruithill Park, totally oblivious to the fact that anything had happened that afternoon. To each of them, everything had to be put into proper perspective. That cool, calculating type of balance and inner determination was to propel both men into the national consciousness during the course of the next 40-odd years. The Armagh man, Séamus Mallon, was to become one of the country's most able and distinguished politicians. Having joined the SDLP (Social Democratic and Labour Party), shortly after its foundation, the Markethill man became the party's deputy leader and a Westminster MP (member of Parliament in London representing Newry and Mourne). In July 1998, Mallon, deeply committed to a peaceful resolution of Ireland's political problems, got his due reward when he was appointed Deputy First Minister of the new Northern Ireland Executive. Meanwhile, the Derry man, Seán O'Connell, had long been recognised as one of the most skilful and respected Gaelic footballers to emerge from the historic province of Ulster.

Seán O'Connell was born in 1937 in Garvagh where there was no tradition of Gaelic football. Though born just inside the parish of Kilrea, where he played underage football, Seán was geographically much closer to Ballerin which had become a bastion of Gaelic football since its foundation in 1944. In 1948, Seán went as a boarder to St Columb's College in Derry City. As students in earlier years had misbehaved during an inter-college game, the then President of the college forbade students from entering any Ulster Colleges' competitions. However, thanks to the tremendous input from students, particularly from the rural areas of counties Derry and Donegal, internal leagues, which proved exceptionally competitive, were organised on a regular basis. The young O'Connell soon realised that playing Gaelic football came naturally to him so he eagerly looked forward to playing club football. It did not take much persuasion from Ballerin officials such as Brian Mullan and Barney McNicholl to entice the now strapping six footer to transfer his club allegiance to them.

At the age of 15, Seán made his debut for the club's minor and senior teams within days of each other. That year, 1953, they reached both the minor and senior county finals. Played at Magherafelt the minor game was the curtain raiser to the senior decider. Seán O'Connell and seven others who played in the minor final returned 15 minutes after its conclusion to participate in the senior match. Little did anyone then think that 24 years later O'Connell would play for his club in an All-Ireland final.

In 1955, Seán made his debut with Derry minors and the following year he graduated to the Derry junior team. 1957 was the year that Seán made his first major impact at senior inter-county level. Having made his initial appearance against Donegal in the McKenna Cup, O'Connell, who was now a student at St Mary's Teacher Training College, made his senior championship debut against Antrim in June 1957. Derry exorcised many past humiliations at the hands of the same opposition when they heavily defeated the Glensmen on a 4-14 to 0-8 scoreline at Ballinascreen. In the semi-final, they faced Cavan, for so long worthy standard bearers of Ulster football, on the Croke Park stage. With the game evenly balanced at 1-9 each, O'Connell calmly slotted over the winning point just before the referee blew the full time whistle. Derry had beaten Cavan for the first time ever in the Ulster championship and the young right half forward from Ballerin had added a much needed scoring edge to Derry's play. The final was against neighbours and then Ulster champions Tyrone who had only lost by two points to eventual All-Ireland champions, Galway in the previous year's All-Ireland semi-final. It was the first Ulster final pairing between two teams from the political jurisdiction of Northern Ireland.

Played at a furious pace, the football was of the highest order. In the end the O'Neill county emerged victorious by two points. Though beaten, the future of Derry football looked very promising indeed. The Gribben brothers, Hugh, Francis, Owen and Roddy possessed skill and determination. Patsy Breen and Peter Smith were tenacious tacklers, each with an uncanny eye to spot an opening. Also, they had one of the all time greats of Gaelic football – Jim McKeever – to direct them from either midfield or the centre half back positions. Now, for the first time in many years, they had, in Seán O'Connell, an outstanding forward both from play and frees. His eight points in the final against Tyrone was surely an omen of greater things to come. At club level the fantastic work and dedication of men like Brian Mullan, Barney McNicholl and Paddy Deigham (who was never to miss a club game at any level for over 40 years) was to reap its just reward when Ballerin qualified for the 1957 Derry senior county final against Ballymaguigan. In the week prior to the final a serious 'flu virus known as the Asian 'flu was rampant throughout most of Ireland. One victim, who was badly stricken, was Seán O'Connell. As Saturday evening arrived, a feverish O'Connell was resigned to not playing. As he lay in bed in his Belfast 'digs,' he thought he heard a noise in the gathering autumn darkness. Drifting restlessly between sleep and semi-consciousness, the sharp tap of pebbles on his bedroom window told Seán that something was awry. The voices of Brian Mullan and Barney McNicholl rended the Belfast air. 'Seán, we're coming to bring you to play in the county final tomorrow.' Despite protestations to the contrary, a compromise was reached. They would take him to see Dr McGurk in Kilrea and accept his judgement in the matter as final. 'I would be somewhat dubious as to what exactly went on between the doctor and my two noble clubmen. The doctor told me that I would be able to play if I took plenty of barley sugar to keep up my energy levels! After the game I was to take a hot bath. In the final analysis, everything turned out fine. We won our first county final by defeating hot favourites Ballymaguigan and I had my hot bath in O'Connor's Pub in Drumsurn just a few miles from the match venue in Dungiven. Though I had responded to the good doctor's cure, several other players were not so lucky and were in bed afterwards for two months,' Seán informed me when I met him at his home in Limavady.

In the spring of 1958, a special incentive awaited the contestants of the previous year's Ulster final. The winners of a rematch between those Derry and Tyrone teams would qualify to play Connacht winners, Galway, in the first GAA tournament game ever to be staged at the home of international soccer – Wembley Stadium in London. With midfielder Jim McKeever lording it over Tyrone's Jody O'Neill and left half back Peter Smith blotting out the ever-dangerous Tyrone wing half forward Iggy Jones, Derry played splendidly to defeat the Ulster champions by ten points. Thus Tyrone's enviable record of never having been beaten in an Ulster competitive match for two years was unceremoniously broken. Derry and Seán O'Connell were about to make history along with Galway to be the first GAA sides to adorn that famous stadium. It was a particularly happy occasion for O'Connell as three of his clubmates Brian Mullan, Seoirse McKinney and Michael Mullan joined him in the Derry team. Played in front of 33,000 spectators Seán became the first GAA player to score at Wembley when he flighted over the first point. Though beaten in the end by a superior and more experienced Galway side, O'Connell reflects on that Saturday, 24 May 1958. 'At last we were making an impact. There was a great bonding between all the members of the team. A certain cavalier attitude permeated the minds of some players. This was typified by our goalkeeper Patsy Gormley. As he surveyed the beautifully manicured surface of Wembley preparing a kick-out, he shouted to corner back Tommy Doherty where to place the ball – 'put her up on a good rush bush!'

The following month of June was to see Derry embark on what was to be their most successful championship season for the next 35 years. In the first round, Derry played very poorly to beat Antrim by three points. The Ulster semi-final against Cavan, for the second successive year however, was to see Derry play superbly. In an impeccable display of catching and passing, Jim McKeever continually supplied his forward line. Six different Cavan players were switched in an attempt to thwart the aerial dominance and passing prowess of the Ballymaguigan man. It was all to no avail as Derry eased their way into their second consecutive Ulster decider. This 1958 final was to feature the novel pairing of Derry and Down – the first Ulster final since 1890 in which neither team had previously won the Ulster championship. This final was to witness the aforementioned McKeever give yet another outstanding display in a career of so many top quality performances. Jim McKeever, his brother Denis, Leo O'Neill (brother of Martin O'Neill of Northern Ireland soccer fame), Owen Gribben, Charlie Higgins and the elegant O'Connell were the scorers as Derry eked out a four point victory to claim their first Ulster senior football title.

One of the wettest years on record did not deter Derry as they prepared diligently to meet the might of Kerry in the All-Ireland semi-final. Immediately before the game, the rain forced the cancellation of the pre-match parade. Though Kerry had gone into a 1-2 to 0-1 lead, a purple patch of unparalleled dominance by the Derrymen, inspired by their captain, the marvellous Jim McKeever, clawed back three points to leave the score 1-2 to 0-4. Now, with 28 minutes gone, Radio Eireann listeners tuned in to the game for the first time (the first part of the game coincided with live commentary of Ronnie Delaney's fruitless attempt to win the 1500 metres title in Stockholm). They heard Micheál O'Hehir excitedly remark. 'And now the ball is with Denis McKeever. A goal! A goal! Derry are sensationally leading the Kingdom 1-4 to 1-2.'

In the second half, Kerry switched wing forward Mick O'Connell for the first time, to try and curb the majestic midfielder from Derry. Those who witnessed the ensuing contest will never forget the titanic battle of skill and endeavour between two of the game's most purely talented footballers of all time. Though Derry's Seán O'Connell pointed a free in the second minute of the second half to give the Oak Leaf County a three-point advantage, Kerry tenaciously fought back with two fabulous scores from Paudie Sheehy to reduce the deficit to the minimum. When Gary McMahon brought the sides level, it appeared that Derry's initial Croke Park appearance would disappear into the realms of history and that the Kingdom would go on to claim victory. The Derry defence, however, had not read the script. With Patsy McLarnon and Hugh F. Gribben especially commanding at right full back and full back respectively and the whole half back line of Patsy Breen, Colm Mulholland and Peter Smith giving a superlative performance, the game was not yet over. A continuous 13-minute Kerry siege was finally lifted when Jim McKeever's very able midfield partner, the high catching Phil Stuart was fouled in possession. Seán O'Connell coolly pointed the resultant free to edge his team ahead. Three minutes later and the same time from the end, Peter Smith sent a Derry free from 60 yards out into a cluster of players. The ball broke free in front of Seán O'Connell. He trapped it, soccer style, pushed it to his right and sent it rocketing to the net from the 14-yard line. Just before the final whistle, the tireless Tadhgie Lyne burst through the Derry defence for a dramatic goal. However, from the kick-out, referee Mickey McArdle of Louth blew the full time whistle. One of the greatest ever upsets in the history of Gaelic football had just occurred. The Derry players could not believe that they had won 2-6 to 2-5 and that they were really in the All-Ireland final. Seán O'Connell, who had contributed 1-5 of the total, was an instant hero. His goal will always be looked on as one of the classic goals that Croke Park has ever seen. It is hard to credit but the same O'Connell was to score an equally dramatic and skilful goal 18 years later in an All-Ireland semi-final against the same opposition. As Derry arrived home to a tumultuous reception in Magherafelt the whole team but especially McKeever and O'Connell were cult heroes.

The All-Ireland final against Dublin was to see the end of Derry's dream. With 20 minutes to go, the sides were level but a defensive slip allowed Dublin in for an opportunist goal and the Metropolitans went on to record a somewhat flattering six-point victory to claim their first All-Ireland triumph since 1942. However, the game was not without its controversy. For all Derry fans and many neutrals, the fact that Derry were not awarded close-in frees when full forward Owen Gribben appeared to be repeatedly fouled was the chief talking point in the aftermath of the game. Former Cavan star, Simon Deignan, who refereed the game was accused of being too lenient. One incident in particular galled the Derry supporters. Dublin goalkeeper Paddy O'Flaherty seemed to foul the ball on the ground inside the square but no penalty was awarded.

'As the following day's papers clearly illustrated, it was a definite penalty. We were really getting on top when the referee ignored O'Flaherty's foul. Retrospectively, if we had focused properly we could have won the game. If Owen Gribben had been a less honest player he would have made the continual fouls more obvious. Still the whole summer had been a great adventure. Most of our team had never seen Dublin before and only three had ever previously played in Croke Park.'

That 1958 Derry campaign seemed to herald a bright new future for the Oak Leaf County. Still, for the next 34 years, Derry's undoubted potential was never fulfilled. Seán O'Connell was to play for Derry for a further 18 years without experiencing any national success. During that time, he played in three All-Ireland semi-finals in 1970, 1975 and 1976 and three National League finals in 1959, 1961 and 1976. Heartbreaking defeat was his lot on each of those occasions. In that 1976 All-Ireland semi-final, the evergreen O'Connell, now 38 years of age, scored one of the greatest goals of all time. Corner forward Johnny O'Leary crossed the ball into the Kerry goalmouth and O'Connell volleyed it into the corner of the Kingdom net. Despite his age, Seán was to appear again in Croke Park the following spring with his club Ballerin in the All-Ireland club final against Austin Stacks of Tralee. O'Connell, in a team that included former All Star, Peter Stevenson and fellow county men Malachy and James McAfee, played terrifically for a man approaching his 40th birthday. The powerful Tralee team which included Kerry All-Ireland winners Ger Power, Ger O'Keeffe, John O'Keeffe and Mike Sheehy only overcame the Derry champions by three points. Seán O'Connell, the 6´2˝ footballing artist with deceptive speed and a marvellous sidestep had played his last game at Croke Park. Such length of service at such a consistently high standard was testimony to the skill, fitness and determination of one of Derry's and Ulster's most talented forwards.

Like so many other great footballers who did not get many opportunities to display the vast repertoire of their skills for their counties in major games, Seán O'Connell's distinguished career with the Ulster Railway Cup side presented such an opportunity. Between 1959 and 1971, he represented his province 15 times winning five medals and captaining the 1971 team. It was most appropriate that three Derrymen whom he had coached as minors and U-21s to All-Ireland success in 1965 and 1968 respectively had played alongside him in that 1971 provincial success. Malachy McAfee, Mickey Niblock and Eamon Coleman (substitute) were the players involved.

During his playing career, O'Connell notched up many exceptional scoring feats enabling him to amass a total well in excess of 600 points in his county and inter-provincial careers. In 1970 he topped the national charts. The man who played over 200 games for Derry once scored 0-11 out of his club's total of 0-12 in a county semi-final. In addition, on successive Sundays, he notched 3-4 and 2-4 against Armagh and Donegal respectively.

Not content with his huge commitment to playing for Derry, Seán also became heavily involved in coaching. In the spring of 1965, a brilliant St Columb's College (now back in competitive colleges' football) not only won the MacRory Cup but went on to become only the second Ulster side to win the All-Ireland Colleges' title when they defeated Belcamp for the coveted Hogan Cup. Meanwhile, Fr Séamus Shields, a curate in Swatragh who was responsible for the setting up of a very well organised co-operative society in the south Derry village, wanted to do something for Derry minor football. As a result of his promptings, St Columb's coach Fr Ignatius McQuillan, his teaching colleague Raymond Gallagher and Fr Shields came together to co-ordinate a more sophisticated approach to the preparation of Derry minor sides. Having been appointed as coach and manager, the Ballerin man soon realised the exceptional potential within the minor panel. With a nucleus of college stars such as Tom Quinn, Malachy McAfee, Séamus Lagan, Colm P. Mullan, Chris Browne and 15-year-old Brendan Mullan to supplement the other non-St-Columb's outstanding prospects like captain Tommy Diamond, Eamon Coleman, Adrian McGuckin and

Mickey Niblock, O'Connell set to work. The rookie coach brought a sense of pattern to their play and they went on to win not only the Ulster final but the All-Ireland as well. Brilliant displays in the final against Kerry by goalkeeper Eugene McCaul, Séamus McCloskey and Philip Friel brought Derry their first All-Ireland minor title in 1965. Three years later, with O'Connell still at the helm, basically the same side won the All-Ireland U-21 title when they defeated Offaly in the decider. Seán O'Connell would have loved an opportunity to manage that team at senior level but he was a victim of his own high playing standards. At the time it was not considered appropriate that a current player could also act as manager.

Seán O'Connell has always been an outstanding sportsman, never having incurred the wrath of any referee during his playing days. He has also been a man of high principles. In 1973, Derry drew with Kerry in a National League semi-final and had two players sent off. Later, a Kerry player alleged, in writing, that he had been struck by the Ballerin man. O'Connell was summoned to Croke Park but refused to go on the basis that if players started making written allegations against each other, disciplinary procedures would break down. His principles cost him a three-month suspension but he did not mind. When he returned to play, he consistently maintained his high standards. Moreover, his integrity was intact and his reputation unbowed.

That same concept of fair play and social justice surfaced 14 years earlier when he was suspended by the Derry County board for playing soccer. As a child in Garvagh, O'Connell had played soccer as his father Pat had done before him in what was essentially a soccer-oriented community. Seán's cousin, Séamus O'Connell, had played first division soccer with Chelsea, won an amateur FA cup medal with Bishop Auckland and had represented England as an amateur international. When Seán was approached by Coleraine FC in the autumn of 1959 he agreed to join them. A vociferous opponent of the GAA's foreign games rule, O'Connell always believed the rule to be extremely negative and counter-productive. 'I was delighted to see the abolition of Rule 27 but there are still bans in the GAA. The GAA should be ban-free, the games should be available to all who wish to play them and the organisation should be mature enough to allow them to do so. However, back to my soccer days.'

I played centre half for Coleraine from October 1959 until March 1961. I really enjoyed playing with such stars as Fay Coyle (an Irish international), Harry McCormack and Clancy McDermott. But I missed playing Gaelic, so because of the ridiculous ban I had to give up soccer.'

When Seán was suspended for playing soccer, a GAA writer under the *nom de plume* 'Linesman' continually castigated the Ballerin player in his column in one of the weekly provincial papers. 'It really was a very scurrilous campaign against me because I played soccer.' However, the whole saga was not without its funny side. So many people were blaming local GAA official, Willie John Halferty for actually writing under the 'Linesman' by-line that he was forced to issue a disclaimer stating that

'Willie John Halferty wishes it to be known that he is not 'Linesman.'' At the same time, in Maghera, a local broadsheet appeared periodically. It related news of current social, political and sporting events. Its editor, popular Maghera businessman Michael McKeefrey, was an ardent supporter of Seán O'Connell. His broadsheet known as 'The Mid Ulster Muckserver' became a forum for supporters of the Ballerin man. In the week after Halferty's disclaimer McKeefrey penned the following humorous retort. 'Linesman wishes it to be known that he is not Willie John Halferty'!

Having taken early retirement from his position as headmaster of St Patrick's Secondary school in Dungiven he spends his time watching all sports particularly golf which he also plays regularly. All kinds of music especially the works of Beethoven and Gilbert and Sullivan, musical film themes and tenors like Pavarotti and Mario Lanza occupy his leisure time.

Seán O'Connell thinks that today there is an over emphasis on physical fitness at the expense of the game's skills. 'I am not particularly happy with modern Gaelic football. We need to get the balance right between handpassing and footpassing. I also think that the status of the National Football League needs to be considerably upgraded. Play-offs, semi-finals and finals should be eliminated. There should be three divisions with the top team in each winning that particular section. A proper league would do much more to promote the game in the weaker counties than a championship system which makes it exceedingly difficult for them to progress especially in Leinster and Ulster.'

In 1971, the GAA instituted an All Stars awards scheme for those outstanding footballers and hurlers whom the selectors considered to be the best players in their particular position during the course of that year. Several years earlier the *Gaelic Weekly* which was a very prestigious paper dealing exclusively with Gaelic games initiated their own All Stars awards. In 1967 the genial giant from Ballerin, Seán O'Connell was nominated at right corner forward. It was a tribute both to the *Gaelic Weekly* and O'Connell that he was the only nominee not to have at least won a provincial medal in the 1960s. The 'big fellow' as he was colloquially known had at last received national recognition for a lifetime of service, skill and dedication to the club and county he loved so well. The peerless prince of Derry forwards was further honoured when he was selected on the 1984 *Sunday Independent*/Irish Nationwide team for footballers who had never won All-Ireland medals. Married to Margaret, they have a family of four children, Joanne (25), James (22), Máire (17), and Seán (15) who is a very promising footballer.

When selecting his Ulster and Ireland teams he made the following nominations:

IRELAND (1955–1999)

John O'Leary
(Dublin)

| Robbie O'Malley | John O'Keeffe | Tom O'Hare |
| *(Meath)* | *(Kerry)* | *(Down)* |

| Michael Donnellan | Kevin Moran | Stephen White |
| *(Galway)* | *(Dublin)* | *(Louth)* |

Brian Mullins   Jack O'Shea
(Dublin)   *(Kerry)*

| Michael Kearins | Seán Purcell | Pat Spillane |
| *(Sligo)* | *(Galway)* | *(Kerry)* |

| Seán O'Neill | Eoin Liston | Kevin Heffernan |
| *(Down)* | *(Kerry)* | *(Dublin)* |

ULSTER (1955–1999)

Finbarr McConnell
(Tyrone)

| Gabriel Kelly | Tony Scullion | Tom O'Hare |
| *(Cavan)* | *(Derry)* | *(Down)* |

| Henry Downey | Paddy Moriarty | Jim McDonnell |
| *(Derry)* | *(Armagh)* | *(Cavan)* |

Jim McKeever   Colm McAlarney
(Derry)   *(Down)*

| Peter McGinnity | Greg Blaney | Paddy Doherty |
| *(Fermanagh)* | *(Down)* | *(Down)* |

| Frank McGuigan | Seán O'Neill | Peter Canavan |
| *(Tyrone)* | *(Down)* | *(Tyrone)* |

When it came to loyalty, length of service, marksmanship, skill, coaching ability, versatility and dedication, no one came any bigger than the sporting Gael from Garvagh. Ballerin Sarsfields GAC are entitled to feel proud to have had Seán O'Connell among their playing ranks for 25 years of football delight. He has done his club, county and province much service.

Anthony Daly

IN 1977 AND 1978, Clare won successive National Hurling League titles. These feats generated a great buzz around the county. Perhaps at last, their supporters thought, Clare would make their first provincial championship breakthrough since they previously won the Munster title in 1932. Eighteen years earlier, in 1914, Clare, represented by Quin, had won their only All-Ireland hurling title when they defeated Laois in the final. Now they had a team of exceptional talent powered by a magnificent half back line of Ger Loughnane, Seán Stack and Seán Hehir. In the attack, interprovincial player Johnny Callinan was a never-say-die supreme hurling artist. It was the latter's consistent performances that won the admiration of a certain eight-year-old Clarecastle boy.

Johnny Callinan was the sole Clarecastle member of that double-winning league side. He, more than anyone else, inspired his youthful fellow parishioner to wield the camán with increasing fervour. Thus, Anthony Daly became inducted into the game that later would propel him into the national hurling consciousness. When the victorious Clare team of those years brought the League trophy to Anthony's local school, his teacher John Hanley, a top hurling coach himself, took the opportunity to impress upon his pupils the importance of practising the skills of hurling. No pupil was more serious or more dedicated in his quest for hurling perfection than Anthony Daly who had an impressive family tradition of hurling to draw on. Two of his uncles were members of the Clare team that defeated Dublin in the National Hurling League final of 1946. His father had also won three county championships playing for Clarecastle in the 1940s.

As a player, Anthony was a slow starter, even failing to make the mid-Clare U-16 panel in a district competition. The fact that his close friend and future county colleague Fergus Tuohy did make that team made him more determined to work at his game. A student, however, at the famed Munster hurling nursery of St Flannan's College in Ennis, Daly developed his skills and was a star figure on his club side, which won the 1986 county minor hurling championship. That team, incidentally, was coached by Michael Slattery who had refereed the 1973 All-Ireland senior hurling final between Limerick and Kilkenny.

The St Flannan's selectors witnessed Daly giving a wonderful display at right corner back in that decider and immediately drafted him into the college's senior hurling squad for the 1986–1987 season. Daly became their regular corner back and was in that position when St Flannan's defeated Midleton CBS in the Dr Harty Cup final.

Played before an attendance of over 5,000, Daly gave a truly impressive display of first class hurling. In the All-Ireland semi-final, St Flannan's easily overcame St Joseph's of Garbally before scoring a comprehensive victory in the All-Ireland college's final against St Kieran's of Kilkenny whose outstanding forward was one Denis Joseph Carey. By now, Daly had developed pace and strength commensurate with a player of senior county standard and it was no surprise that he was selected to play for the Clare minor side of that year. 1987 brought further honour to Anthony when he was a member of the panel that won a county club senior championship with Clarecastle. His burgeoning talent was further recognised when he made his debut with the senior county side, at left corner back, in a hurling tournament held in Kilmallock in the late autumn. Though he played well and won his first inter-county medal in that tournament he was not part of the 1988 senior championship squad. In the 1989 championship game against Waterford when Clare were hammered in Thurles, Daly was a substitute. Still he was relatively happy as he knew he had developed tremendously since his omission from the mid-Clare U-16 team of a few years earlier.

The breakthrough that Anthony had long awaited came in October 1989 when, along with goalkeeper David Fitzgerald, he made his official competitive debut in a league game against Waterford in Dungarvan. Great displays also in his three years with the county U-21 side in 1988, 1989 and 1990 enhanced his position as an integral part of the Clare senior team.

Successive championship defeats to Limerick in both 1990 and 1991 did not offer any prospect of future glory even though they did win Division Two of the league in the latter year, only to be relegated the following season. Just before the 1992 championship game with Waterford, Clare's captain and outstanding forward Tommy Guilfoyle suffered a severe hand injury whilst mowing his lawn. Spotting Daly's inherent leadership qualities, Clare manager Len Gaynor immediately promoted the 22-year-old Clarecastle man to captain. Clare were eventually eliminated by Waterford after a replay in which the Decies scored a controversial winning free in the latter stages of the game. Under his captaincy, Clare reached both the 1993 and 1994 Munster finals only to suffer humiliating defeats to Tipperary and Limerick respectively.

Those barren years of inter-county frustration were eased considerably by the achievements of Daly's club, Clarecastle, who won further senior championships in 1991 and 1994. In the autumn of 1994, Len Gaynor stepped down and a new management team comprising Michael McNamara and Tony Considine, under the tutelage of current selector and former All Star, Ger Loughnane took control of the county's fortunes. Enthusiastic and totally dedicated, Loughnane upped the training schedule to previously unheard of heights and his infectious belief in the men under his control was rewarded by Clare leading Division One of the league at Christmas. In the last game before the Christmas recess, Clare defeated Limerick. This victory proved to be a psychological watershed for the Banner County as practically the same Limerick personnel had trounced Clare just four months earlier in the Munster final.

Clare's good form continued after Christmas when they defeated Tipperary and then Waterford in the league semi-final. In the league decider, however, they were defeated by double scores by Kilkenny, 2-12 to 0-9. As Clare supporters walked disconsolately from this latest debacle, the players hung their heads dejectedly in the dressing room. One man, however, had no doubts about what his team were capable of achieving if they applied themselves. With all players seated and all doors shut, heads gradually started to lift to listen to the messianic voice of Ger Loughnane.

'I guarantee you lads one thing. We're going to win this year's Munster championship which begins in a few weeks time. We might or mightn't win the All-Ireland but we will most definitely win the Munster title. The work is only starting now. You may think that we have done a lot of work but I tell you now we haven't done anything yet.' Anthony Daly and all the players thought that Ger was being over-optimistic but as the weeks passed all knew that Ger's words were beginning to permeate.

The championship began with a Munster semi-final clash with Cork in June. Clare played superbly and appeared to be on their way to their third consecutive Munster final when Cork staged a dramatic comeback. Half a minute from the end, the Rebel County edged in front when Cork forward Kevin Murray sent the sliotar to the Clare net. Then, into the breach stepped the indomitable Seán McMahon, Clare's commanding centre half back. Fifteen minutes earlier, Seán had suffered a broken collar bone but he could not be replaced because Clare had already used their quota of three substitutes. Now playing at corner forward and in obvious pain McMahon somehow managed to win a sideline ball, not far from the corner flag. Fergus Tuohy adroitly crossed the resultant sideline cut into substitute Ollie Baker who connected with the ball to send it to the net for a sensational winning goal.

Displaying fantastic character and resilience, Clare's Munster final performance against Limerick was a magnificent team effort. Their speed and support play truly pulverised the Treatymen who had unluckily lost the previous year's All-Ireland final against Offaly. In the end, Clare, for the first time in 63 years, had won the Munster senior hurling championship. They did it in style, overcoming their neighbours on a 1-17 to 0-11 scoreline. Ironically Clare supporters, in their thousands, had stayed away from this game. They simply could not believe it as they listened to the final minutes of the radio commentary on the game. From the pitch to the victory podium was a long but happy walk for Anthony Daly.

'As the game neared its end and despite the fact that we had a good lead I kept thinking of what happened to Limerick against Offaly in the previous year's All-Ireland. So I just kept totally focused on the ball. It was only when one of the

Limerick players turned round and said, "Fair play to you," that I realised we had at last won that elusive trophy.'

This result banished negativity and inferiority complexes from the county. A huge psychological barrier to success was now gone. Ger Loughnane had been the catalyst for its removal. It was only after this provincial success that the same Ger fully realised that, to gain national respect, Clare must go on to win the All-Ireland. The All-Ireland semi-final against Galway was to see Clare translate that new-found confidence onto a much bigger stage. Seán McMahon, now fully recovered from injury (he had, miraculously, been able to take his place in the Munster final) played stupendously against the Tribesmen in Clare's penultimate game of the 1995 championship. In fact, so good was he that Galway were forced to take off his direct opponent, All Star Joe Rabbitte after only ten minutes of the second half. McMahon's exhibition was emblematic of a brilliant, cohesive performance as the whole Clare team, for the first time, showed their power, skill and determination in the greatest GAA stadium of all. Playing their best hurling of the year, the Banner County went on to record another famous victory as they convincingly defeated the Westerners 3-12 to 1-13. After the humiliation of the previous two years, Clare were now, for the first time since they were beaten by Kilkenny in 1932, in an All-Ireland senior hurling final.

The preparations for the final against Offaly were planned down to the minutest detail, by Loughnane and his management team. As a player, Ger Loughnane had lost five Munster finals and as a manager or selector at Colleges, U-21 and senior level he had lost an incredible 12 finals in a row. The Munster final of 1995 had reversed his fortunes. It had been his lucky 13th final. It was because of all those disappointments that Loughnane left nothing to chance for the greatest day in the history of Clare hurling for 63 years. Every hour in the lead-up to the game would see the players usefully occupied. On the morning of the final, the players assembled in Ennis, took a coach to Shannon Airport and flew to Dublin where they had breakfast in a hotel near Dublin Airport. They then slept for two hours, had a light training session and a snack before watching the first half of the minor game. They were extremely relaxed and ultra-confident as Ger Loughnane addressed them with his deliberately repetitive mantra before they left the Croke Park dressing room. 'Lads,' he said, 'we are going to do it'.

As Offaly apparently controlled much of the game itself, Anthony Daly and his colleagues did not panic as they might have in the past. They kept totally focused on the task in hand, remembering at all times the belief and trust that their extraordinary manager had placed in them. As the game entered its closing stages, Offaly were leading by two points when Clare were awarded a free deep inside their own half. Seán McMahon, who had scored many wonderful long-range frees during the year moved across to take the free. Oozing confidence, his captain Anthony Daly waved his colleague aside and took the free himself. He struck the sliotar hard and sent it high into the Offaly goalmouth. The ball rebounded off an upright. Eamonn Taaffe, who had come on as a substitute a short time before, anticipated the deflected ball and sent it crashing to the net. Clare, the no-hopers, were dramatically leading the odds-on favourites by a point. It was a particularly sweet moment for Taaffe as he had missed the whole championship campaign up to this because of injury. Clare, spurred on by this glorious goal, were now in the ascendant. Two minutes from the end, Clare were awarded a '65' and Daly, again leading by example, sent the ball all the way over the bar to put his side two points ahead. Shortly afterwards, referee Dickie Murphy of Wexford blew the full-time whistle. Thousands of overjoyed Clare supporters rushed on to the pitch to laud their team's wondrous achievement. Victory had been snatched from a gallant Offaly side by a herculean effort from a team obsessed with the idea of obliterating years of constant failure.

The whole team were heroes. Agile goalkeeper David Fitzgerald was inspirational. Defenders, full back Brian Lohan and the magnificent half back line of Liam Doyle, McMahon and Daly were especially cool and collected as their forwards, for much of the game, struggled to score. Ollie Baker was a tower of strength at midfield while Fergus Tuohy, with four marvellous points, and the jinking speedster Jamesie O' Connor were the star performers in the forward line. The anguish and disappointment of past failures were suddenly forgotten as Anthony Daly went up the steps of the Hogan Stand to receive the Liam McCarthy Cup. It was exactly 81 years since last a Clareman had led his side to hurling's holy grail in 1914.

'At first, when that final whistle went there was no emotion, just disbelief. For me, the Munster final had been more emotional as all our efforts had then been concentrated on winning the Munster title. Then slowly the whole significance of what we had achieved really sank in. When I reached the rostrum I knew that things in Clare would never be the same again,' Anthony told me when I met him in his Ennis home.

In one of the most inspiring speeches ever given by an All-Ireland winning captain Daly captured the minds and hearts of a nation by constantly referring to what the occasion and the result would mean to a county starved of success for so long and bedevilled by the ravages of emigration. However, as Daly so eloquently described the unfulfilled ambitions of previous generations, the memory of one incident continually surfaced. 'During my speech my thoughts kept wandering back to my first championship season as captain with Clare in 1992. We had played fantastically well to draw with Waterford in the first game and as the replay neared its end the sides were level. Then, in my opinion, Waterford were unjustly awarded a free which their free-taker duly pointed. With time almost up, Waterford were leading and our chance of success had gone. Their free-taker than raced back after scoring, towards me. I was still lambasting what I considered to be a very unfair decision. Sarcastically the Decies player taunted me. "Stick to your so-and-so music, boy." That remark had always galled me, so on that victory rostrum I just let out everything that was in my head. It really was not only a joyous occasion but also a chance for me to purge the mind of all sneering jibes or sardonic comments. The thing that mattered most was that Clare were All-Ireland hurling champions. Our pride had been restored.'

The celebrations that night in Dublin reverberated through every street, hotel and pub. Young and old from every corner of Clare who were at the game converged on the city's main hostelries playing music and singing the songs of a county long remembered as a haven of Irish culture. Granted, the people of Clare were 'sticking to their traditional music' but it was the deeds of Ger Loughnane's men on the fields which forged together the totality of Michael Cusack's dream. Cusack, who was born in Carron near Burren, Co. Clare, was one of the founders of the GAA in 1884 and its first secretary. To him, the GAA should be the guardian and fulcrum of all things Gaelic. Anthony Daly's speech had encapsulated very clearly all the various strands of those noble sentiments.

As the victorious cavalcade of Clare's hurling heroes made their way to Dublin Airport on the Monday evening after the game, Clare revellers and neutrals alike waved them on their way. Everyone likes to see the underdog succeed and Clare were almost immediately dubbed the People's Champions. The Clare team became the first players to fly the Liam McCarthy Cup across the Shannon for that special homecoming to Shannon Airport.

15,000 flag-waving fans greeted Anthony Daly and his team mates when they arrived in Shannon Airport. Moving by coach through his native Clarecastle where he first discovered the wonder and beauty of the world's fastest field game was a particular source of satisfaction. When they eventually arrived in the county town, Ennis, all Anthony Daly could see was a mass of cheering, flag-waving, singing people. The plane journey from Dublin had only taken 25 minutes but the coach trip from Shannon to Ennis took four hours of sheer bedlam and joy. Daly held the cup aloft to a crescendo of tumultuous cheering. Silence descended on the vast throng as Ger Loughnane stood to address them. Adopting one of the slogans of the sponsors 'Hell for Leather' as his theme, Loughnane reflected. 'Our endless hell began just a year ago for the players when they began training in the hills near Shannon and in the muck at Crusheen. The leather began in April following our defeat in the league final when I know a lot of you lost faith in us. But the players never contemplated defeat. This year we were going to go all the way and no one was going to stop us. After having gone through the pain and torture of a ferocious winter training programme no one was going to put us down,' he concluded to thunderous applause.

In the 1996 Munster championship, Clare played Limerick in a brilliant game of top-class hurling. With three minutes left and three points ahead Clare appeared secure but Limerick's Barry Foley, Gary Kirby and Foley again notched three points to equalise the game. Then came the score that Anthony Daly nominates as the best he has ever seen. Limerick's commanding centre half back Ciarán Carey grabbed the ball deep inside his own half and soloed fifty yards. From very far out, on his weak side and with severe pressure from players behind him, Carey magnificently sent the ball over the bar for the lead point. The final whistle then sounded and Clare's year of triumph had ended. The celebrations of their national success which had continued onto March and their deserved holiday abroad had dulled their appetite somewhat.

1997 was to present, in the words of Loughnane, a new challenge to Clare. His message was simple. 'Good teams win one All-Ireland. Great teams win two. Now prove yourselves great.' Though subsequently relegated in the league, Loughnane was not unduly perturbed. There was only one focus, one target. The Liam McCarthy Cup had to be won again to prove that Clare were not just one-season wonders. Easily defeating Kerry in the first round of the championship, they eventually emerged victorious by a four-point margin over a great Cork side in the Munster semi-final. For the first time in a championship final, Clare defeated Tipperary by three points to regain their provincial crown. Superb displays by Jamesie O'Connor (he scored nine points), Seán McMahon and Daly enabled Clare to defeat Kilkenny in the All-Ireland semi-final much more convincingly than the final winning margin of four points would suggest.

The introduction of the 'back door' system in hurling had allowed beaten Munster finalists, Tipperary, to re-enter the championship at the quarter-final stage where they easily defeated Down. When they defeated Wexford in the All-Ireland semi-final, it meant that the 1997 All-Ireland final between Clare and Tipperary would be a replay of the Munster final. The first all-Munster All-Ireland final had everything: great defensive hurling, brilliant scores and impeccable sportsmanship. In the first half, Tipperary were the better 15 and they led at the interval 0-10 to 0-6. In the second half, Clare came out with renewed vigour and points from Liam Doyle, Conor Clancy, Ger 'Sparrow' O'Loughlin and Colm Lynch had brought the sides level by the seventh minute. Thanks then to a virtuoso performance by Jamesie O'Connor, Clare went into a five-point lead only to be pegged back by a resurgent Tipperary. Just before the end Eugene O'Neill goaled for Tipperary to give the Premier county a one-point advantage. However, a majestic point under the most tense circumstances by the unflappable Ollie Baker brought the sides level. Just when everyone had settled for a draw, Jamesie O'Connor secured possession to loft over the winning point. Soon after, the full-time whistle blew. Anthony Daly then had the signal honour of leading his county to two All-Ireland titles in three years. They had now, beyond all doubt, proven themselves a great side.

In 1998 and 1999, Clare, again under Daly's captaincy made bold efforts to clinch another All-Ireland. Having won the Munster title in 1998 Clare became the unfortunate victims of a time-keeping error by the referee when their winning result in the All-Ireland semi-final replay against Offaly was declared null and void. In the second replay, a very tired Clare team were beaten by the midlanders who went on to become the first 'back door' winners of the All-Ireland hurling championship. After a replay, victory against Tipperary in the 1999 Munster championship, Clare surrendered their Munster title to eventual All-Ireland winners Cork in the Munster final. Thanks again to the 'back door' system, Clare beat Galway, after a replay in the All-Ireland quarter-final only to lose to Kilkenny in the semi-final. Emotionally drained and physically tired, Clare bowed out to a much sharper, fresher and skilful Kilkenny side. Though disappointed, Anthony Daly would not have imagined in 1994 that he would be the proud holder of two All-Ireland and three Munster medals five years later.

Despite his provincial success with Clare, Anthony would like to see the current hurling championship restructured to accommodate just 14 counties in an open draw system.

'I would include all Munster counties with the exception of Kerry: Offaly, Kilkenny, Laois, Wexford and Dublin from Leinster; Galway, Antrim and possibly Down and Derry in an open draw 'A' Championship for the Liam McCarthy Cup. Every year, two teams from a separate 'B' Championship could replace two teams from the previous year's 'A' Championship. Just imagine how exciting it would be to see a packed Semple Stadium with Wexford and Clare meeting in the first round. A televised draw like the FA Cup system after each round would make for compulsive viewing and increased interest. To give additional impetus to the league which is fast fading away, the league finalists could be given a bye into the second round.'

Daly, who loves Gaelic football, won an intermediate championship medal with Clarecastle. 'The Kerry team of the 1980s and the Meath side of the late 1980s and early 1990s were tremendous. Bernard Flynn, Mick Lyons, Colm O'Rourke and Liam Hayes were fantastic footballers,' the former bank official who now has his own sports shop in Ennis stated.

One event in the chequered history of Anthony Daly's climb to fame has always irritated him. It concerns Babs Keating whom he alleges did not give due credit to the Clare team that beat Tipperary in the first round of the 1994 Munster championship.

'After the 1993 Munster final when Tipperary annihilated Clare, Babs came into our dressing room and gave a brilliant speech in which he praised Clare hurling telling us that if we stuck manfully to our task some day we would succeed. After we defeated Tipperary the following year by four points we were all emotional in the dressing room waiting for Babs to come to congratulate us. Instead he sent up Tommy Barrett, the county secretary. Later that evening, on 'The Sunday Game', he made excuses about not having the injured John Leahy available. He should have given us credit for changing an 18-point deficit in 1993 into a four-point advantage in 1994. I will never forget that,' a disappointed Daly ruefully added.

Anthony, who is a Tottenham Hotspurs fan sees his future in the GAA as a coach or manager. 'Ger Loughnane has been a terrific role model in this regard. I would also like to win an All-Ireland club championship title with Clarecastle. As for continuing to play, I just cannot see myself playing for much longer.'

Anthony and his wife, Eilís, have one dauther, Orlaith. When picking his Ireland and Munster selections Anthony made the following choices:

IRELAND

David Fitzgerald
(Clare)

Sylvie Linnane	Brian Lohan	Brian Corcoran
(Galway)	*(Clare)*	*(Cork)*

Peter Finnerty	Seán McMahon	Brian Whelehan
(Galway)	*(Clare)*	*(Offaly)*

Joe Cooney   Frank Cummins
(Galway)   *(Kilkenny)*

Jamesie O'Connor	Martin Storey	DJ Carey
(Clare)	*(Wexford)*	*(Kilkenny)*

Pat Fox	Joe McKenna	Nicholas English
(Tipperary)	*(Limerick)*	*(Tipperary)*

MUNSTER

David Fitzgerald
(Clare)

Denis Mulcahy	Brian Lohan	Brian Corcoran
(Cork)	*(Clare)*	*(Cork)*

Liam Doyle	Seán McMahon	Dermot McCurtain
(Clare)	*(Clare)*	*(Cork)*

Ciarán Carey   John Fenton
(Limerick)   *(Cork)*

Jamesie O'Connor	Gary Kirby	Johnny Callinan
(Clare)	*(Limerick)*	*(Clare)*

Pat Fox	Joe McKenna	Nicholas English
(Tipperary)	*(Limerick)*	*(Tipperary)*

Clare have produced many fine hurlers over the years. Their successful All-Ireland winning team of 1914 had the legendary 'Fowler' McInerney and 'Spam' Spellisey as its anchormen. Dr Tommy Daly's heroics (he won four All-Irelands in 1917, 1920, 1924 and 1927 with Dublin) in the early 1930s with his native county are recalled in song and story. Tull Considine and JJ 'Goggles' Doyle the captain who nearly won the 1932 All-Ireland for the Banner County. In the 1950s and early 1960s, Clare possessed, in Jimmy Smith, one of the greatest scoring (especially goals) forwards of any era. Against Limerick in the 1954 championship, he scored a massive 6-4. Two years later, he totalled 13 goals for the 1956 season – a feat he himself bettered in 1963 when he amassed 17 green flags. Yet, this man, who won six Railway Cup medals, never won any major honour with Clare. It is therefore, perhaps, fitting that his own words should sum up the air of condescension and disappointment that prevailed in Clare over 80 years. In the 1978 *Our Games Annual* he penned the following sentiments:

'The years of defeat and the agonies of ill luck lives with them. It is fine to seem proud. The neighbouring counties smiled knowingly: no spoken word but the condescending smile was always tantalising. We admire your courage, we appreciate your worth; your loyalties are unquestionable, but where are your victories?'

Clare's All-Ireland successes in 1995 and 1997 answered that oft repeated belittling rhetorical question in the most affirmative way possible. On those historic days, the first Clare winner to put his hand up was the pride of Clarecastle, Anthony Daly, tall in stature and taller in spirit – a real captain fantastic.

Peter McGinnity

As A YOUNG GAELIC footballer, Peter McGinnity had three ambitions: to play in Croke Park, to represent his province and for his native Fermanagh to win their first Ulster senior football championship during his playing career. Having already played in Croke Park with the county's Ulster U-21 championship-winning sides of 1970 and 1971, it was a proud and exceptionally excited 19 year-old who entered the dressing rooms of Cavan's Breffni Park prior to his first Railway Cup engagement with the Combined Universities. Not only was his second ambition about to be accomplished but he was to play in a team of stars which included Donegal's brilliant Brian McEniff and legendary full forward, the great Seán O'Neill of Down. There was an additional personal cause for celebration. Four years earlier, Cavan icon Mick Higgins, who had won three All-Ireland medals in 1947, 1948 and 1952 as captain, had come along to coach Peter's native Roslea's U-16 team. 'He picked me out on that occasion for special free-taking coaching. He told me when taking frees to place the ball with the laces facing the goals. In this way the weight of the ball, when kicked, would naturally carry it towards the goals. I took him at his word and had continued to place the ball as he told me with much success, whenever I took frees. Now the same Mick was manager of the Ulster team. My county colleagues Ciarán Campbell and Phil Sheridan were also selected to play for Ulster. So it was a very happy Fermanagh trio who dawdled into the Ulster dressing room. However, any delusions of greatness that any of us may have aspired to were suddenly dashed when Mick came over and said to me. 'Ciarán, here's your number three jersey!' before turning to Ciarán and adding 'Peter, here's your number ten jersey!' Whether or not Mick Higgins made a deliberate faux pas is not important. The fact was I felt terribly disappointed that the man whose coaching I profited from did not apparently recognise me,' Peter told me when I met him in his home in Enniskillen where he lives with his wife Marian and family Tanya, Aidan and Carine.

Peter McGinnity, who was born in Roslea in 1953, inherited his love of Gaelic football from his grandfather, Frank McGinnity, who had won a junior county championship with Roslea in 1932. Apart from regular coaching in the skills of catching and kicking by his grandfather, in Peter's backyard every Sunday after Mass, he did not play any competitive football until he entered St Michael's College Enniskillen. It' was here that Peter gradually developed a love for the game that was to take up most of his spare time for the next 25 years. Coming under the tuition of the then Fermanagh star Mick Brewster who coached the college's team Peter rapidly improved and made the college's Corn na nÓg (U-14$^1/_2$) side as a full back in his second year. Mick Brewster, sensing the special talent he had in his ranks, placed him at midfield on the following year's Corn na nÓg side. 'I really was not much good, just tall at this stage. However, in my fourth year I knew I was getting better and I was picked on the MacRory Cup team (senior colleges football) at right corner back. The prestige of playing for the college was great and because a great footballer like Mick Brewster placed so much trust in me I resolved to practise and practise until I would achieve my potential. I took all the kick-outs and I believe that this practice was to stand me in good stead in later years when I became the county's regular place kicker.

After that college season of 1968 had ended, Peter went home fully enthused. When he played for his club in that year's Fermanagh minor competition the 15-year-old could not believe how he had improved. 'Those competitions were 11-a-side which meant that there was plenty of space and I seemed always to be where the ball was. My kicking and passing had also vastly improved.'

The following year, 1969, the St Michael's College MacRory Cup team played fantastically to reach the Ulster final only to suffer a three-point defeat to one of Ireland's most famous GAA nurseries, St Colman's College, Newry. Despite giving a magnificent exhibition of catching, kicking and passing, McGinnity was sobbing uncontrollably just after the final whistle sounded. Back defending, he had dropped the ball on the edge of the square to allow Newry in for what proved to be the winning goal. 'I felt terrible but I will never forget the kindness of Joe Pat Prunty who raced across the field to console me. Joe Pat, now the managing director of Prunty Pitches told me I was the best footballer on the field and I should not worry as he threw his arms around me. Ironically, in the programme for the 1999 MacRory Cup final there was a report of the 1989, 1979 and 1969 MacRory finals. Whoever wrote those reports must have forgotten the true facts or were just being kind to me because they attributed my mistake of 1969 to my team mate John Courtney,' Peter added.

1970 was to be a vintage year in Peter McGinnity's life as he won an Ulster Rannafast Cup (Under 16$^1/_2$) medal with St Michael's and a minor league medal with Roslea as well as his first medal with the county team when Fermanagh won that year's Ulster minor league. In November 1970, at the age of 17, McGinnity made his senior inter-county debut, against Westmeath, in the National Football League. Thanks to a certain connivance between his mother and himself, the local paper which featured the Fermanagh line out was conveniently concealed from his father who was against anyone underage playing at senior inter-county level. When there was a very favourable report of Peter's debut, in the following week's paper there were no family tricks and Frank was exceptionally proud of his son's display. Thus, an inter-county career that was to last 20 years began. 1970 had been extra special as the budding talent that was Peter had also won an Ulster U-21 medal with Fermanagh when they beat Cavan in the Ulster final, going on to reach the All-Ireland final only to be beaten by Cork. McGinnity, in the one year, had won a medal at club, colleges and two at county level. The future looked promising for the young man who also played soccer with Distillery reserves when he later went to Belfast.

In 1971, Peter and Fermanagh won their second successive Ulster U-21 title when they defeated Tyrone in the decider. Again they reached the final and again they were defeated by a Cork team which included future senior stars, dual player Brian Murphy, John Coleman and Declan Barron in their team. Another dual player in that Rebel county team was full back Martin O'Doherty who was destined to captain Cork to All-Ireland hurling success six years later in 1977. For the next eleven years, McGinnity consistently appeared for the Ernesiders in league and championship games. During all this time, Fermanagh only won one championship game when they recorded a narrow two-point victory over fellow strugglers, Antrim, in 1973. The 6´3¹/₂˝ Roslea man only experienced one achievement of note during this period in the green and white of Fermanagh when they overcame Donegal by 1-8 to 1-7 in the 1977 McKenna Cup final. This was the first time since 1934 that this particular competition had been won by Fermanagh. But for great stalwarts like McGinnity and fellow U-21 Ulster championship colleagues Ciarán Campbell, Phil Sheridan and Barney Reilly, this barren period was inexplicable. Those U-21 successes had promised much, but, in the final analysis, no accomplishment of note had been achieved at senior level.

In 1982, however, with McGinnity, Campbell and Reilly still on board, Fermanagh shocked everyone when they defeated Derry by a point in the first round of the Ulster championship. Their semi-final joust with Tyrone was to see Peter McGinnity giving his best ever display in a Fermanagh jersey. Fetching superbly, defending when required and scoring points from all angles and distances, McGinnity inspired his team to a historic 1-8 to 0-10 victory over the O'Neill county. Fermanagh were in their first Ulster final since they were beaten by Cavan 37 years earlier in 1945.

In the final against Armagh, the Orchard county took an early lead and seemed to be on their way to an easy victory until Peter McGinnity intervened. A magnificent second-half goal by McGinnity brought the teams to level terms and when Fermanagh scored a point to go into the lead shortly afterwards, an upset looked on the cards. All Fermanagh supporters and every neutral desperately urged the Ernesiders on as they sought to consolidate their lead. Maybe that elusive first Ulster championship was on its way to Fermanagh. However, it was Armagh that dug deepest, retook command of the game and went on to record a three-point victory 0-10 to 1-4. Peter McGinnity's third ambition had vanished. Even though McGinnity has tended to get most of the plaudits for that near success, he himself points to the great endeavours by all his colleagues during that 1982 campaign. 'Ciarán Campbell at full back, my midfield partner Philip Courtney and forwards including our team captain Arthur McCaffrey, Barney Reilly, Aidan Jones and Dominic Corrigan were especially effective. At the end of the day we lost and the result was all that mattered. We did not have the self-belief or confidence to build on our lead. A team like Fermanagh only gets very few opportunities to play in an Ulster final. You must take all your chances when that opportunity arises. We did not and so we lost. When I look back on it, even yet, I often think that we could have won that game,' Peter sadly recalled.

Though Fermanagh sensationally knocked out then National League champions Down in the first round of the following year's Ulster championship Peter McGinnity was never again to experience another championship victory before he retired, for the first time, after the 1988 championship exit to Armagh. A badly damaged knee had forced Peter to make his decision

'Initially, after I injured my knee in 1985, I reluctantly agreed to act as player/ manager for the following two years, 1986–1987. This did not work out as I was too young and too close to the players. I had hoped that I would curtail my playing activity but lack of numbers meant that I carried on. Even after I retired in 1988, a combination of injuries and unavailability of some players made me play in some league games in the 1989–1990 season. However, my long-term injury made me decide finally early in 1990 to retire for good.' The man who had graced the playing fields of Ireland for 20 years had hung up his boots for the last time.

After Peter McGinnity qualified as a PE teacher in 1976 from St Joseph's College of Education in Belfast, he was appointed to the staff of St Augustine's secondary school in the city. At the same time, he transferred his club allegiance to leading Belfast side, St Johns. This transfer had a major impact on his football life because he played with a lot of good players and faced many tough opponents. In a three-year spell with St Johns of Antrim, Peter won three county championships, three county league titles and several ancillary competitions. The outstanding highlight of this period was St Johns winning the Ulster club championship in 1977 when they defeated Cavan Gaels in the Ulster final. They went on to contest the 1978 All-Ireland club final only to be defeated by a powerful Thomond College of Limerick. The Limerick college included such brilliant footballers as the Spillane brothers, Pat and Mick of Kerry, Brian Talty of Galway and Richard Bell of Mayo. St Johns too had very capable performers in Gerry McCann, Joe McGuinness, Liam Jennings, Mick Darragh and 1971 All Star Andy McCallion. It must be said that this successful period with St John's was primarily responsible for developing Peter McGinnity into one the foremost midfielders in the country.

In 1979, when Peter was appointed as a PE teacher to his old alma mater in St Michael's Enniskillen he transferred back to his native Roslea club. His return was the main catalyst for the phenomenal rise in the fortunes of Roslea. Six successive league titles (1981-1986) as well as three county championships in 1982, 1984 and 1986 were chalked up. 1984, when Roslea won the double and the Centenary Cup, stands out in Peter's memory as his club's most noteworthy achievement during all his years of playing with them.

His return to Fermanagh heralded another facet of Peter McGinnity's contribution to county football. Along with Dominic Corrigan, Peter set out to improve the standard of football within the college. 'We looked at what the top Ulster colleges like St Patrick's of Maghera and St Colman's of Newry had achieved and how meticulous the preparation of their teams was. We tried to copy the marvellous work that Adrian McGuckin was doing at St Pat's and Ray Morgan was undertaking at St Colman's. I also decided to become manager of the county minor team. Thus, there would be no conflict of interest between college and county and we could maximise and synchronise the commitments of both. Having been in the McLarnon Cup (the Ulster colleges 'B' championship), we decided to enter the MacRory Cup (Ulster colleges 'A' championship). Playing against better teams would improve our standards and this was proven when we won the Ulster Colleges Corn na nÓg (U-$14^1/_2$) in 1988. Now we knew that we had the nucleus of a great senior side. That side fulfilled their earlier promise when we won the MacRory Cup in 1992. The satisfaction of planning for something over a period of years and then achieving it was tremendous. This victory was not just for those who played in that winning side but also for those other great players like Paul Brewster and Paddy McGuinness who had starred for St Michael's in earlier years and who had won nothing.' The effort that Peter and Dominic had put in was finally rewarded. When St Michael's again won the MacRory Cup in 1999, no one in Fermanagh was in any doubt but that their seniors would one day soon reap the reward of St Michael's success.

In September 1997, McGinnity was appointed manager of the Leitrim county team. Leitrim were in a transition period after many of their successful Connacht championship winning team of 1994 were either retired or reaching the veteran stage. When Leitrim were heavily beaten in the 1998 Connacht championship by a very good Galway side which went on to win the All-Ireland, their morale reached a new low. After a subsequent poor league campaign in the 1998–1999 season, Peter decided to resign his position. 'A combination of injuries, illness and the retirement of some players made my job more difficult. As well as that I had two eye operations during my time with Leitrim and that certainly did not help the continuity of my preparations. My outstanding memory is of a great Leitrim performance when they defeated Louth, to retain their Division One league status, in the spring of 1998. We saw the real Leitrim that day. Nevertheless, I have many happy memories even though the fact that so many players lived far from home made team-planning very difficult. However, when I saw that the mutual respect and the necessary effort to achieve success was being eroded I decided to retire after the league in order that someone else would have time to prepare them for the 1999 Connacht championship,' Peter concluded.

The BBC in Belfast launched a new comprehensive coverage of Gaelic games in 1990. With the increasing popularity of Gaelic Games throughout Ireland, they responded magnificently to the expectations of GAA supporters in the province of Ulster by introducing 'The Championship' series. Former Armagh All Star and captain of their 1977 All-Ireland team, Jimmy Smyth was selected as commentator. Peter McGinnity was chosen as match analyst. 'I really enjoyed the experience. It was not too serious. I did not see myself as an expert, I just told it as I saw it. My job was a lot easier than Jimmy's. He had to do all the research. The BBC, it must be said, did a fantastic job in raising the profile of Gaelic Games. The fact that their saturation coverage coincided with three Ulster teams, Down, Donegal and Derry winning All-Irelands certainly helped.'

McGinnity would like to see radical change in the present format of the championship football.

'For the fruitful development of Gaelic football, the institution of a round-robin series in each province is essential. Each county should be guaranteed at least three championship games. There is something radically wrong with a system whereby I only played 22 championship games in 18 years of championship football with Fermanagh. Many other players have had similar experiences. Being continually knocked out in the first round of the championship, as Antrim have experienced for the last 17 years, does nothing for the promotion of Gaelic football.'

During the course of his career, Peter McGinnity was selected as an All Star in 1982 and as a replacement All Star in 1973 and 1977. He also played for Ireland against Australia in the Compromise Rules series of 1984 but it is as a star performer for Ulster in the Railway Cup for which he will be most remembered. For fourteen years (1973–1975 and 1977–1987) he continuously gave peerless performances in the Ulster jersey successfully captaining his province on two occasions, in 1980 and 1983.

At club level, his most difficult opponent was his county colleague Paddy Reilly of Teemore Shamrocks. The best player he ever faced was Dublin's Brian Mullins when he played against him at colleges, county and interprovincial levels. McGinnity, who rates Séamus Moynihan and Maurice Fitzgerald of Kerry, Anthony Tohill (Derry) and Peter Canavan (Tyrone) as the leading players of today will never forget the best individual performance he ever saw. 'It was a Railway Cup semi-final against Leinster at Breffni Park. Time was almost up and Ulster were leading by three points. Matt Connor of Offaly got possession just outside his own 21-yard line and passed the ball to a colleague. After a four-man passing movement, Connor, who had run the whole length of the field, received the final pass and sent a rocket of a shot to the Ulster net from 24 yards out. This brought the game level and sent it into extra time. It was a marvellous score by the most fantastic footballer I have ever seen.' Incidentally, Ulster went on to win that game.

McGinnity credits three GAA coaches for maximising his potential as a Gaelic footballer of renown. 'Mick Brewster of Fermanagh and Ulster first gave me the confidence to utilise whatever ability I had. It was he also who made me practise my free taking when he allotted me to take the kick outs under his tutelage at St Michael's. When I attended St Joseph's College of Education in Belfast (1972–1976) I came under the influence of one of the greatest footballers of all time, Jim McKeever. As a young boy I remember Micheál Ó Hehir on the radio lauding the exploits of McKeever with such comment as 'the great Jim McKeever goes highest in the air and plucks the ball from the clouds'. He was the head of the PE department at St Joseph's and I never saw a man who could catch the ball so majestically or kick it so gracefully as Jim.'

Peter made his all time national and provincial selections as follows:

IRELAND

Billy Morgan
(Cork)

| Tony Scullion | John O'Keeffe | Eugene Hughes |
| *(Derry)* | *(Kerry)* | *(Monaghan)* |

| Tommy Drumm | Kevin Moran | Paudie Lynch |
| *(Dublin)* | *(Dublin)* | *(Kerry)* |

Brian Mullins   Jack O'Shea
(Dublin)   *(Kerry)*

| Matt Connor | Colm McAlarney | Pat Spillane |
| *(Offaly)* | *(Down)* | *(Kerry)* |

| Mike Sheehy | Eoin Liston | Peter Canavan |
| *(Kerry)* | *(Kerry)* | *(Tyrone)* |

ULSTER

(selected mainly from his Railway Cup playing days 1973-1987)

Brian McAlinden
(Armagh)

| Tommy McGovern | Gerry McCarville | Tony Scullion |
| *(Down)* | *(Monaghan)* | *(Derry)* |

| Kevin McCabe | Paddy Moriarty | Finian Ward |
| *(Tyrone)* | *(Armagh)* | *(Donegal)* |

Liam Austin   Colm McAlarney
(Down)   *(Down)*

| Eugene McKenna | Joe Kernan | Eugene Hughes |
| *(Tyrone)* | *(Armagh)* | *(Monaghan)* |

| Martin McHugh | Frank McGuigan | Andy McCallion |
| *(Donegal)* | *(Tyrone)* | *(Antrim)* |

It was once said, rather cynically, that Fermanagh would never win anything as half of the county was water and that 50 percent of the remaining half consisted of people who did not play Gaelic Games! Whatever about that, no one can deny the fact that they have a very small playing base of only 18 clubs. That, however, has not prevented Fermanagh teams, officials and supporters from contributing handsomely to the enrichment of the GAA. Players like star forward of the 1950s and 1960s, Kevin Sreenan and Railway Cup stars such as PJ Treacy and the late Mick Brewster have made significant contributions. Treacy, who played in Ulster's four-in-a-row Railway Cup successes (1963-1966) received a man-of-the-match accolade for his 1-4 in the 1963 provincial final success. Many Fermanagh county board officials, in the past, have given long and loyal service to the GAA in extremely difficult social and political circumstances. Men like John Joe McElholm, Gerry Magee, Malachy Mahon and Tom Fee fall into that category as do present-day officials John Vesey, Eddie Traynor, Joe McGurn and Paddy Donnelly.

The greatest administrative accomplishment of all was brought to the county when Teemore Shamrocks member, Peter Quinn, was elected President of the GAA for the term 1991 to 1994. The former Ulster Council GAA President and a top financial consultant in his professional life was nationally recognised as a person of exceptional ability who very worthily represented the GAA at home and abroad.

Despite its size, the spirit of the founding fathers of the GAA is alive and prospering in the picturesque Lakeside county. Each generation of GAA people has produced people of extraordinary ability who have successfully passed the GAA torch to the next generation. With present stars such as Raymond Gallagher, Paul Brewster, Paddy McGuinness and Shane King, the future looks bright. Shortly, young outstanding talent from St Michael's like Colm Bradley, Colm Monahan and Ciarán Smith will supplement Fermanagh's quest for that first ever senior Ulster championship title. As a player, Peter McGinnity almost achieved his third and most important ambition. Given his record of 20 years of coaching at St Michael's, that day will come sooner rather than later. No man will be happier than Peter McGinnity to see Ulster champions Fermanagh playing in Croke Park in an All-Ireland semi-final.

Jimmy Keaveney

JIMMY KEAVENEY WAS SITTING at the bar drinking a pint in the old St Vincent's Clubhouse in Raheny. It was a Friday night in May 1974. Suddenly he was conscious of a gentle tap on the shoulder and a very familiar voice. 'So you're not taking this training seriously. If you were, you wouldn't be drinking on a night prior to a training session,' stated his St Vincent's colleague and Dublin manager, Kevin Heffernan.

Jimmy, at first, adopted a very casual attitude to this comment and dutifully returned to the club on the following three Friday nights. On each of those nights, the abstemious Heffernan also came and to all intents and purposes he ignored the presence of the rotund, 15-stone Keaveney. Eventually, Heffernan had enough. He marched up to Keaveney and beseeched him, 'Look, Jimmy, will you do me a favour? Would you ever go home and look after yourself?'

Having always respected Heffernan and his tremendous dedication, Keaveney decided to eliminate his socialising and concentrate solely on making himself superbly fit for the championship ahead.

To understand fully the importance of the above anecdote, one must go back to the first round of that year's Leinster championship. In that game, Dublin had defeated Wexford. Despite winning the game rather easily, Heffernan realised that it was imperative that his team obtain a reliable place kicker and target man. So, on the night after the game he called on an old retired friend – Jimmy Keaveney.

Keaveney, even though he was only 28 years of age had become totally disillusioned with Gaelic football in Dublin. From 1964 to 1972, he had worn the county colours. With the exception of a National League home final win against Down in 1964, a thrilling Leinster final success against Longford in 1965 and an unsuccessful National League home final against Galway in 1967, those years had been essentially barren on the inter-county front for Keaveney. So, when Dublin were knocked out of the 1972 Leinster championship in Navan, the then burly St Vincent's man decided to hang up his boots.

'When Kevin asked me to rejoin the panel in 1974, there was no point in arguing with him. As he was such a persuasive individual, I just told him that I would come to training on the following evening,' stated Jimmy when I met him in the Sunnybank Hotel in Glasnevin.

What Keaveney had not bargained for, however, was the intensity and regularity of the physical fitness programme that Heffernan had mapped out for his players. In addition, the dietary and alcohol habits of all players had to be altered in order to maximise their fitness. Kevin Heffernan, who along with Kerry's Mick O'Dwyer, was destined to change the format of Gaelic football in the 1970s, had just introduced the most strict and regimental physical programme that one could imagine. Part of this entailed a training session each Saturday morning at 10.00 a.m. Previously, very few, if any, teams trained on a Saturday morning. So, one could readily understand Keaveney's reluctance to change his Friday night trips to the St Vincent's Club Social Rooms.

When Jimmy Keaveney played his first match in the second round of the 1974 Leinster championship, Dublin faced Louth. It was Jimmy's all-round leadership as well as his deadly accuracy from frees which was primarily responsible for Dublin emerging victorious on a 2-11 to 1-9 scoreline. For Heffernan, the final and most important piece in his championship jigsaw was firmly in place. This was to prove vital in the five championship campaigns from 1974 to 1978 when Keaveney was to amass the colossal total of 12 goals and 142 points.

After the Louth game, Keaveney was beginning to see some tangible reward for his rededication to the cause. He looked forward eagerly to a quarter-final match against Offaly who had won successive All-Ireland senior football titles in 1971 and 1972. They were the team against which Dublin could measure their progress. In the game itself, Dublin played brilliantly throughout. As a roving target man, Keaveney became the fulcrum of every attack. Also, as a free taker par excellence he became the outward face of a great Dublin inner determination and newly found confidence. On the other hand, Offaly had not won the three previous Leinster championships and two All-Irelands without an outstanding football pedigree. They maintained this high standard to the very end of this exciting and totally absorbing contest. With time running out, the sides were level. Then, Dublin substitute Leslie Deegan, despite being surrounded by several Offaly defenders, scored a marvellous winning point. Dublin had won by the narrowest of margins 1-11 to 0-13. They were now in the semi-final against Kildare and thanks to a mercurial display by the ever-accurate Keaveney, Dublin triumphed by a six-point margin. Now Keaveney and Dublin were in the Leinster senior football final for the first time in nine years. In a tough, dour and uncompromising game, with little quality football, Dublin overcame their adversaries, Meath by 1-14 to 1-9.

Simultaneously, a new GAA culture was about to emerge. Young Dublin sports followers had been starved of success in any sport for many years. The Dublin Gaelic football side was to fill that vacuum. Gaelic football, particularly in Dublin, now became an accepted game in the eyes of the hitherto uncommitted or even avid followers of other codes such as rugby or soccer. Dublin supporters, in dramatically increasing numbers, adopted Croke Park's Hill 16 as their hallowed territory. More than any other player, Jimmy Keaveney epitomised their newfound Gaelic spirit. In essence, he became the focal point of their hero worship – the real darling of the Hill. Kevin Heffernan was popularly and correctly acknowledged as the calculating architect of this euphoria. It was, however, Jimmy Keaveney who was the master engineer of all the glory on the field of play.

In the All-Ireland semi-final, Dublin met the then All-Ireland champions, Cork. Until now, the majority of the Dublin players had been content to win the Leinster title. Few, if any, had any ambition to win the 1974 Sam Maguire Cup. Heffernan, as always, had his own definite ideas and targets. Immediately prior to the Cork game he told his men that, not only were they going to defeat the red-hot favourites, Cork, in the semi-final but that they were going on to win the coveted All-Ireland title as well. Jimmy Keaveney will never forget how, Heffernan, in a passionate five-minute address, convinced his team that the ultimate prize was theirs if they wanted it.

Thus when they faced Cork, each Dublin player was totally focused on the task in hand. Giving a wonderful exhibition of fast creative football, Dublin tore the Cork defence to shreds. They exploited the use of space magnificently, with much running off the ball when the game demanded it. This concept of total football mesmerised the opposition. Thanks to this overall game plan and Keaveney's pinpoint accuracy, Dublin ran out convincing winners 2-11 to 1-8. Jimmy Keaveney was about to appear in his first All-Ireland senior football final.

In that final, Dublin were pitted against a Galway side, the nucleus of which had lost both the 1971 and 1973 All-Ireland finals. Aided by a strong breeze in the opening half, Galway seized the initiative. Despite their outfield supremacy, however, Galway failed to capitalise and missed two clear goal chances in the process. Indeed, when the sides retired at half time, Galway only held a two point advantage, 1-4 to 0-5. When Jimmy Keaveney pointed a free in the eighth minute of the second half the deficit was reduced to the minimum.

It was four minutes later that the turning point in this game came. Galway were awarded a penalty when ace forward Liam Sammon was hauled down in the square. However, the resultant penalty was stopped by the alert Dublin goalkeeper, Paddy Cullen. The psychological impact of this save galvanised Dublin. Along with Leslie Deegan's winning point against Offaly in the Leinster quarter-final, one could say, retrospectively, that Cullen's save was another defining moment in Dublin's quest for acceptability as a great footballing team. For the remainder of the game, Dublin totally dominated proceedings. Football fans now saw a cameo of Dublin's style of play which was to become their trademark for the next four years. Magnificent combination football played at a blistering pace was central to this system. On that historic day Dublin had many stars such as defender Robbie Kelleher, 19-year-old midfielder Brian Mullins and netminder Paddy Cullen. The roving tactics and penetrative runs of forwards Bobby Doyle and David Hickey confused the whole

Galway defence. Nevertheless, it was the craft, guile and skill of Jimmy Keaveney that converted his colleagues' excellent approach work into scores. Due to his unerring free taking and one fabulous point from play, Jimmy was chiefly responsible for Dublin's convincing victory on a score of 1-14 to 1-6.

'When the final whistle sounded, the greatest and proudest moment of my life had arrived. Fantastic subsequent achievements in 1976 and 1977 could not compare to that magic moment when our captain Seán Doherty raised the Sam Maguire Cup. What made me especially happy was that Paddy Cullen, Gay O'Driscoll, Seán Doherty and Tony Hanahoe who had given such long and loyal service were there to share this great moment with me,' said Keaveney.

Rarely in the history of Gaelic Games were there such emotional scenes as Dublin fans rushed onto the field to greet their new heroes. The sacred sod of Croke Park was immediately draped in a sea of light and navy blue. Another outstanding and unusual memory from that victory continually pervades the mind of Jimmy Keaveney. On the night following the game, a civic reception was held for the team in the Mansion House. Prior to that, the Dublin team were paraded around the streets of the capital on an open top double-decker bus. As an elated Keaveney stood along with his colleagues on that bus, it suddenly occurred to him that the man who made it all possible was not on board. Then as the bus snaked its way through the vast crowds in O'Connell Street, Keaveney spotted Kevin Heffernan down below, standing amongst the cheering thousands. There he was smiling, watching and savouring the beauty of the hour just like any ordinary Dublin supporter. To Jimmy Keaveney that gesture encapsulated both the greatness and simplicity of Kevin Heffernan.

Jimmy Keaveney was to earn further All-Ireland success in 1976 and 1977 when Dublin defeated Kerry and Armagh respectively. That 1976 victory was Dublin's first championship success over Kerry since 1934. This was another highlight as Keaveney looks back on his second coming! Keaveney also feels privileged to have played in what is commonly acknowledged as one of the outstanding games of all time - the 1977 All-Ireland football semi-final between Dublin and Kerry. The whole game, but particularly the last ten minutes, will be forever etched in his memory.

Jimmy Keaveney was born in Dublin in 1945. He credits his Belfast-born father and the Christian Brothers, especially the late Brother Coughlan in Scoil Mhuire, Marino, for fostering within him a love of Gaelic Games. His debut in Croke Park was in a primary schools competition when he played against a Laurence O'Toole's side which included future colleague, Paddy Cullen. The great Dublin teams of 1955 and 1958, most of whom were stars with the club he had joined – St Vincent's – were his boyhood heroes. The 1959 Colleges' victory of his secondary school, St Joseph's, Fairview, simply reinforced this. As he observed the skills of such Dublin notables as Kevin Heffernan, Denis O'Mahoney, Ollie Freaney, Blackie Coen and dual stars 'Snitchy' Ferguson and Des Foley, Keaveney's burning ambition to wear the then blue and white of his native Dublin, was fuelled. From his minor year of 1963 until he retired in 1979, Jimmy Keaveney was to play in all grades in both hurling and football at inter-county level.

Like all truly great players, Keaveney has a special affinity for his club, St Vincents. This doyen of clubs which had 14 players on the successful Dublin side which won the 1953 National Football League is still Jimmy's pride and joy. Currently involved with coaching underage players at the club, Keaveney is particularly proud to recall the day that St Vincent's won the All-Ireland football club championship in 1976. Three years previously, they had reached the final but after a replay they had to succumb to a wonderful Nemo Rangers side. The Cork side included such stalwarts as Billy Morgan, Frank Cogan and Jimmy Barrett. The St Vincent's side of 1976 had such household names as Gay O'Driscoll, Brian Mullins, Fran Ryder, Tony Hanahoe and Bobby Doyle. Playing superbly under the captaincy of Jimmy Keaveney, St Vincent's strolled to a comprehensive victory over their opponents Roscommon Gaels. 'It was a bitter, wet and miserable day in Portlaoise. I remember the then President of the GAA, Dr Donal Keenan, coming over to me after the game. He was wearing a big, heavy overcoat and was carrying the Andy Merrigan Cup underneath it. Then, he took the cup out and said, "Congratulations, here you are Jimmy." After the game all the players went their separate ways. We did not have a meal. By the way, there was nothing unusual about that at that time. For example, when we won the 1974 All-Ireland, I was so tired that I went home immediately after the game and went to bed for two and a half hours. Admittedly, I came back into town for the team celebration, later. Times have certainly changed since then,' concluded Jimmy.

Two of Jimmy's greatest disappointments in his playing career occurred in consecutive years in 1978 and 1979. For the first 20 minutes of the 1978 All-Ireland final against Kerry, Dublin were not only playing superbly but leading comfortably. However, a series of bizarre incidents and elementary defensive errors contributed to Kerry notching three goals in rapid succession. Jimmy recalls the day with some uncharacteristic sadness. 'During the first quarter we were totally dominant. For the first time in my life I saw the Kerry defence so rattled that they were arguing amongst themselves. Then we became too casual. If we had held our discipline I have no doubt that we would have won.'

When 1979 began, Jimmy had decided that whatever the circumstance this would be his last season with his native county. But Jimmy's career did not end in the manner that he either expected or wanted it. In that year's Leinster final against Offaly, he was sent off. As he was suspended for two months he missed both the All-Ireland semi-final and final. Jimmy's career was effectively over. It was his personal experience of those particular circumstances which allows him to hold such definite views on one of the most contentious issues in the GAA today – match suspensions or time suspensions. Jimmy assesses the controversy.

'I believe that the GAA should have match suspensions instead of time suspensions as it is a much fairer system. If this had been like this in 1979 I would have been eligible to play in the All-Ireland final. Incidentally, if the GAA had stuck to the original date for that final I would have been eligible anyhow. The final was brought forward a week that year to facilitate the Pope's visit to Ireland.'

Keaveney, who is very much against the so-called back-door system in championship hurling and the possible introduction of a round-robin system in championship football, has some very interesting views on how major GAA competitions should progress as we enter a new millennium.

'Counties do not have enough meaningful competitive games. I would have a fixed inter-county season from the first of February to the last day in September. This would commence with the National Football League which I would divide into two divisions of sixteen teams. Operating a proper league, with promotion and relegation, I would eliminate play-offs, semi-finals and a final as we have at present. To avoid a clash with club fixtures I would envisage many of these games being played either under floodlights on Friday nights or on Saturdays.

Following the end of the League, I would run off, within a much shorter time span, the current provincial championships in both football and hurling. After the completion of the interprovincial championship I would hold an open draw for the All-Ireland championship in both codes.

As I see it, the present championships are too predictable. One can readily assume the names of six or seven counties that will feature in the concluding stages of the All-Irelands at present. Under my plan, weaker counties could have a greater opportunity of progressing to round two or round three, thus guaranteeing them at least three games, e.g. Waterford could be drawn against Antrim in football or Roscommon against Kerry in hurling. We could also have the unusual spectacle of teams from the same province playing in the All-Ireland final.' Jimmy opined.

Keaveney, who won two Texaco Footballer of the Year Awards in 1976 and 1977, feels that there is far too much short passing in the modern football game. In his opinion this leads to too much fouling and thus the game suffers in terms of spectator appeal. 'When a forward breaks quickly from his marker he is entitled to get the ball as very few such opportunities present themselves in any given game. What annoys me about this over-indulgence in short passing is that when a movement breaks down, as often it will the selectors blame the full forward line and one of them is replaced. This is patently unfair, as frequently it is not the forward's fault that he did not receive quality ball in the first place. To counteract this tactic and to eliminate the pulling and dragging in the game I would make three suggestions:

1. Award two points for any free given for a personal foul inside the 45-metre line.
2. Allow the pick up off the ground with the hands.

3. Adopt the Australian type challenge where the player in possession must release the ball when tackled.'

To complete the professional development of Gaelic games, Keaveney would install an efficient hooter type system at all major games, introduce a marketing saturation of Gaelic games exposure, particularly in Europe, and play Railway Cup finals in a foreign country each year.

Jimmy Keaveney, whose uncle, Paddy Dyer, won an FAI Cup medal with Drumcondra in the 1940s, is a lover of all sports. He attended the 1990 and 1994 soccer World Cup finals in Italy and America respectively. Every year along with several of his former team-mates he visits Listowel Races where he meets such friendly adversaries of old as Kerry's Eoin Liston and 'Ogie' Moran. When the die is cast, however, it is Gaelic games in general and hurling in particular which takes pride of place. 'I love hurling and the many wonderful players who have contributed so much to its popularity – Christy Ring (Cork), Donie Nealon (Tipperary), Jimmy Barry Murphy (Cork), Gerald McCarthy (Cork), the Quigley Brothers (Wexford), Eddie Keher (Kilkenny), Eamon Cregan (Limerick) and Joe Salmon (Galway) are but some of the outstanding exponents of the sliotar who have impressed me,' added Jimmy.

During his time watching and playing Keaveney has admired the skills, dedication and tenacity of many brilliant Gaelic footballers from every county in Ireland.

'Dublin's Paddy O'Flaherty, Paddy Cullen and John O'Leary were all fantastic goalkeepers. Billy Morgan (Cork) and Johnny Geraghty (Galway) were extremely alert with a good sense of anticipation. Jack Quinn (Meath), Frank Cogan (Cork), Martin Newell (Galway), Nicholas Clavin (Offaly), Noel Tierney (Galway), along with old team-mates Lar Foley, Gay O'Drisoll, Seán Doherty, Robbie Kelleher and Kevin Moran were defenders of undoubted class. Peter Moore (Meath), Mick Carolan (Kildare), Pat Mangan (Kildare), Brian Mullins (Dublin), Des Foley (Dublin), Mick O'Connell (Kerry), Jim McKeever (Derry) and Jack O'Shea (Kerry) were all great fielders. O'Connell and McKeever were the two most graceful and athletic Gaelic footballers that I ever saw,' said Keaveney.

Jimmy, who once scored 1-11 in a Leinster championship game against Louth, would select Dublin's Kevin Heffernan and Ollie Freaney, Down's Seán O'Neill and Paddy Doherty and Kerry's Pat Spillane, Mike Sheehy, Eoin Liston and John Egan as exceptional talents. 'I would love to have had an opportunity to play with those Kerry forwards. They all simply oozed class in everything that they did. The greatest opponent that I ever faced was another Kerry man – John O'Keeffe. He was a brilliant fielder, had great positional sense and a good turn of speed. The fact that he was selected as an All Star, both at full back and at centrefield, proves how versatile he was.'

Alongside the magnificent playing qualities of O'Keeffe, Keaveney places his former midfield colleague, Brian Mullins. It was Mullins' indomitable spirit, particularly in the face of adversity that tips the scales in Mullins being Keaveney's all-time favourite GAA personality. 'Very few people, outside of Dublin, realise what Brian went through to get back to full fitness after a horrific car crash in 1980. I saw Brian with his forearm stitched to his hip trying to get a skin graft to take. For two weeks, night and day, he lay in that same horizontal position. Only for that injury, I am convinced that Dublin would have won at least two other All-Irelands in the early 1980s. As it was, he was the man who inspired them to their 1983 success,' concluded Keaveney.

When Jimmy decided to forego his weekly visits to St Vincent's Club in 1974 his manager, Kevin Heffernan, being the perfectionist that he was, continued those visitations for the next three weeks just in case Keaveney might return. Eventually, he stopped, happy in the knowledge that his chief lieutenant was deadly serious about his commitment to Dublin.

Almost four years later, on St Patrick's Day 1978 the annual Gaelic football match between a Dublin XV and a Rest of Ireland selection took place in heaven. St Patrick was manager of the Irish side who wore green. St Joseph was the supremo of the Dublin team who were clad in their traditional blue. With ten minutes to go, Ireland were leading by eight points when a rather obese figure with the number 14 on his back entered the fray for Dublin. In a virtuoso performance, the substitute scored one goal and six points to snatch a sensational victory for St Joseph's charges.

After the game an irate St Patrick dashed over to St Joseph and yelled.

'You cheated. You played an illegal player, a player who is not even dead!'

'Stop talking nonsense,' retorted St Joseph.

'I'm complaining about you bringing on Jimmy Keaveney,' replied Patrick.

'That's not true,' Joseph quietly answered.

'Well, who was the fellow who scored one goal and six points?' implored the increasingly frustrated Patrick. 'Was that not Jimmy Keaveney'?

'No, not at all. That was Our Lord himself! He just thinks he is Jimmy Keaveney,' said Joseph.

That story, plucked from the various legends and myths concerning the many remarkable scoring exploits of Jimmy Keaveney, emphasises the enormous esteem in which he is held. All Dublin and indeed all GAA aficionados everywhere would concur. Jimmy's place in GAA folklore is deservedly assured. He, and his wife, Angela, have four children, James, Roisín, Maria and Timothy.

Pakie McGarty

IN THE PRESENTATION BROTHERS primary school in Carrick-on-Shannon, the final-year pupil frantically scanned the 1959 English Primary Certificate examination paper. For weeks he had anxiously hoped that an English essay title appropriate to his interests and aptitudes would appear in the test. An excellent English essay performance would be a passport to a good result. When he saw the composition entitled 'My Hero,' the apprehensive youngster was elated. The previous year, he had watched a Leitrim man giving one of the best ever individual displays in the history of Gaelic football. Pakie McGarty was the man who would make the words 'My Hero' a living reality for the budding academic.

As a young boy growing up in his native Mohill, Pakie McGarty was continually inundated with talk of Gaelic football. His father was club chairman and his brother Willie was an established club player. Their influence, considerable though it was, paled into insignificance when compared to the impact that a new bank clerk had. Leo McAlinden, who had starred for Ulster in the Railway Cup final of 1944, had come to work in the Leitrim town. Pakie vividly recalls the Armagh native's first game for Mohill. 'When Leo announced his availability some locals were rather sceptical. Mohill had a big strong junior team at that time and Leo's light physique did not match their idea of a competent footballer. So they picked Leo at corner forward for a league match against Cloone. Leo, who had played midfield both for Armagh and Ulster asked to be placed at centre field. The selectors reluctantly agreed to his request. I will always remember Leo's terrific display that day. With his pacy, incisive solo runs he literally ran Cloone off the pitch. No one in Mohill had ever seen solo running before. After that game Leo was everybody's hero. He had all the skills, could kick 50s with either foot straight over the bar and I wanted to imitate him. I used to follow him around the town as he went solo running with a shilling piece or an apple up the street. Watching this football artist at work made me decide that Gaelic football was the game for me,' Pakie added when I met him at his Clondalkin home. McAlinden, who often trained on his own, soon had a very willing ball boy who himself rapidly developed into a first-rate player, winning his first two medals for the Mohill U-14 schoolboy teams in 1946 and 1947. McGarty credits local teacher Mark Keegan, a native of Offaly, for developing their individual and team skills. However the midfield pairing of Pakie and his future county colleague, the late Eddie Rowley, played a pivotal role in that achievement.

Two years later, in 1949, Pakie had the unusual distinction of playing for the Leitrim senior team before he played at county minor level. The circumstances of his debut were rather bizarre. A week earlier, Pakie had played very well in a club game and as a result had been called up to the panel for the senior league game against Offaly the following Sunday in Mohill. Pakie did not get any personal notification of his promotion but had read it in the paper. Modest youth that he was, he really thought that it was a mistake so he just went along to the game as a spectator. With a few other young lads, Pakie had participated with the county players in a pre-match kick around. When it was discovered that the team was a player short Pakie was immediately drafted into the left corner forward position. But first he had to run home for his football gear, making the return journey just in time for the throw in. Though Leitrim were trounced in the game, the 16-year old McGarty scored a goal and a point. An incomparable career that would span four decades had begun. For the next 22 years, Pakie McGarty would be an automatic choice for the men in green and gold.

As Mohill had no club minor team, they amalgamated with Fenagh with whom Pakie, along with Cathal Flynn, Jimmy McKeon and Eddie Rowley starred in back-to-back county minor title-winning teams in 1950 and 1951. At the same time, Leitrim were experiencing extreme difficulty in fielding a senior side so they were regraded to junior status in 1952. That year's Connacht junior championship was to launch Pakie McGarty onto the national stage after they won the provincial title when they defeated Mayo in the final. Having beaten Tipperary in the All-Ireland semi-final, McGarty and Leitrim faced Meath in the All-Ireland (Home) final. Despite magnificent displays by his boyhood hero, Leo McAlinden, full forward Columba Cryan and McGarty himself, Leitrim succumbed to the Royal County. Unfortunately, failure at this final hurdle was a foretaste of many similar disappointments which McGarty was to experience all his football life.

In 1953, Leitrim regained their senior status and only lost by two points to Galway with whom Jack Mahon, who was to win an All-Ireland medal in 1956, was making his debut. That promising championship performance was further enhanced when Leitrim, with Pakie scoring 1-4 of their total, only lost by a point to Sligo in the 1954 Connacht championship. The following year the Mohill man went to England but returned to score seven points from midfield only to suffer a humiliating defeat at the hands of Mayo.

However, a significant change then took place in the management of Leitrim football. Fr Seán Manning, a highly respected coach who had brought All-Ireland glory to St Mel's College Longford in 1948 as well as numerous Leinster colleges championships, was appointed coach to the Leitrim minor team in 1956. His approach was so thorough and his training so professional that he guided Leitrim to a fantastic provincial success when they defeated Roscommon by four points in the decider. In the All-Ireland semi-final, they beat Donegal before going under to a star studded Dublin 15 which included the Foley brothers Lar and Des in the final. After his minor success Fr Manning was asked to coach the senior team which he did with rare abandon and much success guiding them to four consecutive Connacht finals (all against Galway) from 1957 to 1960. The introduction of one venue for training for the 1957 championship helped to co-ordinate training, improve tactical awareness and create a better team spirit. With more than half of Leitrim's players domiciled in Dublin at any given time, the previous arrangement had been to have two separate training venues one in Dublin and one in Carrick-on-Shannon. This new arrangement meant much greater personal sacrifices for the Dublin-based players as they inevitably did not reach their Dublin homes until two o'clock in the morning after training sessions. When Leitrim defeated Sligo to reach their first Connacht final since 1949, all sacrifices were deemed worthwhile. But when they suffered a heavy defeat to Galway, some cynics were rather sceptical. Undaunted, Fr Manning put down Leitrim's 1957 failure to a certain inborn obsession with failure as well as meeting an exceptionally good Galway side whose terrible twins Purcell and Stockwell tore the Leitrim defence asunder.

A good league run in the 1957–1958 season supported Fr Manning's contention. A great performance by Leitrim when they defeated Roscommon 0-11 to 0-9 in the semi-final of the 1958 Connacht championship added significantly to Leitrim's newfound confidence. In addition, as well as beating Roscommon for the first time in the championship since 1927 they had developed a pattern to their play. Innovation and imagination were the order of the day as Leitrim assiduously prepared for a second successive final against Galway. The Leitrim team had now their own masseur, Bob Brophy, which was an unheard of development at the time. Dublin and Leinster star, Kevin Heffernan who would captain Dublin to All-Ireland glory in 1958, was working with the ESB in Sligo. He gave talks to the Leitrim players on a variety of team and individual skills. The novelty of this approach gave a fresh impetus to Leitrim's search for provincial success.

In Connacht GAA football lore, the 1958 final has always been referred to as the Pakie McGarty Final. Played on a gloriously sunny day, it was the last major game to be staged at the old St Coman's Park in Roscommon. The football was exhilarating and the tension unbearable as both teams displayed total commitment and an abundance of skill. True to form, Galway raced into a 1-3 to 0-1 lead after only seven minutes. But now McGarty, though nominally listed at centre half forward, made himself available in the general midfield area. With radar-like anticipation, he seemed to own the ball. Wherever he went, the magical leather was drawn to him. Time after time, he soloed fearlessly through the heart of the Galway defence earning frees which the ever-reliable free-taker Cathal Flynn duly pointed. Still, despite McGarty's dominance Galway led at half time on a 2-4 to 0-6 scoreline.

The second half started as the first had ended with McGarty orchestrating every foray, and they were many, into the Galway defence. Only wayward finishing by some of his fellow forwards prevented Leitrim from going into a shock lead. After a terrific Leitrim movement which produced a goal, the sides were level. Again McGarty had been the provider as he soloed and sidestepped his way at incredible speed before laying the ball off to corner forward Cathal Flynn to score a great goal. Immediately after that inspirational score, McGarty leapt for possession in the centre of the field but the referee did not spot an obvious push in the back. A Galway player gained possession and sent a long kick downfield which resulted in the lead point for the Tribesmen. With the scores now at 2-8 to 1-10, the psychological advantage had swung Galway's way. Still the inferior and defeatist complex of past years had been forgotten as Leitrim continued to attack. A near miss for a sensational winning goal when full forward Columba Cryan hit the side netting was the nearest, however, that Leitrim came to creating history. Two further points by Galway and one by Leitrim concluded the scoring as gallant Leitrim finally acknowledged defeat 2-10 to 1-11. A combination of wasteful shooting and exceptionally tight marking allowed Galway to escape with a very lucky victory.

The fact that Galway only lost by one point to eventual All-Ireland champions Dublin in the All-Ireland semi-final shows how good Leitrim really were. The organisational skills of Leitrim's management team under the coaching baton of Fr Manning plus the performances of star defenders Tom Colreavy, Josie Murray (captain of the 1956 minor side) and Tony Hayden as well as the astuteness of Columba Cryan and the accuracy of Cathal Flynn had brought Leitrim to a level of football respectability not experienced in the previous 30 years. However, it was the irrepressible McGarty, then at the height of his considerable powers, who was chiefly responsible for this outstanding display. His speed of thought and fleetness of foot combined with his consummate ball skills were qualities which would tear any defence apart. Every team capable of winning any match of consequence needs a player who will lead and inspire. McGarty was the perfect example of such a player.

Leitrim supporters and neutral observers at the game maintained that they never witnessed such an exhibition of high fielding, devastating solo runs and incisive passing as that given by McGarty in the 1958 final. Galway had no answer to his penetrating runs and it was felt by many that the 5′7″ McGarty was the subject of much rough treatment by the Galway defence. This thesis was substantiated by the fact that Pakie's jersey was in shreds after the game. One Galway player in particular was alleged to have continually dragged and pulled McGarty repeatedly to the ground but he did not receive any serious admonition from the referee. Despite such tactics McGarty never retaliated. 'I decided shortly after I started playing that I would never foul or retaliate. I would leave the control of the game to the referee and I would just keep playing as hard and as fairly as I could.' This only proved him to be the great sportsman that he was always acknowledged to be. It was felt that if McGarty had got the requisite number of frees that he undoubtedly deserved then Leitrim would have won their first Connacht title since 1927. Be that as it may, however, all who were privileged to be at St Coman's Park that July day in 1958 still wonder how any human being could rise so often to the heights of athletic perfection that one Pakie McGarty attained in that Connacht final. In spite of the anguish of defeat, Leitrim supporters and some Galway followers as well raced onto the pitch after the game and spontaneously carried McGarty shoulder high around the pitch.

The National League of 1958-1959 saw Leitrim, from a section which included Mayo, Meath, Cavan, Sligo, Longford, and Westmeath, qualify for the semi-final against Derry. However a bad Leitrim defence, where only Eddie Duffy and Josie Murray played up to their usual high standards, allowed Derry star forward Seán O'Connell to score 2-2 and thus ended, Leitrim's quest for league glory. Leitrim reached further Connacht finals in 1959 and 1960 only to again suffer the fate of the vanquished. Four successive finals and four defeats for McGarty and Leitrim. One could say that Leitrim were extremely unlucky to come up against a great Galway side which won five titles in a row (1956-1960) and were unlucky not to win a second All-Ireland during that period. The 1958 final apart, it must be said that Galway were far superior to their Leitrim counterparts in the other finals.

For eleven more years, Pakie McGarty played for Leitrim, reaching another two Connacht finals in 1963 and 1967, again experiencing heavy defeats to Galway and Mayo respectively. The 1967 decider was to be the last of Pakie's six unsuccessful appearances in a Connacht final. When Pakie's wife was injured in a car crash, he was forced to spend more time in his thriving mini-market shop in Clondalkin. Family duty had to take precedence over the green and gold of Leitrim. So, at the age of 38, Pakie played his last county match in 1971. One of the longest inter-county careers of all time had come to an end. No league or championship trophies adorned his cabinet but a host of marvellous footballing memories and enduring friendships have stood the test of time.

In 1954, at the age of 20, Pakie was selected on the Connacht team to play Munster in the Railway Cup semi-final at Tralee. McGarty was working with the ESB in Donegal helping them to build a power line between Letterkenny and Gweedore. Two days prior to the game, Pakie badly hurt his hand pulling a pole up a mountain. Still undaunted by the pain he put on a protective glove and travelled the 295 miles to Tralee. McGarty turned in a scintillating performance in his provincial debut scoring 1-4 before an estimated 20,000 people. McGarty's favourite memory of this game was Mayo's flying doctor Pádraig Carney coming up to him after he scored the first point and saying 'Good man, Junior!' McGarty was also exceptionally pleased that he had scored so much off his marker, right full back Jas Murphy who had captained Kerry to win the 1953 All-Ireland against Armagh.

McGarty, who played in the Railway Cup series for a further 13 years until 1967 won three medals, two at left half forward in 1957 and 1958 and one as a substitute in 1967. The 1958 Railway Cup semi-final against Leinster in Ballinasloe was to be McGarty's best ever provincial display. Four men including Stephen White and Jim McDonnell of Louth and Wicklow's Gerry O'Reilly were in turn switched on the Mohill man in an effort to curb the elusive Pakie but all to no avail as Pakie, who formed a dynamic left wing partnership with county colleague Cathal Flynn, literally ran riot. The two Leitrim players astonishingly accounted for 1-9 out of Connacht's final tally of 1-11. Ironically Pakie and Cathal nearly missed that match. It was their understanding that some Dublin-based Galway players were to give them a lift to the game. However, an obvious breakdown in communication meant that Flynn and McGarty were not collected. They had no option but to hire a car which cost them £5. When they arrived in their hotel in Ballinasloe, Pakie remembered that he had left his football gear outside his 'digs' in Dublin. Thanks to Jim Moran, father of former Dublin footballer and Manchester United soccer star Kevin Moran, Pakie's predicament was solved. Gerry O'Malley lent him a pair of togs, Liam Good supplied a pair of boots and his direct opponent Gerry O'Reilly, provided him with stockings.

In 1955, McGarty went to work in Dublin where he stayed until 1958. During that period he played for the well known Dublin club Seán McDermotts. With them, he got to a county final in 1958 only to lose to a star-studded St Vincent's team. That 1958 McDermotts team was a very cosmopolitan side which included within its ranks Seán Quinn of Armagh, Patsy Devlin of Tyrone, Mickey Brady of Offaly, Kevin Beahan (Louth), Kevin Sreenan (Fermanagh) as well as McGarty himself and county colleague Cathal Flynn. In 1958, Pakie went to England to work. By 1964, Pakie had saved enough money to come home and buy his own shop in Clondalkin where he worked until he retired in 1998. After 34 years of beginning work each morning at seven o'clock and stopping at 10 p.m. Pakie decided to take things easier. At work and at play he had served both his colleagues and customers to the utmost of his ability. He and his wife, Ellen, have seven children – Christine, Jean, Padraic, Michael, Aileen and Eamonn.

Regarding Gaelic football at present McGarty is not reticent about presenting his views:

1. First of all managers of county teams should be natives of the county that they manage because they have a better knowledge of the clubs and players. Also, it is much cheaper for a county board to have a management team which is home-based.

2. There is too much emphasis on physical fitness today and not enough on the skills of the game. One only has to look at the number of deplorable wides in any match to realise this.

3. Referees should apply the rules consistently so that pulling and dragging are eliminated from the game. If this were done, the game would be a greater spectacle. Nevertheless, refereeing is a very tough job and they should not have to tolerate any kind of verbal abuse.

Despite these shortcomings as perceived by McGarty he still admires the skills of many of today's players. 'Séamus Moynihan (Kerry) – the best back in the country and Darren Fay (Meath) are fabulous defenders. Finbarr McConnell (Tyrone) has great presence as a goalkeeper. Anthony Tohill (Derry), Niall Buckley (Kildare) and John McDermott (Meath) are excellent midfielders. Peter Canavan (Tyrone), Maurice Fitzgerald (Kerry), Joe Brolly (Derry), Declan Browne (Tipperary) and Michael Donnellan (Galway) are exceptionally skilful forwards. My favourite forward in the past few years was Enda Gormley of Derry. He was a very stylish and accurate kicker of the ball both from frees and play.'

McGarty is also deeply appreciative of the immense role journalists and television analysts have played in Gaelic games. 'The late John D. Hickey of the *Irish Independent* was superb in his summary of any game. Amongst today's journalists, no one is as precise in his judgement of games and players as Eugene McGee. Down the years, all the television analysts on 'The Sunday Game' and 'The Championship' were very good. Enda Colleran, Liam Austin, Martin McHugh and Colm O'Rourke have been particularly accurate in their views.

McGarty who has an encyclopaedic knowledge of games, teams, venues, dates and journalistic reports of matches loves reminiscing about the past. One anecdote he recalls with particular gusto is the following.

A friend of Pakie's, Jim McGlynn from Donegal was a well known inter-county referee who had worked with him in the ESB. Jim was driving through Dublin when he was stopped by a garda for a minor motoring offence. The Garda, Tom Langan of Mayo, then one of the most feared forwards in the country (who was selected on both the 1984 Centenary and 1999 Millennium All Time teams) asked the offending motorist his name:

'Jim McGlynn,' came the instant reply.

'Are you the referee?'

'Yes, I am.'

'Well you can go on but remember if I'm going through any defence, don't blow that whistle,' the Mayo man concluded.

Another dual Centenary and Millennium All Star who featured prominently in McGarty's life was the renowned Kerry half back Seán Murphy. In all their many encounters in the Railway Cup series, Murphy could never get the better of McGarty. On St Patrick's Day in 1957, McGarty won his first Railway Cup medal when

Connacht defeated Munster. The legendary half back simply could not handle the indomitable McGarty. Twenty-four hours later, McGarty marked Murphy again in the then annual Ireland versus Combined Universities series. McGarty, who played three times for Ireland, totally outplayed the Kerry man. Murphy later admitted that McGarty was the one player he simply could not watch. He just could not mark the man with the electrifying burst of speed, the unbeatable sidestep and unerring boot.

McGarty who played for the Tara Club in London from 1958 to 1964 and for Clondalkin Round Towers from 1964 to 1971 only had one serious injury in 22 years of top-class football. It occurred in his last game for the Tara club when an opponent deliberately and repeatedly struck him in the face, requiring Pakie to have 11 stitches. That isolated incident did not diminish Pakie's obsessive love of playing football or instil any animosity in one of the most talented and humane men ever to tog out on a Gaelic football field.

'I just enjoyed playing the game and making friends. Similarly, I love watching all sports, especially soccer and boxing. Cruyff of Holland, Eusebio of Portugal and Best of Manchester United were the best soccer players that I ever saw. I also loved to go to the National Stadium in Dublin in the halcyon days of Ireland's outstanding Olympians Fred Teidt, Freddie Gilroy and John Caldwell. They were very skilful. On the professional front, former World Heavyweight Champion Rocky Marciano was my favourite,' concluded Pakie.

When it came to making his Ireland and Connacht selections Pakie chose the following players:

IRELAND (1949–1971)

Johnny Geraghty
(Galway)

Jerome O'Shea *(Kerry)*	Paddy Prendergast *(Mayo)*	Tom O'Hare *(Down)*
Seán Murphy *(Kerry)*	Gerry O'Malley *(Roscommon)*	Stephen White *(Louth)*

Pádraig Carney *(Mayo)*		Jim McKeever *(Derry)*

Seán O'Neill *(Down)*	Seán Purcell *(Galway)*	Paddy Doherty *(Down)*
Denis Kelleher *(Cork)*	Tom Langan *(Mayo)*	Kevin Heffernan *(Dublin)*

CONNACHT (1949–1971)

Johnny Geraghty
(Galway)

Willie Casey   Paddy Prendergast   Tom Dillon
(Mayo)   *(Mayo)*   *(Galway)*

Jack Mahon   Gerry O'Malley   Martin Newell
(Galway)   *(Roscommon)*   *(Galway)*

Pádraig Carney   John Nallen
(Mayo)   *(Mayo)*

Mattie McDonagh   Seán Purcell   Micheál Kearins
(Galway)   *(Galway)*   *(Sligo)*

Frankie Stockwell   Tom Langan   Cathal Flynn
(Galway)   *(Mayo)*   *(Leitrim)*

Born in a county with such a small population and few job opportunities, Pakie's chances of ever winning a provincial championship were slim from the outset. It says much for McGarty's loyalty to his native heath that he made countless yearly sacrifices to return to play for his beloved Leitrim. For 22 years, Pakie McGarty travelled thousands of miles just for the honour of donning the green and gold. In an interview with John D. Hickey in 1958 Pakie said, 'no matter where I am, I will never play for any county only Leitrim as long as they will have me. Winning is not everything. Not for anything would I part from my Leitrim team-mates.'

That young Carrick-on-Shannon schoolboy of 1959 chose very wisely when he decided to write about the great Pakie McGarty. Today that youthful scribe, popular Longford GP Mel Gorman, is one of Leitrim's most avid and enthusiastic supporters. He and many others have reciprocated that innate loyalty which Pakie McGarty possessed in such abundance.

Paddy Collins

ON THE MORNING OF the 1984 All-Ireland senior football final Paddy Collins awoke at 8.30 a.m. The normally cool and unflappable individual was a little more exuberant and excited than usual. True, he had refereed two previous senior All-Ireland finals but this one was extra special. Known as the Centenary All-Ireland, it was a day that the GAA were going to commemorate, in a distinctive manner, the fact that they were celebrating their 100th birthday. In addition, on this historic day, the two sides that had dominated Gaelic football in the previous decade – Kerry and Dublin – were paired against each other. It was to be a real gala day of remembrance with golden-voiced commentator, Micheál Ó Hehir, introducing to the assembled thousands in Croke Park, all the surviving winning senior football captains of previous All-Ireland days. In addition, those players who had been selected on the *Sunday Independent*/Irish Nationwide team of the century were also scheduled to appear in Ireland's most famous sporting arena. It was as much a tribute to the democracy of the GAA as it was to the undoubted competence of Paddy Collins that a man from a so-called weaker county should hold centre-stage on this most auspicious of occasions.

As he leapt out of bed, the psychiatric nurse was justifiably proud. Then, accidentally, he hit his foot off the side of the bed and immediately an excruciating pain pierced through his toes. Living in the hope that the pain would disappear as quickly as it had arrived, a shaken Paddy limped into his car, collected his four umpires and sped to Croke Park. With a swollen foot and pronounced limp his umpires escorted him far away from the madding crowd as he entered the stadium at the Nally Stand end. Having received a combination of injections and tablets from former GAA President, the late Dr Donal Keenan, Paddy pronounced himself fit to officiate a mere half an hour before the throw-in. Just prior to his final injection Paddy, hobbling in obvious pain, met Micheál Ó Hehir on a corridor.

'I begged him not to mention my injury in his commentary until the game was over. When the medication began to have the desired effect my only problem was a psychological one! Would something happen that I would not be able to finish the game? As it turned out, the game was essentially uneventful and everything went well regarding my toe, which was diagnosed as broken, and Micheál Ó Hehir kept his promise. The whole episode just shows how a simple accident could have destroyed my dreams,' stated Paddy when I met him at Westmeath's GAA headquarters in Cusack Park, Mullingar.

Born in Athboy, Co. Meath in 1942, Paddy Collins' earliest GAA influences stemmed from his father, Bob, and his primary school teacher Master Keenan. They were responsible for inculcating a love of football and hurling in the young Collins who proudly remembers being told that his father was the first Meath man to represent Leinster in the Railway Cup in hurling. This he did as a goalkeeper in 1929.

The enthusiastic youngster played both codes for Athboy at underage level before graduating to play at senior level in hurling and football for the Royal County. One occasion from his senior playing days with Meath stands out. On a cold murky day in the depths of winter he played against Antrim in a National Hurling League game at Navan. Thirty minutes after that game he appeared on the same pitch for the second half of a weekly Gaelic football tournament match between Meath and Galway. In a spectacular scoring spree, he notched 1-5 against no less a man than all-time great Enda Colleran. Pat Reynolds, the much travelled John Nallen and 'Red' Pat Collier, whom he rates as his most difficult opponent, are just some of the well known players he played alongside in a Meath jersey.

Paddy came to work as a psychiatric nurse in St Loman's Hospital in Mullingar in 1960. That was the beginning of a lifelong affinity with his adopted county of Westmeath and led to Paddy transferring his inter-county allegiance to the Lakeside county with which he played hurling and football.

Though winning county championships with his new local club, St Loman's, in 1961 and 1963, Paddy retired as a player while still in his mid-twenties. One day, work colleague and then existing county secretary, Paddy Flanagan, asked him to do a favour, which was to launch Paddy Collins into the career of refereeing. This was to make him into one of the household names in the world of refereeing. No referee was available for a colleges' game between St Finian's of Mullingar and St Mel's of Longford, so one Paddy coerced another to officiate. His performance was so satisfactory that he immediately became a club referee within the county. 'Even though I had never read a rule book I seemed to have an aptitude for refereeing,' stated the genial Paddy. 'My first inter-county game was a National Football League fixture between Dublin and Longford and my first major game was the 1974 All-Ireland minor football final between Cork and Mayo. Having officiated at the following year's Railway Cup final, I was subsequently appointed to take charge of the 1976 Sigerson Cup final and the 1976 All-Ireland club football championship final. I must have done okay because I was asked to take charge of that year's All-Ireland senior football final between Dublin and Kerry. That was a great honour and I went on to take charge of three more All-Irelands in 1981, 1984 and 1989. Several All-Ireland semi-finals, Leinster finals, one Munster final and many important National League encounters also came my way,' concluded Paddy.

When Paddy Collins sent off Dublin's Jimmy Keaveney for a striking offence in the Dublin/Offaly Leinster final of 1979, he incurred the wrath of many Dublin supporters. What annoyed them most was, not Paddy's decision, but that the penalty for such an offence was a two-month suspension. This meant that Keaveney would miss both that year's All-Ireland semi-final and final. When the Leinster council, as per rule, adopted the referee's report there was a concerted effort to have Jimmy's suspension reduced. Dublin appealed his case to the Management Committee of the GAA in Croke Park. Prominent people such as Paddy Moriarty, Chief Executive of the ESB and Chairman of the RTE Authority, 'Sunday Game' panellist Liz Howard and the player he was alleged to have struck, Offaly's Ollie Minnock, interceded on Keaveney's behalf. Despite all of this, however, the appeal was unsuccessful.

'I was disappointed for Jimmy as his misdemeanour was totally out of character. I always found him a very sporting player. Nevertheless, it was my job to enforce the rules on the field of play,' stated Paddy.

Collins, who actually sent off very few players in his career, has been popularly acknowledged as one of the greatest referees of all time. The modest Paddy does not dwell on all the accolades that have come his way. Instead, he prefers to emphasise what he perceives are the necessary qualities that a good referee should possess.

1. He needs to have a natural 'feel' for the game.
2. He must have a sense of fairness.
3. He must display good judgement. Good judgement is very often acquired from learning from previous bad judgement.
4. The capable referee must have the ability, in religious parlance, to separate the mortal sin from the venial sin. Players and supporters do not want referees to be preoccupied with what they see as minor matters while at the same time not being able to deal adequately with major offences.
5. The efficient referee is able to make a judgement between a player who has malice aforethought when committing an offence and one who fouls spontaneously.

Having outlined the parameters for good refereeing standards, I asked him why he always appeared to be so much in control of every situation even when gross breaches of discipline appeared imminent. 'Even though I worried before every game, when it began I knew I would be able to handle it. A journalist once wrote that no game was too big or too small for me. Without sounding cocky or arrogant that journalist was probably correct. It was just the way that I was.' What I really like to see in a referee is the ability to move up a gear when the occasion demands it. Most referees can cope when everything is going well. However, when some player decides to play outside the rules, the excellent referee will adjust to the new situation, take the appropriate action and then go back to controlling the game as he did prior to the incident. An efficient referee always gets the balance right between the minimum of stoppages and the maximum of control.'

Collins also stresses the importance of treating players as adults while still letting them know who is boss. 'Players do not want to be brought to the sideline, lectured and finger wagged in front of thousands of people. Players always know when they have done wrong. It is essential that players are not publicly humiliated while at the same time they are left in no doubt what will happen if they commit the same offence again. There is a very subtle difference between public admonition and a severe private warning. A quick, quiet word which makes the transgressor feel guilty is much more effective.'

Paddy, who continued to referee at inter-county level until early 1996, had his swansong on the big stage when he refereed the 1990 Leinster final between Dublin and Meath. No greater tribute could be paid to the esteem in which he was held than to be asked by a Leinster chairman who was a native of Dublin, to officiate in a provincial final in which Collins' native Meath were playing.

'My first reaction was what would Dublin and the general public think if I accept?' Collins wondered. The persuasive chairman, Dublin's Jimmy Gray, soon dispelled those doubts and Paddy accepted.

Just a minute into the game he had his doubts about the validity of his decision. A high ball dropped into the Dublin square. Goalie John O'Leary fumbled the catch. The inrushing Meath forward Colm O'Rourke sent the loose ball to the net and in the process made physical contact with O'Leary. Collins had no doubts about the legality of the goal. He immediately and definitely acknowledged its validity. A crescendo of booing amongst Dublin's vast army of supporters rent the air. 'For a split second I wondered would the whole game be like this and why did I listen to the plaintive pleadings of Jimmy Gray? Why did I not say to him, Jimmy, sorry, get someone else. Thankfully all the players just got on with the game. There were no further controversies', Collins added. Next day the papers were, as always, fulsome in their praise of the man in black. No other referee, they ventured, would have had the courage to award that first-minute goal. Once again Collins' decision was vindicated.

For the next six years Paddy Collins' refereeing career was severely curtailed by a combination of injury and advancing years. 'In 1991 I got a frozen shoulder which was extremely painful. I couldn't lift my arm properly for over a year. Just after my recovery, the GAA had taken a decision to introduce younger referees. While I didn't appreciate it at the time, I can now fully understand their thinking.' The days of officiating in front of 60,000 people were over for Paddy Collins. So, when he refereed a National Football League game between Mayo and Roscommon in the 1995–1996 competition Paddy knew his time had come. Thirty years (1967–1996) for the GAA's most famous man in the middle had come to an end.

Being such a perfectionist on the field of play one wondered had Collins himself any refereeing role models. The answers were forthcoming. 'Even though I didn't pass any remarks on who was refereeing when I was a player I, nevertheless, had great regard for John Dowling (Offaly) and Jimmy Hatton (Wicklow). I always had great admiration for John Moloney (Tipperary) as both a top-class hurling and football referee. Frank Murphy of Cork was a brilliant hurling referee. He had this almost unique ability to let the game flow while maintaining control.'

Collins was assiduous in his physical and mental preparation for games. A pioneer and non-smoker, he was particularly careful about his diet. The physical training was more regular than strenuous. He trained four times a week, allocating a half an hour per session. This consisted of sprinting and jogging procedures plus body exercises.

Collins' club, St Loman's, have provided Westmeath with its last four County Secretaries. One of them, the long serving Paddy Flanagan, retired in 1970 to be replaced by another colleague, Tony Gilligan. Paddy Collins, who had never been any kind of club official before, was elected Assistant County Secretary at that year's Annual Convention. Since 1976 he has been County Secretary. As well as carrying out his secretarial duties in a thoroughly professional manner, he has served on various GAA national and provincial committees especially those dealing with the rules of the game and the administration of those rules by referees. In 1996, the then President of the GAA, Jack Boothman, asked him to chair a new national referees authority. In 1999 this body became responsible for the appointment of all referees for National League and championship games. Heretofore, the GAA's Central Council only appointed referees for the three major championship games each year – the All-Ireland semi-finals and final. All other games had been under the aegis of the relevant Provincial Councils.

The three-man executive of this authority, Collins, Frank Murphy of Cork and the incoming GAA president, Seán McCague, basically decide who referees which games. Assisted by two representatives from each province, in an advisory capacity, they draw up a national referees' panel and a supplementary panel as well as providing necessary training, fitness tests and examinations for them. They also organise a national panel of assessors who monitor the referee's performance in each game. When the GAA decided in 1999 to have one central referees appointments body, Collins was especially delighted as he had been canvassing for this for the previous ten years. 'This new, central body provides a better opportunity for consistent, ongoing assessment and a more scientific base for the appointment of referees. It is also important that the referees themselves see progression in the number and status of the games that they are asked to do,' Collins stated.

He is also very articulate when discussing the new rules to deal with personal fouling. 'People have been crying out for years to curb the excessive number of personal fouls in our games. Negative, destructive players who were continually indulging in jersey pulling, pushing and holding were preventing positive constructive and skilful players from realising the potential that their talents should permit. Now,

I believe, this new three-tiered system of the implementation of the personal fouling rule should have the desired results:

1. For the first offence, the offending player's number is noted.
2. The guilty player's name is taken and a yellow card is issued for the second offence.
3. For the third offence a yellow card accompanied by a red card is issued and the player is sent off.

Referring to the type of football played nowadays, Paddy thinks that we need a proper balance between the number of kick passes and hand passes in Gaelic football. People have tried to legislate for this by curbing a skill such as the hand pass or solo run. In my estimation, a more positive way of dealing with this dilemma would be the introduction of a limited form of Australian Rules 'mark'. I would permit a mark for a kick pass of 20 metres, for kick outs and general play. I would not allow it for frees or sideline kicks as a team could play a tall man on the edge of the square and he could score easily from such a ploy. On the other hand Collins is very much against the introduction of another Australian Rules rule which states that a player must release the ball when tackled. 'In other codes such as Australian Rules, Rugby Union and Rugby League tackling really means grabbing your opponent. In Gaelic Football the tackle is on the ball, not the man. If we introduced this rule into our game it would pave the way for various interpretations of what a tackle is.'

While in agreement with retaining the National Football League as it is, Collins would love to separate our current provincial senior football championship from the All-Ireland championship. 'I would run off the provincial championships as separate entities and then have an open draw for the All-Ireland championship. This would have three important advantages:

1. It would guarantee each county at least two competitive games in the summer.
2. Many of the weaker counties would look upon the winning of a provincial championship as a more realistic target.
3. The possibility of playing different teams would create an exciting dimension to the championship.'

Like many GAA officials and fans Paddy has a tremendous regard for the talents of GAA President, Joe McDonagh. 'Joe McDonagh is one of the most inspirational people I have ever seen. He has the capacity to make people listen to his every word. This is not confined merely to GAA people.

A few months ago, I was at a GAA function which also included many people who were there in a commercial capacity and who only had a fleeting interest in GAA affairs. They were absolutely enthralled by what he said, how he said it and his fantastic powers of recall.'

Paddy Collins travelled the length of Ireland and even as far as Australia during those marvellous 30 years of officiating. 'In 1986 and 1990 I was the Irish referee in the Compromise Rules series. I enjoyed the country but not the games under the rules that then existed. The subsequent adjustment to the rules made the 1998 series much more palatable.'

The games, its players, its officials and supporters have made the GAA an integral part of Paddy Collins' life. The exposure which television, radio and the print media alike have given to Gaelic Games has enriched and embellished them. Such journalists as the late John D. Hickey *(Irish Independent)*, the late Pádraig Puirséal *(Irish Press)*, Jim O'Sullivan *(Cork Examiner)* and Con Houlihan *(Evening Press)*, in particular, impressed Collins with their incisive contributions. 'They all had a great "feel" for the games. The demands on journalists from editors are slightly different now. Nevertheless, I feel that present GAA *Irish Independent* reporters such as Liam Horan and Vincent Hogan would have been outstanding in any era. I am a great admirer of Vincent's, I always marvel at his command of words.'

Collins, who considers Mike Sheehy (Kerry) and Matt Connor (Offaly) as the two most skilful footballers he has ever seen, also has great respect for the work and competence that GAA managers have brought to the game. He does concede, however, that they are extraordinarily influential people whose major responsibility is to ensure that Gaelic Games must be played within the spirit of the rules. They can make the referee's job much easier if they do this.

When selecting his Ireland and Leinster sides, Collins stressed that they were based almost entirely on players that he had witnessed at the height of his refereeing days. During that time, Kerry and Cork dominated in Munster. Likewise, Dublin, Meath and Offaly were the influential sides in Leinster. Ulster and Connacht football were essentially in the doldrums. Consequently, great players like Martin McHugh (Donegal), Tony Scullion (Derry), Mickey Linden (Down) and Liam McHale (Mayo) were not considered. Collins, who loves to watch horse-racing and rates steeplechaser 'Arkle' and his jockey Pat Taaffe amongst his all-time sporting heroes, made the following choices:

IRELAND

John O'Leary
(Dublin)

Robbie O'Malley *(Meath)*	John O'Keeffe *(Kerry)*	Robbie Kelleher *(Dublin)*
Páidí Ó Sé *(Kerry)*	Kevin Moran *(Dublin)*	Martin O'Connell *(Meath)*

Brian Mullins
(Dublin)   Jack O'Shea
(Kerry)

Matt Connor *(Offaly)*	Larry Tompkins *(Cork)*	Pat Spillane *(Kerry)*
Colm O'Rourke *(Meath)*	Eoin Liston *(Kerry)*	Mike Sheehy *(Kerry)*

LEINSTER

John O'Leary
(Dublin)

Robbie O'Malley *(Meath)*	Mick Lyons *(Meath)*	Robbie Kelleher *(Dublin)*
Paul Curran *(Dublin)*	Kevin Moran *(Dublin)*	Martin O'Connell *(Meath)*

Brian Mullins
(Dublin)   Willie Bryan
(Offaly)

Matt Connor *(Offaly)*	Colm O'Rourke *(Meath)*	Tony McTague *(Offaly)*
Kevin O'Brien *(Wicklow)*	Brian Stafford *(Meath)*	Bernard Flynn *(Meath)*

In March 1999, Paddy Collins, once more, strode across the green sward of Croke Park. This time there were no thousands of people cheering nor bands playing. Instead, only a few stray squawking seagulls hovered overhead. Paddy, in the company of ace RTE Radio and TV commentator Marty Morrissey, stood ten yards from the centre of that famous pitch. Marty asked him did he not miss those great moments when he held centre-stage.

'Those words of Marty made me remember what I missed most. I just loved standing in Croke Park for the national anthem on All-Ireland final day. Here I was an ordinary person representing St Loman's, Westmeath, my wife Anne, my son Enda and myself. Those were the moments of great joy that I will never forget. Knowing that I was the person in charge of the game for the ensuing seventy minutes was a salutary yet humbling experience. Unfortunately, my birth certificate decided that I was surplus to requirements.' Paddy Collins may have taken his last curtain call on Ireland's most important sporting days but the memory of his many 'Man of the Match' performances live on. The GAA is eternally grateful that Paddy has passed its way.

Eamon Cregan

EAMON CREGAN OR 'NED' as he was popularly called played for Limerick in three successive All-Ireland senior hurling finals in 1933, 1934 and 1935, winning the 1934 final after a replay with Dublin. He had also won four Munster senior championship medals as well as three National League medals. Reared on a daily diet, from his father's knee, of tales about the great men of the 30s made young Eamon Cregan want to emulate his father 'Ned' and play this wonderful mysterious game. Though Eamon and his older brother, Michael, played the game at their primary school it was not until they joined local club  Claughaun that they established a proper affinity with hurling. Though small in stature, young Eamon showed exceptional promise and was selected as goalkeeper on the club's U-16 team at the age of ten. One year later Eamon won his first medal, ironically, for Gaelic football, when his school team St Patrick's won the U-12 schools league. In that same year, 1957, the then eleven-year-old won both the county and city U-16 hurling championship with Claughaun.

As he grew older, Cregan became bigger, stronger and better. Now recognised as a midfielder of outstanding quality and vision, the blossoming hurler was quickly promoted to the school team when he went to Limerick CBS for his secondary education. This school, in Sexton Street, was renowned not only as a seat of learning but as an academy of hurling excellence. The Christian Brothers in general, and Br Burke in particular, imparted the Gaelic Games ethos with a passion and enthusiasm rarely equalled and seldom surpassed within the 32 counties of Ireland.

In 1964, Limerick CBS, with Eamon Cregan captaining the side at midfield, made history when they became the first Limerick team since 1932 to win the Dr Harty Cup (Munster senior hurling cup for secondary schools). The All-Ireland semi-final against St Mary's Galway was a close encounter with the Sexton Street boys eventually winning by a three-point margin. The All-Ireland final against famed St Peter's of Wexford was Eamon Cregan's passport to greatness. Now dubbed the blond bombshell, the 18-year-old with a wonderful turn of speed and exuding class in everything that he did, orchestrated every move. All hurling followers who witnessed his flair and finesse, on that April day, instantly knew that a new hurling star had arrived. The years of fatherly advice and daily practice during the summer holidays on his uncle's farm in Newcastle West had come to fruition.

Three years prior to this colleges' victory – the first ever by a Limerick team – Eamon made his debut for the Limerick county minor team when he came on as a sub against Cork in the Munster championship. The following year he played in goals for the minors against Galway who then played in the Munster championship. In the first half, five goals were scored by Galway and he was taken off at half time. His brother Michael, incidentally, was also on that team. In 1963, Eamon Cregan played for his third campaign in the Munster minor hurling championship in which Limerick defeated Tipperary 4-12 to 5-4 in the provincial final. However, in the All-Ireland final, with Cregan now at centrefield, the Treatymen slumped to a six-point defeat to Wexford. Eamon was exceptionally nervous and did not play to his full potential. The whole Croke Park atmosphere with its massive crowds just got to him on this occasion. This experience, nevertheless, was to stand him in good stead when, only seven months later, he turned in a superlative performance in the 1964 All-Ireland colleges' final.

After watching the budding, elegant hurling stylist during the colleges' campaign, the Limerick senior hurling mentors invited Eamon to join the county panel. He made his senior inter-county debut when he came on as a sub in a National League game against Dublin in November 1964. His abiding memory of that game was when he dummied the defence and hit a magnificent angled shot towards the far corner of the net. Seemingly out of nowhere, Dublin goalkeeper and future Leinster Council Chairman Jimmy Gray spreadeagled himself across the goal line to stop the shot and prevent Cregan from making an illustrious start to his inter-county career. Though he was selected to start in the following league game, he was replaced during it. After that, except when he was injured, Eamon was a permanent member of the Limerick senior teams until he retired, eighteen years later, in 1982.

Nothing spectacular happened in terms of Limerick hurling at the outset of Cregan's inter-county career. However, two games during 1965 and 1966 gave a glimpse of possible future success. With Eamon Cregan, despite marking Waterford's brilliant Larry Guinan, giving an excellent exhibition at midfield, Limerick only lost by a point in the 1965 championship. One year later, in the first round of the Munster championship Eamon Cregan scored a thundering 3-5 when Limerick knocked out Tipperary, the then All-Ireland champions. Nevertheless, these were only spasmodic displays of potential. It was not until the league campaign of 1970–1971 that Limerick had developed a consistent pattern of high quality hurling. Mentors, Br Burke and Jimmy Hennessey worked particularly hard as Limerick developed a unique style of diagonal passing. This style was particularly effective against strong and slowish full back lines, who relished the idea of man-to-man marking. The concentration on stickwork and the use of open space was anathema to most defences. This style had first been successfully practised in that famous 1966 championship game against Tipperary. Nevertheless, it was five years later before the sweet, freeflowing, scientific, hurling men of Limerick tasted national success. By now every member of the team was automatically aware of how the team's main game plan was panning out. In 1971, in a wonderful league final, Limerick beat Tipperary 3-12 to 3-11, won the Oireachtas competition and only lost to Tipperary by a point in the Munster hurling final.

Though naturally disappointed, Eamon Cregan and Limerick were quite philosophical as they looked positively towards the future. They had, after all, won their first League title since 1947 and their Munster final conquerors, Tipperary, went on to win that year's All-Ireland. All and sundry reckoned that 1972 would be Limerick's year. Dermot Kelly, a wonderfully skilful hurling artist had scored 1-12 when Limerick last won the Munster title in 1955. As it happened, 1972 turned out to be an unmitigated disaster as far as Limerick hurling was concerned. Firstly, they lost their National League crown to Cork, by three points. That was bad enough in itself but when it was allied to an untimely and unexpected championship exit to Clare, in their first game, it became a crisis. Disappointment led to dissension, which quickly turned into animosity over alleged wrong training techniques. The whole unseemly situation was eventually resolved when Eamon's brother Michael, who had retired after the 1972 championship, agreed to train the side.

In January 1973, Michael Cregan devised the most rigid, tough and regimented training programme devised for any group of athletes. With Michael's army experience in physical education, he outlined a programme that was so intense that many players initially found it hard to cope with. Even yet, his brother Eamon squirms with anguish when he thinks of what they went through. As events on the playing field developed during that season, Limerick were to undergo this physical endurance and stamina work programme thrice weekly from January to mid-August. Only then did Michael Cregan stop so that the team could rest as they prepared tactically and mentally for the biggest day of their lives.

They played well in the league and reached the final for the fourth successive year only to be well beaten by Wexford. This time there was no despondency as all their preparations were geared towards a good championship campaign. Some cynics were not so sure. They maintained that Limerick's perceived allergy to winning in Croke Park was epitomised by that dismal league final performance. Team management and players knew that they could and would prove their detractors wrong.

Having overcome their internal difficulties and with a fantastic response to the new training regime, Limerick had shown a new resolve, not hitherto associated with Limerick sides. This was particularly evident when they beat both Cork and Tipperary in the league (the latter after a draw and a replay in the semi-final). The good work nearly came to nought again when Limerick could only scrape a victory against Clare in the provincial semi-final with the winning score procured by captain Eamon Grimes. In the final against Tipperary, the Premier county initially looked more likely to take the honours. The selectors asked Cregan to move out from his corner forward role to the general midfield area. This Eamon did successfully, gaining much necessary possession and moving the ball forward to considerable effect. With Ned Rea (who had moved from defence) in his new full forward role wreaking havoc as a result of Cregan's promptings, Limerick recovered and the sides were level as the end approached. Then Limerick were awarded a '70' which was hotly disputed by the Tipperary defence. Long-serving midfielder Richie Bennis took the puck. He sent it long, high and apparently over the bar for a sensational winning point as the referee blew the full-time whistle. Though the referee allowed the last-gasp point, many Tipperary folk still query, to this day, whether the ball went over the bar or not. Nevertheless, the score stood and the record books show that Limerick beat Tipperary to win their first Munster title in 18 years, the score being Limerick 6-7, Tipperary 2-18.

In the All-Ireland semi-final, Limerick easily disposed of London by 1-15 to 0-7. During that game, Eamon badly damaged a cartilage which required intensive physiotherapy before he was pronounced fit for the greatest day of his life. For the final, against Kilkenny, Limerick selectors decided to carefully plan their match strategy. Kilkenny were missing four key players through injury, Eddie Keher, Jim Treacy, Eamon Morrissey and Kieran Purcell. Limerick now knew that Kilkenny would be totally relying on their captain and centre half forward Pat Delaney to run at the Limerick defence. Eamon Cregan, though a recognised forward or midfielder, was earmarked as the man capable of stopping Delaney from going on his searing runs. To do this, Cregan would have to play centre half back instead of the incumbent Jim O'Donnell who was considered not as mobile as the Claughaun speedster. Being sensitive to Jim's feelings, Eamon advised the selectors to explain to him the tactical reasons for such a switch. Psychologically, Limerick were now at an advantage. Having watched Delaney play in the Leinster final, Cregan knew exactly what to expect. On the other hand, Cregan who had played successfully at centre half back when his club won the 1968 county senior championship final was an unknown, in this position, in the eyes of the Kilkenny team.

There were two distinct and specific tactics employed by Limerick for the final. Number One was that Cregan's primary role was to ensure that Delaney would not gain possession. It did not matter if he himself did not touch the ball. Secondly, full back Pat Hartigan who was famous for spectacular high catches was told to forget about catching and to concentrate on the less exciting but safer policy of preventing his man from gaining possession.

Displaying fierce determination and scintillating, exciting hurling, Limerick seized the initiative from the moment the final began. Hartigan, Cregan and Seán Foley were phenomenal in defence and captain Eamon Grimes and Bernie Hartigan were dominant in the midfield sector. Ned Rea and Offaly born Joe McKenna were simply flawless in their stickwork in the attack. Limerick were leading by seven points when Pat Hartigan discovered that there were only two and a half minutes left in this 80-minute final. Excitedly, Hartigan ran up to the more serious minded Cregan. 'We have it. We have it'. 'I told him to be careful as anything could happen in two and a half minutes. However, Pat was in his element and wanted just one opportunity to show his aerial prowess. Within a minute he had a chance to do so. A long, high ball floated dangerously towards the Limerick square. Ignoring both life and limb and the possibility of conceding a goal the mighty man soared into the air and plucked the ball from a forest of hurleys and drove the sliotar at least 80 yards downfield. Pat smiled happily and smirked at me. Soon after, the full-time whistle sounded, Limerick 1-21, Kilkenny 1-14. For the first time since 1940, we were All-Ireland champions.

'My first thoughts were of my father who had not lived to see his two sons play their part in Limerick's success. Unfortunately, he had died of a brain haemorrhage the previous year. For me it was a dream come true because since I was a little boy I was infatuated with the belief that some day, somehow, I would win an All-Ireland senior medal.

From that historic year a host of golden memories continually cross my mind. The homecoming to Limerick was unforgettable. Mick Herbert, a former county hurler and then a TD, could not understand how cool and calm the team were when they entered the city to a tumultuous welcome. To me this was understandable because a lot of us had been playing a long time and had seen so many bad days. We just felt strange and shell shocked that the good days had actually arrived. Deep down, all of us realised that the high standard of coaching within all our schools but especially in my old alma mater Limerick CBS had been very influential in our triumph. Limerick CBS had won four Harty Cups in successive years (1964, 1965, 1966 and 1967). Our captain Eamon Grimes, who had won two All-Ireland colleges' medals (Croke Cup) with Limerick CBS in 1964 and 1966, Seán Foley, Bernie Hartigan, Michael and myself were all past pupils of Sexton Street. In addition, Richie Bennis had been captain of the Limerick City team, which won the first Senior Vocational School title at All-Ireland level in 1961.'

Having won the Liam McCarthy cup in 1973, Eamon Cregan continued in the pivotal centre half back position when Limerick reached the Munster final in the following year, beating Clare in the final and then overwhelming Galway in the All-Ireland semi-final. In that year's final, Limerick were disappointing as Kilkenny exacted revenge for the previous year's defeat with a convincing 12-point victory. By 1978, Cregan had reverted to a corner forward role where he was to remain for the rest of his career. In 1980 and 1981 he won two further Munster championships only to fail to Galway in the 1980 All-Ireland final. (This was Galway's first senior success since 1923). Limerick lost to the same opposition, after a replay, in the 1981 All-Ireland semi-final. The latter game has been repeatedly documented as one of the greatest games of hurling ever witnessed. Fast and furious it was exhilarating throughout with the inventiveness of the Limerick attack a joy to behold. Many pundits would say that, were it not for a combination of unfortunate circumstances (three injuries and a controversial sending off of Seán Foley in the drawn game), Limerick would not only have beaten Galway but would also have annexed the All-Ireland title that year. Limerick had a fabulous forward line that year of pacy, diminutive stylist, Ollie O'Connor, the roving target man, Joe McKenna and the inimitable, evergreen Eamon Cregan.

When Limerick were beaten by Waterford in the first round of the 1982 Munster championship by the minimum of margins, 37-year-old Eamon Cregan decided to retire. He had given long service, had played in three All-Irelands, five National League finals and eight Munster finals. In a remarkable, distinguished career he had received three Carrolls' All Star Awards.

Intermittently, during the course of the next few years Eamon developed his own coaching skills and had two separate spells, in 1984–1985 and in 1987–1988 with the county's U-21 side. RTE then invited him to become an analyst with their weekly 'Sunday Game' programme. His views on the merits and demerits of hurling as a game, his quick analysis of live performances on the field of play and his after-match post mortems are anxiously awaited. They bring a fresh and invigorating approach to the game and considerably enlighten the average hurling follower.

In January 1993, Eamon Cregan was appointed Offaly senior hurling manager. Realising the potential of the players and the fact that Offaly were in Leinster were his prime motives for accepting the post. Bringing in Gerry O'Donovan to train the side while he concentrated on skill training and tactical awareness, the team prepared diligently for the 1993 Leinster championship. Even though Offaly played really well against Kilkenny in the first round of that year's campaign, they were defeated, somewhat controversially, by two points. The legality of Kilkenny's winning goal was hotly disputed as ace forward DJ Carey appeared to run too many steps with the sliotar in his hand before he dispatched it to the net. As well, many neutrals deemed the sending off of Offaly's Rory Mannion to be rather harsh. When Offaly were drawn against Kilkenny in the 1994 Leinster championship semi-final, Cregan did not require any extra motivational incentives. The fact that Kilkenny were going for three All-Irelands in a row and four successive Leinster titles only added spice to the confrontation.

Aided by a stiff breeze in the first half of the game, Offaly surged ahead to lead by seven points at half time. In the second half, with Brian Whelehan and Kevin Kinahan superb in defence and the three Dooley brothers dictating matters throughout the rest of the team, Offaly won by four points. Showing tremendous grit as well as the usual combination of pace and skill, Offaly defeated Wexford 1–18 to 0–14 in the Leinster final. Again, Kinahan starred with excellent support coming from Hubert Rigney, Johnny Pilkington, Daithi Regan and Billy Dooley. Debutante championship goalkeeper, David Hughes, made a marvellous contribution with two high-class saves.

It was then that a terrible thought struck Eamon Cregan. His native Limerick had beaten Clare in the Munster final the previous Sunday. 'What if...?' he pondered, before switching his mind to the impending All-Ireland semi-final with Galway. In a superlative display of tight marking and the quick release of the ball, Offaly convincingly defeated the Tribesmen, much more comprehensively than the six-point winning margin would suggest. Rigney, John Troy, Whelehan, Kevin Martin and Billy Dooley were again outstanding in what was essentially a great team performance.

Now, what Eamon had hoped would never come to pass was a living reality. He would be managing Offaly against his beloved native county of Limerick in an All-Ireland final! 'I had to separate my personal affiliation from my role of planning for an Offaly success. I had marvellous experienced selectors who gave me great advice. Pat McLoughney, Andy Gallagher, Mick Spain and Paudge Mulhaire helped me immensely as we plotted for an Offaly win.'

In the final itself, Limerick totally dominated for the vast portion of the game. Hurling superbly, no one, not even Offaly supporters, would have begrudged them the McCarthy cup as the game moved into its last five minutes. Limerick were leading, justifiably, by five points. Offaly were then awarded a free which Johnny Dooley slammed, unexpectedly, to the net. Shortly afterwards Offaly substitute Pat O'Connor seized the ball and scored a goal from close range. Unbelievably, Offaly were now a point up and there were still three minutes to go. Playing like men possessed, Offaly then scored a further five points (three of them per the excellent Billy Dooley) to record a sensational 3-16 to 2-13 victory. Croke Park had just witnessed one of the most amazing comebacks in the history of hurling.

'Offaly just kept plugging and plugging away. Limerick, I believe, felt the game was over, so they relaxed. But really, it was not in the last five minutes that they lost the game. They actually lost the game in the first half when they shot 12 wides. I felt strange when the game was over but I had a job to do for Offaly and I was delighted for them,' said Eamon.

Closely watching the downfall of his native Limerick, in the most dramatic of circumstances, left conflicting thoughts his mind. Seeing friends and familiar faces shed tears of sorrow still preys on Eamon's mind.

Now, however, there is a great passion lurking within him to bring honour to his native Limerick. Two years after Offaly's success, Eamon retired as Offaly manager and at the beginning of 1998 he became manager of the Shannonsiders. 'I feel there is an All-Ireland in Limerick. There is a great blend of young and experienced players. We can win possession but we must be able to convert that into scores,' Eamon told me when I met him in Nenagh where he works as manager with the Irish Nationwide Building Society.

Whichever new system the GAA introduces, if any, at competitive inter-county level it must guarantee top quality games in the summer according to Cregan. 'We cannot allow a system to continue where, for example, Limerick were knocked out of the 1999 championship in May and do not have another major game until the National League campaign in the year 2000. A league-type system should be introduced for the championship in each province, guaranteeing each county at least three games,' added Eamon who rates Brian Murphy (Cork), Jackie O'Gorman (Clare) and 'Fan' Larkin (Kilkenny) as his most difficult opponents.

In selecting Ireland and Munster teams, Eamon chose from as wide a base as possible in order to facilitate the inclusion of as many outstanding hurlers that he saw. The sheer class of Christy Ring, Phil Grimes and Jimmy Smith made him select them on both teams. Otherwise, he tried to accommodate as many players as possible. He did not consider any players whose careers coincided with his own.

IRELAND

Ollie Walsh
(Kilkenny)

| Bobby Rackard *(Wexford)* | Nick O'Donnell *(Wexford)* | John Doyle *(Tipperary)* |

Jimmy Finn
(Tipperary)

Tony Wall
(Tipperary)

Séamus Cleere
(Kilkenny)

Joe Salmon
(Galway)

Ned Wheeler
(Wexford)

| Jimmy Doyle *(Tipperary)* | Phil Grimes *(Waterford)* | Christy Ring *(Cork)* |

| Jimmy Smith *(Clare)* | Nicky Rackard *(Wexford)* | Paddy Molloy *(Offaly)* |

MUNSTER

Tony Reddan
(Tipperary)

| Jim Brohan *(Cork)* | Austin Flynn *(Waterford)* | Tony O'Shaughnessy *(Cork)* |

| Tom McGarry *(Limerick)* | Martin Óg Morrissey *(Waterford)* | Con Roche *(Cork)* |

Séamus Power
(Waterford)

Mick Roche
(Cork)

| Frankie Walsh *(Waterford)* | Phil Grimes *(Waterford)* | Liam Devaney *(Tipperary)* |

| Donie Nealon *(Tipperary)* | Jimmy Smith *(Clare)* | Christy Ring *(Cork)* |

Cregan recalls with glee a story told by his former club and county colleague Jim Hogan.

'It was the opening of a new pitch in Drumcollogher. Hogan had played hurling in Cork and was familiar with the style of Cork's Christy Ring. Limerick were playing Cork and Hogan was the Limerick goalkeeper. A new 6´4 inch gangly youth called

JJ Brosnan would be marking Ring. Hogan told him how to mark Ring. 'You're faster than he is, so make sure you get out in front.' As the game was about to begin, the becapped Ring approached Brosnan and said. 'Are you new, boy?' JJ nodded, muttering through his teeth, 'I won't be long letting you know whether I'm new or not.' As the game progressed and entered its final two minutes, JJ was a happy man. He had played a blinder. Ring had been curtailed and Limerick were leading by two points. Suddenly, a long ball dropped between Ring and Brosnan. Both pulled on it. As Hogan stood in the goal, something whizzed past him followed by something else. In amazement, Hogan saw the sliotar and the cap nestling beside each other in the net. Brosnan's pull had connected with the cap and Ring's with the ball. Brosnan had held Ring scoreless for 58 minutes but in a flash, a swivel of the hips and an overhead shot the Cork wizard scored the winning goal.'

Eamon Cregan was also a Gaelic footballer of note, winning seven senior football championships with Claughaun between 1967 and 1986 as well as playing for the county side between 1964 and 1968. Finding it difficult to fulfil his dual commitments, he made a choice to concentrate on hurling. The footballing right half forward played for Limerick against Kerry in the Munster final of 1965 marking Mick Morris of future golfing fame. He also played league games against the great three-in-a-row winning Galway side in 1966 and Down in 1967, only losing by small margins on each occasion. 'The greatest footballers that I played against were Mick O'Connell, Mick O'Dwyer and Donie O'Sullivan of Kerry, Seán O'Neill and Paddy Doherty of Down and Noel Tierney, Martin Newell and Enda Colleran of Galway.'

The versatile Cregan who has also won an All-Ireland medal in the Pierce Purcell Shield golf competition with Nenagh Golf Club, believes that there should be no more rule changes in hurling and is of the strong opinion that a third official is required to adjudicate in all championship and league games. 'Younger referees, definitely younger and trained umpires and linesmen are needed to make the game more professional in its presentation and more official in its operation,' says the man who observes that if there is trouble with rules in football the GAA tend to change the rules in both codes.

Eamon does not confine his interests to sport. 'I like reading books of a historical nature especially those dealing with the archaeology and history of Limerick city. Genealogy is a preferred pastime of mine as well. We have studied our family tree and can go back, with a fair degree of accuracy, I think to 1750.'

When it comes to music, Cregan's interests are many and varied. The man who likes the songs that Daniel O'Donnell sings, loves all music, especially the hits of the great showband era of the 1960s and early 70s. Dean Martin is a particular favourite but nobody, in his eyes, compares to the man from Mullingar, Joe Dolan. 'There is no greater way to be entertained than to go to a Joe Dolan concert. I have been at three of them in recent times and they were superb. Joe has a fabulous voice, has recorded wonderful songs and gives great value for money. With the exception of Limerick winning an All-Ireland, I can't think of a better way to enjoy oneself than to go to a Joe Dolan concert,' concluded Eamon.

By universal acclaim, Mick Mackey, from Ahane, was not only Limerick's best ever hurler but one of the all-time greats that this ancient game of Cuchulainn has ever produced. The 1930s and 1940s were the golden eras of Limerick hurling. Between 1933 and 1947 Limerick appeared in eleven Munster finals winning five of them and bringing home the Liam McCarthy Cup in 1934, 1936 and 1940. During all that time Mick Mackey was their star performer, winning three All-Irelands, (two of them as captain in 1936 and 1940) and five consecutive National League titles (1934-1938).

No man, except Cork's Christy Ring, could ignite the imagination of hurling followers or attract extra thousands to Semple Stadium on Munster-final day more than the magnetic Mackey. His forging solo runs had an electrifying effect as the crowds swayed in anticipation of another score. His hurling was from the heart. The instinctive pleasure of striking a sliotar was all that mattered.

Mick Mackey and Eamon Cregan were close friends. Mick, who served both as a county and provincial selector often advised Eamon during his playing career. When Mick Mackey died in 1982, GAA followers everywhere, but especially in Limerick went into mourning. On the morning that he passed away, his widow Kitty informed Eamon that the family were burying Mick in his Munster blazer but they required a GAA tie to put on Mick's shirt in the coffin. That evening Eamon went to the Mackey homestead to pay his respects and to give Kitty his own GAA tie.

That simple request from the widow of Limerick's greatest hurler says it all. Mick Mackey had bestowed his own imprimatur on whom he thought was his worthy successor. Eamon Cregan must feel proud. He and his wife, Ann, have five children, Gary, Ciara, Niamh (a camogie star), Caoimhe and Brian.

Jimmy Smyth

IN JUNE 1983, THE Head of BBC Radio Sport in Northern Ireland rang the recently retired Armagh footballer, Jimmy Smyth, and asked him would he like to join their sports team. His first engagement would be to act as summariser to commentator Paddy O'Hara for the Ulster championship semi-final between Donegal and Monaghan. A surprised Smyth readily accepted and he clearly remembers taking his place beside the legendary Micheál Ó Muircheartaigh who was covering the game for RTE. Jimmy's first official function was to read out the names of the players of each team as well as their club names. Everything was going well until he read out the name Anthony Molloy and then referred to his club. Surrounding eyes immediately looked askance at the novice announcer. He had pronounced Molloy's club as AR-DAR-A, instead of AR-DRA. Though phonetically correct, dialectically he was wrong. Thereafter Jimmy ensured that he would do his homework properly. Despite this obvious faux pas Smyth was retained for the Ulster final and then a bigger 'break' came.

Cork and Dublin had drawn in that year's All-Ireland senior football semi-final. Thanks to a last-minute goal from the irrepressible Dublin forward Barney Rock, the Metropolitans had snatched a last minute equaliser. The replay was scheduled for the last Sunday in August in Cork's Páirc Uí Chaoimh. This time, when the BBC rang Jimmy, it was to ask him to cover the replay live from Cork. What made this honour even more interesting for Jimmy was the fact that the BBC production team were to fly down, in a six-seater plane, to Cork on match day.

As the group reached Cork airport a black stretch limousine awaited and the commentary team were quickly whisked towards Páirc Uí Chaoimh. Meanwhile, unknown to them, An Taoiseach Charles Haughey was expected to attend the game and to arrive much later than Jimmy and company. Many extra gardaí had been drafted in for security purposes. As the day was intensely hot and as the guest celebrity was not scheduled to arrive until an hour later some of the gardaí took some time out. A few casually basked in the sunshine with opened shirt buttons and loosened ties. Others, with cigarettes in mouth and hats by their side, relaxed on the grassy verges, well in advance of the official duty time. Then there was an emergency call to arms as a black limousine appeared. 'When we approached the back entrance to Páirc Uí Chaoimh shirts were quickly buttoned, ties straightened and cigarettes extinguished. Hats were solemnly put on heads and each garda stood to immediate attention as we sidled out of our limousine. The natural embarrassment on the faces of the gardaí and the amusement on ours provided an everlasting memory to a great day. The match had a fantastic carnival atmosphere and Barney Rock was absolutely superb. At the end of the game we got into our limousine with a very friendly and helpful garda escort bringing us through the masses of supporters. As we sped away I will never forget two over exuberant Dublin supporters who were jostling each other to get a better view of the occupants of our car.

"There's CJ", said one.

"No, it's not you idiot, it's the blooming referee," the other assured him.

We smiled as we made our way to Cork airport,' Jimmy added.

Born in Waringstown in Co. Down, Jimmy Smyth's earliest sporting experiences were dominated by the game of cricket, which was the predominant sport in his native environment. The young all-rounder was so good at cricket that he made the Waringstown second eleven at the age of twelve. Among the well-known cricketers playing for Waringstown at that time was Michael Reith who latter went on to represent Ireland.

Jimmy attended the nearest primary school, St Peter's, four miles away in Lurgan. Here he came under the baton of a primary teacher, Gerry Fagan, who was steeped in the GAA tradition. As well as being Armagh County Secretary, he was also a well-known referee. In the same class with Jimmy was another young boy, Colm McKinistry. They were destined to spend many happy hours together both at club and county level. Thanks to Fagan, Smyth immediately became immersed in Gaelic football and eagerly looked forward to playing the game at St Colman's in Newry when he went there as a Grammar school pupil. Though keen and quite handy, in his modest opinion, Smyth did not make the college's Corn na nÓg team (U-15) and his first sample of representative colleges football was when he made the Rannafast team (U-16 $^1/_2$) in his fifth year. 'The one lesson I learned from this whole period was to be sensitive to those boys who were not selected on teams. One of the most lasting memories of my teaching career to date occurred a few years ago. A boy, on the fringes of my school team, walked past me in the corridor, looked shyly backwards and asked was the football panel up on the notice board. I answered in the affirmative but did not tell him he was on it. The boy scanned the notice board intently, saw his name and immediately danced with delight. So, whereas it is nice to see the enjoyment being experienced by those on teams, one must always be conscious of the disappointments of those who do not make it.'

The following year, Jimmy was selected at right half back on the college's MacRory Cup team. In the Ulster semi-final, they defeated a strong St Columb's of Derry who had won the Hogan Cup two years earlier and who included in their side future soccer star, Brendan Mullan, later to score two goals for Fulham in an FA cup match. In the first MacRory Cup final to be held outside Ulster, in Dundalk, St Colman's defeated St Pat's Armagh. When they beat Dublin College, Belcamp OMI in the All-Ireland semi-final they were paired against the kingpins of Colleges' football, St Jarlath's Tuam.

Jimmy clearly recalls the build-up to the final. 'We did an hour's training before breakfast every morning. Our manager, Fr Treanor, insisted that in order to build stamina in a developing body we should take raw eggs every morning. Even though they were mixed with lemonade one could not say that they were very palatable! Fr Treanor left no stone unturned so that we would be physically and mentally prepared for the big day. Fr Treanor had guided St Colman's to five previous MacRory Cup triumphs and had steered them to a Hogan cup final appearance in 1957. Now he wanted us to win the title.'

On the morning of the final, he brought the whole team into the senior dormitory, moved back all the beds except one which he left in the centre of the floor. 'This represents the pitch,' he said as he put his hand in his pocket and took out 15 gleaming silver milk tops. Then he placed the tops, which represented our 15 football positions, one by one, on the bed and named each player on the team as he did so. Then he put his hand in his other pocket and took out another 15 tops, each of which had been squeezed tightly. Putting one beside each of the St Colman's shiny milk tops he uttered the famous words – St Jarlath's, crushed already!'

In a pulsating encounter, St Colman's took the lead thanks to a Martin Murphy goal and a marvellous 40-yard point from Smyth. However, in typical fashion, St Jarlath's came fighting back in the second half, to draw level. As St Jarlath's then advanced goalwards, Smyth made a crucial block to prevent a certain score. Just before the end, wing forward, Con Davey, notched, from a free, the winning point for St Colman's. Fr Treanor and St Colman's had achieved the dream of a lifetime. 'Your block was more important than your point,' he told an ecstatic Smyth just after the final whistle.

Jimmy Smyth's father was the best friend of the father of 1960s Down star, James McCartan. So, when Jimmy was young he naturally supported his and his father's native county of Down. However, after the family moved to Lurgan in 1966, Jimmy joined local club Clann na Gael. This really was fortuitous, as Jimmy had actually intended to join Tullylish – the home club of the famous McCartan clan. In fact, ironically, if a Tullylish club official had not forgotten to call for Smyth he would have registered for the Down club and subsequent history would have been turned on its head.

Clann na Gael had an excellent underage structure and they won three successive county minor titles in 1967, 1968 and 1969. This was to form the basis of their All-Ireland club team in the 1970s. Funnily enough, Jimmy was only a sub on the Armagh minor side of 1967 but made his debut with the Armagh senior team in August 1968. His first match was against Antrim, in a special four-county supplementary league between Sligo, Armagh, Dublin and Antrim. Held over three successive Sundays in Casement Park, Belfast, Jimmy's most noteworthy memory of that series concerns Sligo star Mickey Kearins. He sent a magnificent long low trajectory drop kick, which never rose more than a foot above the ground screaming into the corner of the net.

For the next five years, Armagh county football was in a deplorable condition. Bad organisation, poor turnouts for training and heavy defeats were the norm. What kept Jimmy Smyth going was the phenomenal success of his club side. Between 1971 and 1976, Clann na Gael were in five Ulster club finals, winning three successive titles in 1972, 1973 and 1974. In 1974 they reached the All-Ireland final only to be beaten by UCD after a replay. Incidentally, all club championships after that year were confined to individual county clubs.

Clann na Gael's success inevitably nudged the County board into remedial action. In 1974, the County Chairman Tom Lynch asked Peter Makem (a nephew of folk singer Tommy) to manage the county senior team. Fr Seán Hegarty, a former county minor star, Gerry O'Neill from St Colman's Newry and John Morrison of Armagh were all inveigled to join the new management team. Makem and his fellow selectors drew up their plans for the future of Armagh football, put them to a newly selected panel of players and appointed Jimmy Smyth as team captain.

Prior to this, one half of the county played the conventional catch and kick game, whereas the other half concentrated on the short passing game. Makem ensured that all changed to the latter system. It was almost 18 months before there was any apparent difference in terms of results. In 1976, Armagh won Division Three of the National Football League in a campaign which saw them play in Croke Park three weeks in succession. Though there had been limited success in the league, Armagh's poor championship record had not appreciably changed as they lost heavily to Derry both in 1975 and 1976. This problem had to be addressed immediately.

Management and players decided to change their strategy. They would drop their winter training programme and begin an intensive schedule of training for the 1977 Ulster championship. In the first round they were lucky enough, through a Colm McKinistry goal, to defeat Cavan before going on to overcome the challenge of Monaghan in the Ulster semi-final. Now, for the first time since 1961 (when Jimmy Smyth was shouting for Down) Armagh were in an Ulster final. What made them focus intently on this final was the fact that they were facing Derry, their conquerors of the previous two campaigns.

Derry were a tired side after their exertions of the previous years. Armagh, on the other hand, were eager and hungry for success. What is more, they had quality players who could translate that hunger into victory on the playing field. Though missing key forwards Mickey Moran and Brendan Kelly through injury, Derry seized the initiative in the match but missed several easy chances. That was effectively Derry's last positive contribution to this game as Armagh, inspired by veteran full back Tom

McCreesh, scored two opportunist goals per Paddy Moriarty and Noel Marley. Playing superb combination football, the Orchard county went on to record a comprehensive 3-10 to 1-5 victory. For the first time since their initial All-Ireland appearance in 1953, Armagh had won an Ulster title. 'When the final whistle went and I eventually received the cup (one supporter had temporarily hijacked the lid and another the cup itself) I thought about our National League success of the previous year. Then I had brought the cup to an old Lurgan friend Sam Coleman who wept tears of joy. Sadly, early in 1977 Sam had died. I know he would really have appreciated our victory,' added Jimmy.

When Jimmy discusses the huge transformation within Armagh football he credits the imaginative approach and organisational skills of Peter Makem. 'Peter, who now had retired to be replaced by Gerry O'Neill as manager, got us all as united as any club side. Our long-serving full back Tom McCreesh was an inspirational figure. He had won his first Railway Cup medal eleven years previously in 1966. When he spoke everyone listened. Before every game in 1977 he had the same battle cry, "This could be my last game," and immediately the team responded verbally in the dressing room and by deed on the pitch.'

In the All-Ireland semi-final, Armagh met Roscommon, the same county their forebears had defeated at the same stage in 1953. At the All-Ireland semi-final, Croke Park was awash with a sea of saffron and white. An endless selection of banners and flags draped the whole stadium. Initially, the Dublin side of 1974 had ushered in such paraphernalia but it was Armagh fans who by the quality and quantity of their flags, had given a new meaning to the word 'colourful.'

From an early stage, Roscommon took control of the game itself and were six points ahead after 20 minutes. Well into the second half, Roscommon still appeared the more likely team to win but centre half forward Jimmy Smyth had other ideas. Up to this, he had been the game's outstanding player but somehow he managed to dig deeper and inspire his team to draw level as the game entered its final moments. Then suddenly the dynamic Tony McManus cut through the Armagh defence and as he was poised to put Roscommon in front, Paddy Moriarty, who had moved back into the defence, brilliantly blocked his kick for a '45'. As the great Dermot Earley stood up to take the '45', Armagh manager Gerry O'Neill ran across Earley's path and shouted something at him. Earley missed the kick but characteristically did not blame O'Neill for his foray into the field. The whistle then sounded and the game had ended in a draw. The magnificent Jimmy Smyth was primarily responsible for this result. In a sterling performance, he had scored 1-3.

Psychologically, Roscommon were devastated. They felt they had thrown the game away and handed the initiative to Armagh. Even though they only won the replay by a point, a more confident Armagh went through to the All-Ireland final. Roscommon's turn would come again. Armagh had to make the most of the present.

Seldom has any county been as fanatical and euphoric in their preparation for an All-Ireland final as Armagh were in the decider against reigning champions, Dublin. The alleged sayings of ancient Irish prophets were recalled from a thousand years of hibernation. It was then supposedly said, that Armagh would be king of all Ireland when an Armagh native was on the See of St Patrick. Coincidentally, long-time Armagh supporter, future Cardinal Tomás Ó Fiach, had missed the Roscommon match because he had been called to Rome and appointed Archbishop of Armagh. For those clinging to hope, the omens looked promising.

Of all the emotional scenes that occurred in Croke Park down through the years, the pageantry that was headquarters on that day has to rank with the greatest ever. Jimmy Smyth will never forget the explosion of support that took place when he led his team on to the famous pitch, into the driving rain. (Foolishly, from their perspective Armagh came out five minutes earlier than the Dubs and bore the full brunt of the rain. Miraculously the rain stopped when the Dubs came out. Armagh had lost the first battle). The whole arena was festooned with the saffron and white of Armagh and the light blue and navy of Dublin. It was a wonderful spectacle that would surely surpass any festival of sporting excellence anywhere. 'When we came out the Armagh supporters went delirious with joy. I was totally overwhelmed with the tumultuous reception,' said Jimmy. Sadly, that was the end of Armagh's joy as Dublin cruised to a 5-12 to 3-6 victory. The magic boot of Jimmy Keaveney who scored 2-6 plus the skills, speed and experience of the whole Dublin side, especially Bobby Doyle, Tony Hanahoe, Kevin Moran and Tommy Drumm, paved the way for an easy victory.

Only terrific individual performances by Paddy Moriarty, two-goal hero Joe Kernan and captain Jimmy Smyth prevented a greater landslide. The dream, however, for Jimmy and the boys from the County Armagh was over.

Armagh won two further Ulster championships, in 1980 (when Roscommon gained their revenge and beat them in the All-Ireland semi-final), and 1982 when they were easily beaten by Kerry in that year's semi-final. When Armagh surprisingly lost to Antrim in the McKenna Cup final in August 1981, Jimmy retired from playing but became a mentor with the team for the 1982 championship campaign. At that stage, having been involved with his adopted county for a continuous 16 years – 1967–1982, he resigned from that position, Armagh having won another provincial title. It was time to take a break.

One of Jimmy's happiest GAA memories occurred later that year when the Roscommon and Armagh County boards got together and organised a trip to the USA for both teams. They spent two weeks there and played three matches, one each in New York, San Francisco and Los Angeles. Since then, a powerful friendship has developed between the two counties. 'At the end of the day this is an example of how the GAA can create a unifying bond and a mutual friendship,' asserted the Lurgan-based PE teacher.

In 1989, Jimmy Smyth commenced his television commentary career when he presented that year's Ulster semi-final between Donegal and Derry. Producer Rupert Miller gave him very strict instructions when commentating, to leave space for editing and not to speak when kick-outs and frees were being taken. Having adjusted to these parameters Smyth quickly progressed as a commentator and 'The Championship', as the programme was known, has continued to be accepted as an integral and compulsive part of television sports viewing. Jimmy, who looks upon the Down v Derry game, in the first round of the 1994 Ulster championship at Celtic Park, as the finest game he has commentated on, feels personally lucky that his early broadcasting career coincided with so many Ulster successes.

Jimmy would like to see the toe lift abandoned in Gaelic football. 'It slows down the game and most inter-county players do it incorrectly. They just put the toe beside the ball and lift the ball clean off the ground with the hands. Anyhow, Ladies' football has shown that the game is better off without it,' states the man whose wife, Mary, is a former Armagh camogie captain. Like everyone else, Smyth stresses the importance in the consistency of application of rules by referees. 'A referee's first function is to protect the players and if he does this then the game will be protected. He must not listen to pleas of alleged innocence. The rules are there and it is his job to implement them fairly,' says Jimmy whose favourite referees were John Moloney and Paddy Collins.

Smyth, who rates Kevin Moran (Dublin), Anthony McGurk (Derry) and Colm McAlarney (Down) as his most difficult opponents, maintains that the best game he ever played for his club was the 1969 Armagh county final when they defeated Crossmaglen Rangers. Marking such a great player as Tom McCreesh, then a Railway Cup star and scoring six points was a personal triumph for the man who also took part in the Irish Superstars competition.

Jimmy, who has a keen interest in all sports, is particularly fond of hurling. 'The 1973 All-Ireland hurling final between Kilkenny and Limerick was a fantastic occasion. I was especially impressed with the skills displayed by Limerick's Eamon Grimes, Eamon Cregan and Pat Hartigan. Jimmy Barry Murphy's famous goal for Cork when he pulled on an overhead ball and sent it into the net was the best score I have ever seen in any code. I also like to watch free-flowing rugby. The British Lions when they had Willie John McBride, Barry John, JPR Williams and Mike Gibson on board, were a joy to watch.'

One bone of contention that Smyth used to complain about was the lack of publicity for vocational schools football as opposed to colleges' football. For example, there are 96 vocational schools in Ulster and 20-odd colleges. 'Three years ago a committee consisting of Art McRory, Tony McCaffrey and myself decided to redress the situation. We secured a sponsorship deal with the Ulster Bank, decided to hold all vocational finals at one central venue and improved our marketing techniques. Immediately, the press became interested and all the competitions in vocational schools have been elevated to a higher status. Now all second-level competitions, both vocational and colleges, are properly organised and professionally presented. All our students are being equally treated', states the man who is Ulster Vocational Schools GAA Chairman.

Jimmy and his wife Mary have four children, Anne Marie, Paula, Brian and Ciara. They live in Lurgan where I met them on a beautiful May evening in 1999. When making his choices for selecting his Ireland team Jimmy stressed that he only considered those he played against, with one exception, Peter Canavan, whom he rates as an outstanding talent.

IRELAND

Paddy Cullen
(Dublin)

| Donie O'Sullivan *(Kerry)* | Paddy McCormack *(Offaly)* | Tom O'Hare *(Down)* |

| 'Red' Collier *(Meath)* | John O'Keeffe *(Kerry)* | Ger Power *(Kerry)* |

Brian Mullins
(Dublin)   Jack O'Shea
                                       (Kerry)

| Matt Connor *(Offaly)* | Colm O'Rourke *(Meath)* | Pat Spillane *(Kerry)* |

| Peter Canavan *(Tyrone)* | Seán O'Neill *(Down)* | Mike Sheehy *(Kerry)* |

His Ulster selection is based mainly on players who were at their peak between 1965 and 1990:

ULSTER

Brian McAlinden
(Armagh)

| Tom O'Hare *(Down)* | Tom Quinn *(Derry)* | Tony Scullion *(Derry)* |

| Paddy Moriarty *(Armagh)* | Malachy McAfee *(Derry)* | Jim Reilly *(Cavan)* |

Colm McKinstry
(Armagh)   Colm McAlarney
                                      (Down)

| Greg Blaney *(Down)* | Joe Kernan *(Armagh)* | Peter McGinnity *(Fermanagh)* |

| Frank McGuigan *(Tyrone)* | Seán O'Neill *(Down)* | 'Nudie' Hughes *(Monaghan)* |

Armagh is a county which has always been steeped in a rich Gaelic football tradition. For many years, St Patrick's College, Armagh was a bastion of Ulster colleges' football, winning 12 provincial titles between 1917 and 1953. In 1946 they won the first Hogan Cup when they defeated St Jarlath's Tuam in a classic encounter 3-11 to 4-7.

Even though there have not been any successes at senior level, Armagh won an All-Ireland junior football title in 1926 when they defeated Dublin. In 1949 Armagh, in a team that included Jack Bratten, John McKnight, Frank Kernan and Joe Cunningham, won the All-Ireland minor title when they defeated Kerry by two points. At club level, the famed Crossmaglen Rangers won the All-Ireland club championship in 1997 when they defeated Knockmore of Mayo and in 1999 when they overcame Ballina Stephenites.

In addition, Armagh have produced many GAA administrators such as Pádraig McNamee though representing Antrim, who became President of the GAA between 1938 and 1943 and Alf Murray who was President from 1964 to 1967. The late Gerry Arthurs from Keady who was a sub in the 1926 junior side was Ulster Council secretary for 42 years between 1934 and 1976. This amazing man who has the main stand in the revamped St Tiernach's Park in Clones named after him did so much voluntary work on behalf of the GAA that the GAA in Ulster was good humouredly referred to as the Gerry Arthurs Association.

In the 1940s, Eddie McLoughlin and the great Jim McCullagh were outstanding defenders while Alf Murray was one of the games most skilful performers. He was renowned for his speed and handpassing dexterity. All the foregoing represented Ulster with considerable distinction. In the 1950s Mal McEvoy, Seán Quinn and John McKnight were worthy ambassadors of the game. Both McKnight and Quinn were selected on the *Sunday Independent*/Irish Nationwide Centenary team consisting of players who had never won All-Ireland senior medals. The long-serving and stylish Jimmy Whan was one of Ireland's best forwards especially when Ulster did particularly well in the Railway Cup in the 1960s. In the 1970s, Paddy Moriarty had the distinction of winning an All Star both as a forward in 1972 and as a defender in 1977. In the latter year, he was joined on the All Star podium by Joe Kernan and the redoubtable Jimmy Smyth. All of those above, whether footballers or administrators have, in their own way, created a special niche and recognition for the quality of Gaelic games commitment over the decades in the Orchard County.

In September 1979, Jimmy Smyth went to Ballybrit Racecourse in Galway, on the occasion of the Pope's visit to Ireland. The night was decidedly cool and dull when a middle-aged stranger from west Mayo came up to Jimmy standing in the semi-darkness and said to him. 'Would you ever be wearing a number 11 on your back?' Jimmy smiled and graciously acknowledged the remarks. Within such comments is embossed the greatness of the GAA. Jimmy Smyth is indelibly linked to that unique affinity which binds firmly together all GAA people.

Liam Mulvihill

LIAM MULVIHILL, THE ELDEST of ten children, was born in the townland of Knappogue in the parish of Kenagh in County Longford in 1946. As most of the family farm was situated in the neighbouring parish of Ballymahon, Liam went to primary school there where his teacher was Tommy Casey who had been the captain of the first St Mel's College team to win the All-Ireland colleges' championship in 1948. Tommy was a very dedicated and enthusiastic GAA trainer and he organised regular football and hurling leagues within the school. Occasionally he would bring in his All-Ireland colleges' medal to show his budding footballers of the future what could be achieved if they devoted themselves wholeheartedly to playing Gaelic games. As a consequence, no one was more keen to aspire to All-Ireland glory than Liam Mulvihill.

After his initial induction to Gaelic games in Ballymahon, Liam soon turned to Kenagh to further his football education. The introduction of the parish rule, which specified that one must play either in one's native parish or the parish in which they lived, dictated that Liam play for Kenagh. Liam, whose uncles on his mother's side had been prominently associated with the GAA, became more involved when he went as a boarder to St Mel's College in Longford in 1959. Few secondary schools in Ireland held such a proud record as St Mel's, which, in the 1940s alone had won one All-Ireland title, and eight senior Leinster crowns and two junior provincial titles. Though the college experienced little success in the 1950s, that barren period would change dramatically during Liam's time there. During those five years, there was a fantastic revival in the college's fortunes, with the annexing of two All-Irelands, in 1962 and 1963, four successive senior Leinster titles and two junior provincial titles as well as two further All-Ireland appearances in 1961 and 1964. Given his family background and the Gaelic football ethos of St Mel's, it was no wonder that Liam became progressively more interested in a sport that ultimately would be the fulcrum of his life. Liam's love of Gaelic football was far from that of a mere academic as he himself was a very fast and versatile player who could hold his own in any company.

The attack-conscious half back was on the St Mel's junior sides which won back-to-back provincial titles in 1962 and 1963. He was also on the senior panel which won the 1962 All-Ireland final when they beat traditional rivals, St Jarlath's of Tuam. Unfortunately for Liam, he did not get a medal as he was not listed amongst the substitutes who qualified for medals. Nevertheless, that 1962 All-Ireland victory was especially sweet for St Mel's as they not only won the college's second national title but they also prevented their old adversaries from recording a historic three-in-a-row national titles. The captain of that St Mel's team, incidentally, was Dermot Gannon whose father Tom Gannon had led Leitrim to their first senior Connacht title 35 years earlier in 1927.

Early in the 1962–1963 season, Liam was injured but recovered to win provincial medals both at junior and senior level. In the All-Ireland semi-final against St Colman's of Newry, Liam played splendidly at corner back as St Mel's reached their third successive All-Ireland colleges' final. That All-Ireland semi-final was to provide one of the great anecdotes of colleges' football. During the course of the game, a St Colman's player sent a rasping shot towards the St Mel's net. It was blocked in the goalmouth and right full back JJ O'Connor from Annaduff appeared to touch the ball on the ground in the square. Immediately, the umpire, a prominent member of Down's double-winning All-Ireland team of 1960 and 1961, frantically called the referee's attention. Simultaneously, the quick thinking O'Connor handed the ball to St Mel's goalie and cousin of Liam Mulvihill, John Donlon. (Three years earlier the GAA had introduced a rule which allowed the goalkeeper to pick the ball up directly from the ground. They had not at that stage specified that goalkeepers must wear a different colour of jersey from the rest of his colleagues). The referee ran in to see what was wrong. Pointing towards Donlon with ball in hand, the Down man shouted. 'Ref, that's a penalty. He lifted the ball off the ground.'

'There's nothing wrong with that. He's the goalie and all goalies, for the last three years, are allowed to pick the ball off the ground,' asserted the referee. Much to the consternation of the Down man and the relief of the St Mel's defence, the referee awarded a free out! Notwithstanding that incident, St Mel's thoroughly deserved their win as they had played the much better football for most of the game. In the All-Ireland final at Croke Park, St Mel's defeated St Brendan's Killarney by the narrowest of margins 1-6 to 2-2. Liam had won the prize of his dreams – a coveted All-Ireland colleges medal. As captain, John Gilmurray raised the Hogan Cup a satisfied Liam looked around at his happy celebrating colleagues. Each in his own right was a star, but there had been some exceptional performances. Goalkeeper John Donlon brought off one marvellous save. Liam Mulvihill had a tremendous game at corner back and three future county stars, Michael Ryan (later to win All-Ireland medals with Offaly in 1971 and 1972), Mickey Reilly and Jimmy Hannify who were to feature prominently in Longford senior teams a few years afterwards, were truly magnificent. However, it was captain John Gilmurray who really stole the show with a magnificent all-round performance.

Like his predecessors, especially the legendary Fr Seán Manning, St Mel's coach Fr Jimmy McKeon deserved this success. Organisational ability, man management skills and total dedication to the team's preparation were the more obvious abilities the former Leitrim full back brought to his role.

In the 1963–1964 season, Liam Mulvihill for the third successive season was part of the St Mel's senior panel. Dogged by injury for the whole of the Leinster provincial campaign Liam improved sufficiently to regain his place, at left corner forward, for the All-Ireland semi-final against their opponents of the previous year, St Colman's. Again the Longford college emerged victorious to face Connacht champions, St Jarlath's. With time ticking away in the final at Athlone, St Jarlath's were leading by a point when the versatile Mulvihill notched an equalising point. Shortly after, the final whistle sounded. St Mel's, however, were beaten by the Tuam college in the replay at Tullamore. Liam Mulvihill had represented his college for the last time. He had amassed one All-Ireland medal, two Leinster senior medals and two Leinster junior medals during his five-year stay at the famed GAA nursery.

At the age of 14, in 1960, Liam made his inter-county debut, in very unusual circumstances, on the Longford county minor championship team. The then President of St Mel's College refused to allow boarders sitting for public examinations out for the provincial minor championship as it interfered with their study. As a result, many younger students were drafted in as substitutes for the county team. On the day of the game against Meath, in Croke Park, a selected team member cried off and Liam was called in to deputise at corner back and to take the kickouts. Though they lost, Liam was delighted with the honour of playing for his county particularly as the game was in Croke Park. Little did he realise that, 19 years later, his life would be so closely associated with GAA headquarters. However, he only played one further year with the county minors as he himself then came under the college's exclusion orders regarding provincial championship football.

In 1966, Longford had a very good U-21 side which reached the Leinster final only to be defeated by Kildare who had won the All-Ireland, at this level, the previous year. Included in that Longford side were Liam at left corner back and several other players who were destined to become household names in the annals of Longford football. Full back Seán Ryan, half back brothers JP and Mickey Reilly, Jimmy Hannify, Jody Sheridan (Liam's most difficult club opponent) and his own brother, Tom, were the best known of these players. In fact, Tom Mulvihill and Jimmy Hannify were already established senior stars who were members of the great Longford senior side of 1966 who made history by bringing the first senior national trophy to the county when they won the 1966 National Football League. In addition both Ryan and Sheridan were subs on that marvellous side. However, with the exception of a few league games, that was effectively the end of Liam's inter-county career. From those games, he especially remembers how difficult it was to mark Derry's Mickey Moran, now a member of the Management Committee of the Ireland International Rules team.

At club level, the U-21 football championship was introduced for the first time in Longford in 1963. Though his native Kenagh had a very small pool of players they won that first county championship. Unfortunately, Liam missed the final due to injury. Emigration and dwindling numbers prevented Kenagh from building upon that success and by 1966 they were finding it extremely difficult to field a decent junior team. In that year, the Longford County board decided to introduce a separate intermediate grade. This meant that some of the established senior clubs, as well as some recognised junior sides formed the new division. When the County board decided to upgrade Kenagh to this division there was widespread discontent amongst club members and they appealed the decision to Leinster Council. The appeal was turned down and they were forced to play in the new division. Ironically, and much to the delight of both Kenagh and the County board, Kenagh proceeded to win the intermediate championship by defeating neighbouring Cashel 2-8 to 0-7. Within a space of a few months Kenagh had progressed from being a junior club to a senior side. A few years later, the dearth of sufficient playing personnel compelled the club to amalgamate with another neighbouring team, Carrickedmond. Playing under the name of St Martin's they managed to reach a county senior final in the1970s before they each returned to play as separate units. Anyhow, as far as Liam Mulvihill was concerned, his professional career and his ever-increasing GAA administrative duties were considerably reducing his active playing involvement.

In 1964, Liam went to St Patrick's Teacher Training College, Drumcondra in Dublin. After graduating in 1966 he obtained a teaching position in Ballynacargy, Co. Westmeath. One year later, an internal rift occurred in GAA circles in Longford with many existing county officials and delegates resigning. The rift was healed when Ballymahon man, Jimmy Flynn, having been reappointed chairman of the county board used, his considerable diplomatic skills to harmonise relations within the county. Twenty-three-year-old Liam Mulvihill became one of the many new Longford administrators when he was elected vice chairman in 1969. In 1970, on the retirement of Jimmy Flynn, Liam became Ireland's youngest county GAA chairman when he was elected at the Annual Convention. Subsequently, he decided to stop playing competitive club football. Nevertheless, in 1984 he achieved a lifetime ambition when he played for Kenagh against Killashee in a junior league game. Thus he bowed out of the playing scene for the last time having fulfilled his wish to play in the GAA's Centenary Year.

When he was appointed as a School Inspector in 1974, Liam relinquished his chairmanship as his new job was based in Carlow. However his talents were not lost to Longford GAA as he was appointed their Central Council delegate. Unknown to anyone in Longford, and most of all himself, this was the move that was to draw the impressive administrative qualities of Liam to the attention of a much bigger audience.

Incidentally, the title of chairman rested lightly on Liam as it did on his two brothers Tom and Seán who were outstanding senior players for Longford for many years in the 1960s and 1970s. Tom became chairman of UCD and Seán was chairman of St Mary's College Strawberry Hill, London.

When the former Director General of the GAA, Seán Ó Síocháin, retired in 1979 there was much speculation as to who his successor would be. One man who was not mentioned was Longford's Central Council delegate Liam Mulvihill. He had not even thought of applying for the vacancy until friend and colleague former Longford County Secretary, Seán Donnelly mentioned to him that he should 'put his hat in the ring.' Thus, Liam duly applied and was interviewed by a small sub-committee under the chairmanship of GAA President Con Murphy from Cork. Along with some other candidates Liam was recalled for what he presumed was a second interview. Not having given any serious consideration to the possibility that he might get the job, he chatted casually and informally to his fellow Central Council delegates who were gathered in Croke Park. Then suddenly, fellow Central Council delegate and All-Ireland senior hurling medallist of 1959, Donie Whelan of Waterford tapped him on the shoulder. 'You're going to be the new Director General,' he whispered to the Longford man before disappearing into another group of friends. When Liam's turn came to be called into the interview room he briefly wondered what if Donie Whelan's confidential words were right. He had not long to wait as the President informed him at once that it was the unanimous decision of the Appointments Board that he become Ard Stiúrthúir of the GAA. 'How long have I to make up my mind?' asked the surprised Longfordian. 'About ten minutes,' said the President. When Liam then agreed to take up the onerous position he knew that his life would never be the same again. Up to now his whole leisure time had been consumed with his passionate interest in Gaelic games. Now, in addition, his whole working life would be totally occupied with developing the GAA to meet the increasing demands and hopes of all its units. The new 33 year-old Chief Executive Officer of the Association had reached the zenith of administrative positions. He had come a long way in a short time since, at the age of 14 when he was elected an official of the Kenagh Minor club. When the appointment was announced on the radio the next morning Liam was both happy and disappointed. He was delighted that he had been offered such a prestigious position but sorry that he had not time to tell his family before it became public knowledge.

Liam, who is the GAA's longest serving member on the Association's controlling body – the Central Council – is renowned for his diligence, diplomacy and sense of fairness. His annual reports to Congress are masterpieces of innovation and imagination. Liam's views on a whole range of issues pertaining to the future development of Gaelic Games are both catalytic in their intent and measured in their presentation. He is particularly conscious of the massive growth in the population of urban Ireland and the corresponding decrease in the number of people living in rural areas which were, traditionally, the bedrock of Gaelic Games.

Far away from the daily administrative chores and the madding crowds that invade Croke Park on so many summer Sundays, the quietly spoken Kenagh man pursues his other hobbies. 'When I was a child I used to collect stamps from all over the world. Now I collect as many editions as I can of every published book associated with my native Longford. The works of well-known Longford authors such as Maria Edgeworth, Padraic Colum and Leo Casey are among my proudest possessions. Also, I have always accumulated as much information on the local history of the particular area in which I live. As a consequence, local history publications from Longford, Carlow and now Meath have a special section in my library,' Liam told me when I met him in Croke Park.

Liam, who is also a keen reader of political, sporting and religious biographies is a dedicated follower of the American baseball and football leagues. 'Over the years I have become friendly with Dan Rooney who is very involved with the International Fund for Ireland. Dan, who is a native of Newry, Co. Down is a part owner, with other members of his family, of the famous American football side, the Pittsburgh Steelers. So I love meeting Dan to discuss the progress of the 'Steelers.'

At present, the Ard Stiúrthúir feels that the whole structure of the GAA as an organisation is very well balanced between its executive and voluntary officials. 'However, I realise that with increased family commitments and the social pressures in an ever-changing society, the voluntary commitment by so many will inevitably decrease. In terms of administration this may make the GAA more professional while at the same time creating other problems. It will be up to all of us in the Association to rise to these new challenges.'

During his tenure as Director General of the GAA, Liam Mulvihill has presided over an organisation which has contributed immensely to the development of Gaelic Games in every county in Ireland. In order to highlight that massive contribution I asked Liam Mulvihill to give an overview of how the GAA has used its resources, particularly within the last ten years.

HOW THE GAELIC ATHLETIC ASSOCIATION USES ITS RESOURCES

(an extract from an interview with Liam Mulvihill)

'One of the most common comments one hears in a sporting context is the one about the GAA and all its money. It is an easy jibe to make but it shows a serious lack of understanding of how the Association uses its resources.

The most important aspect of the GAA is that it is a trustee organisation which runs the Association on behalf of its members throughout the country and, indeed, abroad. It manages its finances also on behalf of its members and utilises its resources for the benefit of the Association as a whole. This is, in fact, governed by the rules of the Association and how the resources are utilised must comply with the basic aims and the rules of the Association. On this subject, the finances of the GAA are subject to full annual audit and detailed audited accounts and supporting documentation are presented annually to Congress.

Having set the background to the basis of the Association's management, it is worth looking at the figures for the last ten years:

The total revenue of the GAA for that period was £57,607,132. Of this, a total of £29,269,968 was spent on the day-to-day running of the Association including the cost of staging games, teams' expenses, contribution to the Players Injury Scheme and all the administration expenses.

This left a total operating surplus of £28,337,164. While this is a very substantial figure, it only becomes really significant when we look at how this surplus was utilised. This can be broken down as follows:

Croke Park Redevelopment	£14,110,000
Coaching and Games Development	£7,444,306
County Grounds Grants	£1,898,085
Club Ground Grants	£1,784,460
Special Projects	£1,097,000
Provincial Grounds Grants	£900,000
Education Sector Grants	£455,000
Omagh Disaster Fund	£250,000
Urban Development & Job Creation Fund	£70,000

These figures illustrate, quite clearly, the level of contribution, which the Gaelic Athletic Association centrally makes to the national economy. Out of a total income of over £57 million, £29 million is spent on running the organisation and our games and the remainder is spent as above. This means that, over the ten years, the Association has retained only £328,313 or little more than a half of one percent of its total income. This makes it hard to reconcile the myth of the GAA and all its money with the reality as outlined above.

An important aspect of the Association's finances is that each unit operates in an autonomous manner. This means that the provincial councils and the county boards have total control over their own finances. While most counties, except the larger, more successful ones, operate on a close to break-even basis, the total revenue of the counties and provinces and the national leagues would be on a par with Central Council, as shown above. Like Central Council, large amounts are not retained but are re-invested in activities and physical development.

The unavoidable conclusion of this analysis is that, over the last ten years, our Association has contributed well in excess of £100 million to the Irish economy. It is important to realise, also, that since the foundation of the Association in 1884, the members, with the assistance of *Central Council, Provincial Councils and County Boards have provided excellent facilities in every parish in the country without being a burden on the state. In a time of increasing demands on disposable income, the advent of the National Lottery has enabled substantial grants to be given by the state, particularly to county grounds. This has been a welcome development and is one, which the Association is grateful for. It is a tangible recognition by the state of the huge contribution, which the GAA has made, to the social and sporting infrastructure of this country.*

One final point, which is of central importance to any discussion on the finances of the GAA, relates to the redevelopment of Croke Park. This project when completed will have cost in the region of £130 million. This will have been financed by: direct funding from the Association, the long-term sale of seats in the redeveloped stadium and, of course, the well publicised grant from the state. Again, this represents a massive investment in the national economy by an amateur sporting body. Out of the total cost, at least £20 million will go directly to the Exchequer in VAT and PAYE/PRSI remittances.

As a footnote to this review, a table is given below of grants paid to clubs in 1998. A total of 125 clubs were grant-aided, spread over the whole country. This illustrates, not only the spread of clubs, but, also, the level of physical development, which is being undertaken by clubs, of every size, throughout the country. Looking behind these grants reveals that, at any time, development projects, worth in excess of £10 million, are being undertaken by clubs and county boards.'

Club Grants 1998

Connacht	IR£		IR£
Gaillimh		**Maigh Eo**	
Athenry	5,000	Bonniconlon	1,630
Gort	6,700	Ballyhaunis	6,300
Roscomáin		Killala	2,758
Cloonfad Handball	1,000	Davitts	1,520
Eire Óg	1,544	Claremorris	2,000
St Dominic's	3,350	Kiltane	4,000
Ballinameen	1,635	**Liatroim**	
Kilbride	2,000	Allen Gaels	1,200
Sligeach		Drumreilly	2,000
Shamrock Gaels	1,600	**Total**	£46,187
Eastern Harps	1,950	**Funded by Comhairle Chonnachta**	£19,187
		Ard-Chomhairle Grant:	£27,000

Leinster	IR£		IR£
Áth Cliath		Trumera	500
Whitehall Colmcille	2,000	Harps	750
Clontarf	2,500	Camross	1,000
Fingallians	2,500	**Longfort**	
St Finian's, Newcastle	2,500	Dromard	2,200
St Peregrines	500	Mostrim	2,200
Cill Dara		Longford Slashers	2,200
Castlemitchell	1,500	Clonguish	750
Round Towers	2,000	Ardagh	750
Kilcullen	2,000	**An Lú**	
Cill Chainnigh		Naomh Malachaí	1,600
Dunamaggin	1,750	Geraldines	1,600
Graigue-Ballycallan	1,250	**An Mhí**	
Danesfort	750	Kiltale	2,200
Laois		St Brigid's	1,850
Borris-in-Ossory	1,000	Summerhill	1,500
Crettyard	1,850	**Uibh Fháilí**	
Shanahoe	300	Doon	1,100
The Heath	1,150	Carraig & Riverstown	1,430
Timahoe	1,600	Clara	1,500
Portarlington	1,800		

Leinster	IR£		IR£
Iarmhí		**Cill Mhantáin**	
Kilbeggan	1,800	Newtown	2,000
Loch Garman		An Tóchar	1,500
Our Lady's Island	1,150	Kilbride	2,000
St James'	750	**Total**	£74,730
Castletown	2,200		
St Mary's	1,500	**Balance to be distributed**	£270
Sarsfields	1,800	**1988 Ard-Chomhairle Grant**	£75,000
St John's	1,800		
Faythe Harriers	1,650		
Buffers Alley	2,300		
St James, Ramsgrange	1,000		
Ballygarrett	1,500		
Glynn Barntown	1,800		

Munster	IR£		
Corcaigh		**Tiobraid Árann**	
Na Piarsaigh	2,000	Silvermines	2,000
Bantry Blues	2,000	Templederry	1,500
Tracton	2,500	Moyne/Templetouhy	2,000
Eire Óg	2,500	Kilsheelan	2,000
Aghabullogue	2,000	Ballingarry	250
Inniscarra	2,000	Golden/Kilfeacle	250
Rathluirc	2,000	Upperchurch/Drombane	250
Carrigtwohill	1,000	Borrisokane	250
Belgooly	2,000	**Luimneach**	
Kinsale	2,000	Crecora	2,000
Rockchapel	2,000	Effin	2,000
Cobh	2,000	Mungret	1,500
Ciarraí		Old Christians	500
Knocknagoshel	2,000	Newcastle West	250
Knockanure	2,000	Dromcollogher/Broadford	250
Tarbert	2,000	**An Chlár**	
Moyvane	2,000	Nh. Eoin, Cross	1,000
Currow	500	Ennistymon	2,000
Killorglin	500	Miltown Malbay	250
St Pat's Blennerville	250	Newmarket-on-Fergus	250
Lispole	250	Kilmihil	250
Asdee	250	Quilty	250
Cromane	250		

Munster	IR £		
Port Láirge			
Dunhill	250		
Rathgormack	250		
Geraldines	250		
Ballyduff	250		
Total	£54,000		
1998 Ard-Chomhairle Grant	£64,000		

Ulster	IR £		
Aontroim		**Fearmanach**	
Glen Rovers, Armoy	1,250	Belcoo O'Rahillys	2,500
Glenravel (New Pitch)	3,000	Devenish	4,100
Naomh Éanna (Glengormley)	5,500	Teemore	3,000
Loughgiel Shamrocks	4,000	**Muineachán**	
Ard Mhacha		Carrickmacross	1,500
Tullysarron	1,800	**Tir Eoghain**	
An Cabhán		Brockagh (Mountjoy)	3,700
Butlersbridge	1,500	Pomeroy	1,500
An Dún:		**Total**	£39,850
Glassdrummon	2,000	Balance to be distributed	£4,150
Naomh Pól (Holywood)	4,500	**1998 Ard-Chomhairle Grant**	£44 000

The above figures show that the GAA has distributed much of its accruals back down to club, county and provincial level to nurture the grassroots of the GAA. Liam Mulvihill has been pivotal to the vision that has resulted in this sharing and disbursal of funds from Croke Park.

Liam and his wife Máire have three children Daráinne (17), Aonghus (13) and Fionán (11). All three are totally committed Meath supporters. According to their dad, Máire's native Kerry and Longford only came a very poor joint second in their county GAA preferences!

When the new Director General of the GAA came home after his appointment in 1979, he had brought honour to himself, his family, his parish and his county. In the midst of a plethora of well wishers, a well known Longfordian came to wish him well. Any delusions of grandeur that Liam may have had were suddenly shattered. 'How on earth can an intelligent sensible man with a good secure, pensionable job, give it all up to take over an organisation which will be dead in ten years time?' his erstwhile friend enquired.

Liam's term of office is due to expire when he reaches his 60th birthday in 2006. He would like when that time comes, health permitting, to leave the GAA a much more confident, stronger and more modern organisation than it was when he first assumed the reins of office. There is no doubt that the young schoolboy who listened to the words of encouragement of Tom Casey in the 1950s will achieve all of that and much more.

Longford is a small county which will always, through sheer lack of numbers, find it difficult to experience success on the football or hurling fields. Still they have had their hours of glory. They won three Leinster junior provincial titles in 1924, 1937 and 1953. The 1937 side went on to bring home Longford's first national title when they defeated London in the All-Ireland final. Longford also won two Leinster minor titles in 1929 and 1938 when they defeated Dublin and Louth respectively. It was the 1960s that were to provide Longford with their greatest triumphs. In 1966, they defeated Galway and New York in the deciding fixtures to claim the National Football League title. That all-round talented side had outstanding performers in Brendan Barden, Bobby Burns, Jackie Devine and Seán Donnelly. Barden was, arguably, one of Longford's best ever footballers. The subtle, silken skills of wing forward Jackie Devine and the tigerish determined play of corner forward Seán Donnelly embellished the telling contributions of others such as Larry Gillen, Tom Mulvihill (Liam's brother). Jimmy Hannify and Seán Murray. Two years later Longford won their only senior Leinster championship crown when they defeated Laois before losing to Kerry in the All-Ireland semi-final. Though depleted by injury, Longford performed magnificently to lose by only two points to the Kingdom who were making their 50th All-Ireland semi-final appearance as opposed to Longford's first. Many other players, such as Jim Hannify (Snr), Vincent Tierney, Padraic Gearty (his opening point in the 1962 Railway Cup final was the first point to be seen on RTE television) and the long serving Dessie Barry have starred in Railway Cup triumphs. Longford have also produced many eminent officials. Former county and provincial chairman, Albert Fallon, was a candidate for the GAA presidency in 1999 and must rate as one of the favourites for the 2002 presidency. Legan Sarsfields clubman John Bannon had the honour of refereeing the 1998 All-Ireland senior football final between Galway and Kildare. All in all, Longford can be justifiably proud of its contribution, at all levels, to the GAA. Those successes have always encouraged and continue to inspire Liam Mulvihill as he assiduously plans for the future development of the GAA.

When Liam Mulvihill returns to his native county today, he often meets the man who in 1979 expressed grave reservations about his wisdom and the Association's future. Both now look back in laughter and look forward in positive hope as the GAA enters the new millennium stronger and more vibrant than ever. Likewise, all GAA followers throughout the country know that the man chiefly responsible for that new -found confidence is the very able and forward thinking Liam Mulvihill. Longford's individual loss is most definitely the whole Gaelic Athletic Association's gain.

Enda Colleran

AFTER CAPTAINING HIS SIDE to a historic All-Ireland senior football victory against Kerry in the 1964 final, John Donnellan entered the victors' dressing room. His first thoughts were of his father, Mick, who had starred for Galway in the 1920s and 1930s and who had been in the Hogan Stand to see his son play. Prior to the game Mick had expressed the wish, if they were successful, to carry the base of the Sam Maguire Cup back to his native Dunmore. Now an ecstatic John wished to fulfil his father's dream. 'Let's bring the cup across to the old man,' he said excitedly.

An eerie silence descended upon the dressing room. Selector and former Galway star, Brendan Nestor, eased forward and put a consoling hand on John's shoulder. 'It's your father, John, things are not good,' he whispered.

'Is he dead?'

'I am sorry, he is.' Brendan said.

The hour of John's most momentous triumph, simultaneously, was the time of his most poignant sorrow. During the course of the game, Mick Donnellan TD had passed away. Instead of a celebratory return home John Donnellan and his fellow players carried, not the base of the Sam Maguire Cup, but the mortal remains of his father, to his beloved Dunmore.

That mixture of joy and sadness which marked Galway's first All-Ireland triumph in eight years still dominates the mind of Enda Colleran when he recalls his first senior success all those years ago. Human tragedy had put the elation of winning an All-Ireland into proper perspective. When I met Enda in his Barna home he was quick to reflect on the frailties of our human existence and how sport, though important, was just a minuscule part of our earthly journey.

Enda Colleran was born in Moylough and attended one of the most famous GAA nurseries – St Jarlath's College, Tuam. In 1960, he won both an All-Ireland Colleges medal and an All-Ireland minor medal. Sharing that minor victory with Enda were four other outstanding footballers who were to partake in even greater successes. Full back, Noel Tierney, midfielder Seán Cleary and wing forwards Christy Tyrell and Séamus Leyden were names that were to dominate Galway football for the next ten years.

1960 was very much a benchmark year in Enda's football development. As well as those underage victories the words of his boyhood idol were even more catalytic. 'You keep playing and training hard. I have no doubt you will make it to the very top,' were the prophetic words uttered by the one and only Seán Purcell when they met at

Enda's brother's wedding. Armed with those words of encouragement Enda proceeded to train daily, sprinting up and down hills on his father's farm. As a consequence, he was called up to the Galway junior football squad to train for the 1961 Connacht junior championship. When the side to play Sligo was selected, however, Enda was listed only as a substitute. He was furious that he had not been picked on the team because he had performed very well in the pre-match trials. When Galway trainer and captain of their senior All-Ireland winning team of 1938, John 'Tull' Dunne called to collect him he refused to go. Despite being told by his brothers that 'you don't refuse Mr Dunne,' Enda remained stubborn and stayed at home. Thankfully, Dunne, realising Colleran's great potential and his youthful exuberance, forgave him. He was picked on the side that defeated Mayo in that year's junior provincial final and which actually reached the All-Ireland junior (home) final only to be defeated by Louth. Later in the same year, Enda made his senior debut when he came on as a substitute, at left corner back, for the long-serving Jack Mahon. This was Mahon's last game in the maroon and white as he decided, rather prematurely, to retire from inter-county football. From then until he retired, Colleran was a permanent fixture, usually at right full back, on the Galway senior side.

Enda's first senior Connacht final against Roscommon in 1962 has entered GAA folklore for many different reasons. Primarily, it was an exact replica of the 1961 final. The same sides were in opposition, at the same venue (Castlebar) and Roscommon won by a single point on both occasions. Two legendary GAA figures also experienced contrasting fortunes. Seán Purcell, one of the all-time great exponents of Gaelic football, played his last game for Galway on that day. The other, Roscommon's wonderful centre half back, Gerry O'Malley, had one of his most outstanding games for his county.

At half time, the scores were level and by the end of the third quarter Galway had cruised into a 2-6 to 1-4 lead. Then a bizarre incident occurred. In attempting to save a point, Roscommon goalkeeper, Aidan Brady, swung off the crossbar. To the consternation of everyone the crossbar came tumbling down. When the crossbar was repaired, Roscommon had revamped their team, sending O'Malley to midfield. Giving an inspirational display and using his unique high style solo to devastating effect, O'Malley constantly ran at the Galway defence. The Roscommon forwards responded so magnificently to O'Malley's promptings that they pipped Galway by a single point on a scoreline of 3-7 to 2-9. For Enda Colleran, the result was both a terrible disappointment and learning experience which stood him in good stead in the following years.

In 1963, Galway easily overcame Leitrim in the Connacht final before going on to defeat Kerry by two points in the All-Ireland semi-final. The latter victory, courtesy of two late Séamus Leyden points, ensured that Colleran was scheduled to play in his first senior All-Ireland football final, against Dublin. In the final itself, Galway were very profligate in the area of scoring and they succumbed to a two-point defeat.

However, the team had played well as a unit and Enda and his teammates looked forward eagerly to the 1964 championship campaign. Nevertheless, a magical display by Sligo ace, Mickey Kearins nearly put paid to their hopes in the Connacht semi-final. In the end, the accuracy of Cyril Dunne (son of the aforementioned John) and an opportunist goal by Mattie McDonagh ensured a narrow one-goal victory margin. Having easily accounted for Mayo in the Connacht final, Galway qualified to meet Meath in the All-Ireland semi-final. As that game entered its final stages a '50' expertly pointed by midfielder Mick Reynolds and an opportunist Seán Cleary point guaranteed success for the Westerners. 'We were very lucky as Meath's Jack Quinn was unfortunate to have a goal disallowed and our goalkeeper Johnny Geraghty made a fantastic save a short time afterwards. Incidentally, Johnny did not concede a goal in the 1964, 1965 or 1966 finals,' Enda recalled.

In the final, Galway were pitted against Munster champions Kerry. With captain John Donnellan leading by example and Mattie McDonagh wreaking havoc on the '40' in the first half, Galway went in at half time leading 0-7 to 0-3. On the resumption Kerry moved Mick O'Connell from wing forward to his customary midfield position. With the Valentia maestro orchestrating every move with fine fetching and pinpoint foot passes, Kerry began to dominate. It was, however, a fantastic save by Johnny Geraghty from corner forward Jo Joe Barrett which stopped Kerry's momentum. With that save, Galway psychologically lifted the siege and went on to record a fine victory on a score of 0-15 to 0-10.

As the crowds of enthusiastic Galway supporters raced across Croke Park, Enda was overcome with joy. He remembers particularly John Donnellan's rousing speech from the victory rostrum when he said: 'Let's write the name G-A-L-W-A-Y across the sky in large letters of maroon and white.' Little did John or indeed Enda realise that two of Galway's most famous supporters had just died. Along with Mick Donnellan, Galway's captain of their 1934 winning team, Mick Higgins had passed away while watching the game on television.

In the following year, Galway again defeated Kerry, somewhat luckily, in the national football (home) final before going on to defeat New York in the final proper a few weeks later. A tired Galway team just managed to beat Mayo and Sligo on the way to their third consecutive Connacht title. That year's All-Ireland semi-final against Down was Enda Colleran's greatest ever display in a Galway jersey. Ironically, the first six minutes of that game were a nightmare for the UCG student. His direct opponent, Brian Johnstone, scored two points off him in that period.

'I decided I must intensify my mental approach or Brian would be Man of the Match. Luckily, after that, everything seemed to go right for me. Everywhere I went the ball seemed to fall into my hands. On one particular occasion I sprinted after

Down danger man, Paddy Doherty, as he dashed towards goal and robbed him of possession. This made me especially proud as I have always considered Paddy as the best scoring forward in the history of the game,' the man who now teaches in St Enda's College, Salthill revealed.

After securing a three-point victory margin over Down, Galway were now in their third successive All-Ireland final. Of more immediate significance to Enda was the fact that he had been appointed captain for this campaign. 'When my club, Mountbellew, won the 1964 Galway championship, they nominated me, as was the custom of the day, the county captain. Personally, I felt that Mattie McDonagh who had been playing for the previous nine years should have been selected. Initially, I feared that I might not perform my new dual role properly. As it turned out I seemed to get better with every game in the 1965 championship. This self-analysis gave me confidence so I became happy with being captain,' said Enda who was also appointed as the county captain in 1966.

Their opponents in the 1965 final were old rivals, Kerry. Tension filled the air as the teams took the field. Galway had become one of the few teams to inflict three successive defeats in major competitive games against the Kingdom. In the recent League encounter, Galway had snatched victory from the jaws of defeat. During the final stages of that match, Galway were a point in arrears when Mattie McDonagh appeared to pick the ball off the ground before transferring to flying forward Séamus Leyden who sent the ball to the net for a sensational winning goal. Kerry felt cheated. This final presented an ideal opportunity to redress the balance. Nevertheless it was Galway who seized the initiative and they led 0-7 to 0-4 at half time. For the first ten minutes of the second half, the Kingdom's Mick O'Connell was at his majestic best, fetching superbly and sending an array of defence-splitting passes to his forward colleagues who quickly cut the deficit to a single point.

It was then that Galway switched Pat Donnellan to curb O'Connell's superiority. Though small in stature, Donnellan succeeded in breaking the ball from O'Connell. Linking up with the magnificent halfback line of brother John, Seán Meade and Martin Newell, Donnellan controlled the remainder of the game as Galway ran out convincing winners by a three-point margin. Enda Colleran had the honour of leading his native county to their second All-Ireland in a row. When asked about Galway's second half display Colleran was frank in his assessment.

'We played magnificent combination football. Unfortunately, things got out of hand when three men (two Kerry and one Galway) were sent off. Kerry had too many converted backs in their forward line and they relied too heavily on the traditional catch and kick style. Nevertheless it was a great feeling to defeat such a wonderful Gaelic football county in successive All-Irelands.'

Galway again reached the 1966 national football (home) league final only to suffer a surprise one-point defeat to Longford. Though disappointed with the defeat, Enda was pleased for his great friend and former UCG Sigerson colleague, Seán Donnelly, who was a star in the Longford forward line. That defeat nonetheless had the advantage of eliminating any complacency in the Galway camp as they attempted to become the first team since Kerry (1939–1941) to accomplish the historic three-in-a-row championships. Still, they were exceptionally lucky to beat Mayo by one point in the Connacht final before meeting Cork in the All-Ireland semi final. A wasteful Cork forward line in which Niall Fitzgerald missed two open goals enabled the Westerners to fashion out a narrow two-point victory. Luck and experience had contrived to ensure that Galway were on course for that elusive treble.

As their final opponents, Meath, had trounced Down in the other All-Ireland semi-final many pundits were predicting a Royal County success. This was based on the premise that, in football terms, Galway were an old team and that a strong Meath side were thirsty for success. Colleran was determined that Galway would not give in without a fight. To prepare mentally for the occasion, he and colleague Martin Newell decided to spend a few days on the Aran Islands before they commenced their official training programme. Central to Enda's mental preparations was his concentration on the fact that in the final he was marking a Garda 100m champion, Ollie Shanley. So he continually psyched himself as to how he would handle Ollie. Enda himself takes up the story.

'One night in our lodgings Martin Newell was aroused from a deep slumber by an unmerciful roar. I was pacing up and down the room. Then, though sleepwalking, I stood at his bedside, screeching "I can keep up with Shanley, I'll mark him!" It just shows the effect the whole scenario had on me.'

For the final, Galway sensationally dropped their 1964 captain, John Donnellan, replacing him with Coleen McDonagh. Two other rising stars, Jimmy Duggan at midfield and Liam Sammon at corner forward, had replaced Mick Garrett and Christy Tyrell from the 1965 winning combination. In the final itself, Galway played superb, controlled football with tight man-to-man marking being the order of the day. At half time they led by eight points and when the full-time whistle came they were 1-10 to 0-7 in front. This magnificent team had accomplished what no other side had done in the previous 25 years. Enda Colleran, who was again the winning captain, was a particularly happy man. Justifiably, they have since been universally acknowledged as one of the greatest sides in Gaelic football history.

Though Galway won another league title in 1967, they were destined to wait another 32 years before the Sam Maguire cup would cross the River Shannon again. A mixture, in his opinion, of inept selectorial decisions which prompted the breaking up of the three-in-a-row side, plus personal fatigue made Enda give up the game he graced for so long in 1970. At the comparatively young age of 28, Enda played his last game for Galway against Offaly in the National Football League at Ballinasloe.

Incidentally, the man he marked on that occasion – Tony McTague – was himself just 12 months away from winning the first of his two All-Ireland senior football medals.

When Enda Colleran looks back on those halcyon days of Galway football glory, he often thinks of the many brilliant Gaelic footballers that he was privileged to play against. In particular he recalls the tremendous skills of Ray Prendergast, Joe Corcoran and John Morley of Mayo and the Feeley Brothers, Gerry O'Malley and Ronan Creaven of Roscommon. Mickey Kearins (Sligo) and Pakie McGarty (Leitrim) were two of the best forwards that he ever saw. Des and Lar Foley (Dublin), Seán O'Neill and Paddy Doherty of Down, 'Babs' Keating (Tipperary), Mick O'Dwyer (Kerry), Mick Brewster (Fermanagh), Mickey McLoone (Donegal) and Charlie Gallagher (Cavan) were others that he held in the highest regard. 'However, the nicest footballer of all to watch was Mick O'Connell. He was a pure footballer who glided around the field like the super athlete that he was.'

In latter years, he loved to watch Dermot Earley of Roscommon and Bernard Flynn of Meath. 'Earley was a ball winner and playmaker apart and Flynn was the best scoring forward in recent times. The Kerry team of the 1970s and 1980s was the best team that I ever witnessed. Each of them was a star in his own right,' added the soft spoken Galwegian. His favourite present-day footballers are defenders Séamus Moynihan (Kerry), Darren Fay (Meath) and Galway's Seán Óg de Paor. Anthony Tohill (Derry), Liam McHale (Mayo), fellow Galwegians Michael Donnellan and Jarlath Fallon are others he would select in any current All Stars team.

When Enda Colleran retired, he took up rugby and played at full back for Galway Corinthians for several seasons. 'This was a period of my life that I enjoyed immensely. I recall playing against leading side, Wanderers, at Lansdowne Road. It was great to play against such established international players as Kevin Flynn and Paul McNaughton,' admitted Enda.

For a brief term in the 1970s, Colleran was manager of the Galway senior team taking them to a provincial title. Of all the positions in modern sport, he reckons being a manager is the most demanding of all. 'It is the worst job in sport. You are only as good as your last win. Supporters are very fickle and they do not appreciate the amount of time and energy that is expended. I certainly would not undertake such an onerous position again.'

For upwards on ten years, Enda was the television analyst on RTE's 'Sunday Game.' 'This was a fantastic experience. I saw the country by helicopter and renewed many acquaintances.' One anecdote surfaces from his memory.

'For some reason several Tyrone supporters took a great dislike to me because I did not tip them to win any game in the 1986 Ulster championship. When they proved my predictions wrong by reaching that year's Ulster final there were a lot of banners amongst the Tyrone supporters which were rather uncomplimentary to me. After Tyrone won the final I was interviewed by another TV station. The interviewer said,

"Tyrone play Galway in the All-Ireland semi-final? How do you think that match is going to go?"

Being surrounded by Tyrone supporters and with tongue in cheek, I replied. "Only that there are a lot of Tyrone fans listening I would be saying that Galway would beat the pick of the two teams here today." That did not please them and many of them have not forgotten it since. Incidentally, Tyrone were decidedly unlucky not to win that year's All-Ireland against Kerry,' Enda diplomatically concluded.

Regularly, Enda recalls the days of his formative footballing years and how he wanted to emulate his older brothers Séamus, Fr Gabriel and Gerry who was a substitute on the 1956 All-Ireland winning team. Two other men from that era continue to predominate his mind. The undoubted class of Seán Purcell and the opportunism of Frankie Stockwell, who collectively were known as 'the Terrible Twins,' were Colleran's role models. Purcell was the best footballer that he ever saw. His telepathic understanding with full forward Stockwell caused havoc in every defence they faced. Frankie Stockwell's 2-5 in the 1956 All-Ireland still stands as a record score from play in an All-Ireland final.

Another dimension to Gaelic Games that Colleran is especially pleased with is Galway's strong hurling tradition. This latter fact was well emphasised when three Galway men were selected on the *Sunday Independent*/Irish Nationwide GAA Centenary team (confined to players who had never won an All-Ireland senior championship medal) in 1984. Seán Duggan, Joe Salmon and Josie Gallagher had wielded the camán at the highest level for many years but without national success. In 1975 and 1979 Galway reached the All-Ireland hurling final only to be defeated. However, the 1980s proved to be a successful era for Galway hurling when they annexed three titles in 1980, 1987 and 1988. When captain Joe Connolly raised the Liam McCarthy cup in 1980 Enda was elated. As 1979 captain, Joe McDonagh rendered a beautiful version of 'The West's Awake' from the steps of the Hogan Stand, a new hero was born.

'When I started teaching in 1966, Joe was a student in my class. From those early days we could easily see that Joe was destined for greatness. He is one of the most talented individuals that I have ever met. He was a wonderful hurler, is a brilliant actor, beautiful singer and a very capable administrator. I was delighted when he became President of the GAA in 1997. I only hope that when his term comes to an end the GAA will find an important outlet for his undoubted ability,' stated Colleran.

Little did Colleran realise that when he captained the 1966 winning team, Galway would not win another All-Ireland for 32 years. In the interim, they reached four finals only to be unsuccessful on each occasion. With John O'Mahoney at the managerial helm that long sequence was broken when Galway gave an immaculate display to defeat Kildare in the 1998 final. Having played fast, exciting, combination football the final whistle signalled the end of the barren years for the men from the west. In a team of stars one young man stood out as a shining beacon, a real prodigious talent. That man, Michael Donnellan was the third generation of his family to win a coveted All-Ireland medal. Son of 1964 captain John and grandson of 1925 All-Ireland winner Mick, Michael, if he reaches his true potential, has the capacity to become an all-time great.

That 1998 win did not just stand alone in its impact on the GAA national consciousness. In the build-up to the game and in its immediate aftermath, all Gaels also recalled the tremendous achievement of the 1960s Galway team of which Enda Colleran was such an integral part.

'In those years, we took winning for granted. It was only when Galway won the 1998 All-Ireland that I realised the extent of our achievements,' concluded the man who was selected at right corner back on the *Sunday Independent*/Irish Nationwide team of the century in 1984 and on the team of the millenium.

Enda, (he and his wife, Anne have four children, Enda, Orla, Ronan and Shane) was delighted that Seán Purcell had attended his brother's wedding in 1960. Now, almost 40 years later he fully appreciated the magical sequence of sporting successes that meeting and those words of the maestro had triggered. Moylough's most famous son will be forever associated with all that is best in the west.

John Wilson

JOHN WILSON WAS BORN in Mullahoran, a rural Cavan parish steeped in traditional Irish music, songs and games. His father who had played many years for the club and who had been club secretary encouraged John and his other sons Willie, Jimmy, Aidan and Eugene to follow in his footsteps. When Mullahoran won their first Cavan senior championship title in 1935, 12-year-old John's liking for the game and his aptitude for it developed immensely in spite of the fact that there was no underage football structure in his parish. When he was sent as a boarder to one of the country's finest GAA Colleges – St Mel's of Longford – the Cavan youngster's football career quickly flourished. Fr Seán Manning, the college's renowned Gaelic football trainer, was famous for his ability to spot talented players at a very young age and then develop them to their full potential. John Wilson alludes to this when he unequivocally says that the St Mel's priest was the single strongest influence in his development both as a player and as a person.

'I remember my time at St Mel's with great affection. Fr Manning was the most skilled, informed and dedicated trainer that I ever met. We trained arduously seven days a week and he inculcated in us a respect for authority. Under no circumstances were we ever to criticise a referee. Our primary task was to focus on the job in hand – to win the ball, kick it and send it over or under the bar. It was not our function as players to get involved in anything but the playing of the game. In my time there we had some marvellous players. Frank Mitchell of Leitrim played for Connacht in the Railway Cup in the same year that he sat the Leaving Certificate examination. Seán Mitchell, also of Leitrim (no relation to Frank) and Jim Butler of Sligo who went on to play for Galway in an All-Ireland semi-final were both exceptional individuals. Paul Reynolds, also of Leitrim, our winning captain in the 1941 Leinster colleges' final, was a very strong but clean full back. Jimmy O'Brien of Longford was one of the trickiest will o' the wisp type forwards that I ever saw. I was lucky to play in so many successful college teams at St Mel's, at both junior and senior level. I was right half back on their 1941 and 1942 teams and represented Leinster colleges at interprovincial level during those years as well,' John informed me when I met him in the Longford Arms Hotel, Longford.

Wilson, who won his first county club medal when he played for the neighbouring Ballinagh club at minor level in 1941, made his inter-county minor debut the same year. Cavan reached that year's Ulster minor final only to suffer defeat at the hands of Antrim. 'Unlike now, in those days '50s' were rarely scored by any player at any level.

In that final, I remember the late Seán Gallagher who went on to play for Antrim in the 1946 All-Ireland semi-final and who won two Railway Cup medals in 1947 and 1950, sending a '50' over the bar. He really was a very strong young player.'

Three years later, in 1944, John was on the Cavan junior side that defeated Donegal in the Ulster final. Shortly afterwards he was promoted to the Cavan senior team which also won that year's Ulster championship when they beat Monaghan in the final. However, in the All-Ireland semi-final they were well beaten by Roscommon who went on to record their second successive All-Ireland victory. In 1945, Wilson was again on the Cavan team which trounced surprise packets, Fermanagh, in the provincial decider. The All-Ireland semi-final against Wexford was to see Wilson at his best in the Cavan colours. The tough but fair tackling right half back played the proverbial stormer as Cavan edged home on a 1-4 to 0-5 scoreline. Despite good performances by John Joe O'Reilly, Simon Deignan and Tony Tighe, Cork ousted the Ulster champions in John Wilson's first All-Ireland final appearance. That was the day that future Taoiseach and John Wilson's first political leader, the late Jack Lynch, won his sole All-Ireland football medal. The following year would see Lynch win his record breaking sixth successive All-Ireland senior medal.

After their seven consecutive senior provincial successes (1939-1945) no one expected Antrim to defeat the Breffni men in the 1946 Ulster final but that they did. They played very well in the All-Ireland semi-final against Kerry but lost by three points in a game most remembered for the toughness of its physical exchanges.

Wilson who had enrolled as a seminarian in Maynooth College in 1942 graduated with a first class honours degree in Classics in 1946 and then went to UCG to do his Diploma in Education in the academic year 1946–1947. 1947 was to be remembered by most people as the year of the big snow when, for six weeks in late winter/early spring, the whole countryside was heavily covered with snow to a depth of 15 feet in some places. Many people, especially in rural areas were cut off from food supplies. Schools and industries were closed, weddings were postponed and there were many harrowing stories as families struggled under very difficult conditions to bury their loved ones. As the memories of those terrible conditions fade into the mists of time, GAA aficionados recall 1947 as the only year that the All-Ireland football final was played outside the country.

One man did not let the awful spring weather deflect him from seeking the All-Ireland football final being played in New York. For the previous three years, he had unsuccessfully made the same plea that the All-Ireland in 1947 be played in New York to commemorate how the American people had opened their arms to the emigrant Irish a hundred years before. 'Black 47,' as 1847 was known, was the year that the potato blight had driven Irish people in their thousands to America. Canon Hamilton of Clare argued that playing the All-Ireland in New York would be a huge psychological boost for generations of Irish Americans who might never see the 'auld country' again.

At the 1947 Annual GAA congress, it appeared that the Canon's motion was doomed to failure. During an adjournment in the debate, Canon Hamilton again canvassed the delegates for their support. This time, he showed them a heart-rending letter from an exiled priest stating how privileged he would be if the All-Ireland took place in America. When Congress resumed, the motion was passed. Though it subsequently turned out that the exiled priest's letter was a hoax, no one complained and all the necessary arrangements were made for the historic trip.

Because of the prospect of a transatlantic journey, no provincial or All-Ireland semi-final was ever as keenly contested as those of 1947. One incident from that year's Munster final between Cork and Kerry highlights this. Simon Deignan, a Cavan player, who was to feature in that year's final as a wing half back colleague of John Wilson's, was the referee. Raymond Smith in his *Football Immortals* book recalls a controversial incident described to him by Kerry's legendary full back, Joe Keohane, who was selected in that position in the Millennium team of 1999. 'Simon Deignan awarded a penalty to Cork. Kerry protested, claiming it was an unfair decision. At the same time there was a break in the play as an injured player was receiving attention. I had my foot on top of the ball as I argued with the referee and all the time I was pressing the heavy ball deep down into the muddy ground. Jim Ahern, the penalty taker, then, naturally, miskicked the ball which trickled along the ground into the safe hands of our goalkeeper Denis O'Keeffe.' After the game, with tongue in cheek, Keohane told Cork trainer Jim Barry. 'It was awful, Jim, to see 15,000 Corkmen being fooled at three o'clock on a Sunday afternoon in a big field. You should never have allowed it to happen.' Afterwards Keohane admitted to Cork's stalwart midfielder Eamonn Young, 'It was not very sporting I admit but, Eamonn, I could see the Manhattan skyline!'

As events panned out, defending All-Ireland champions Kerry easily accounted for Meath, and Cavan who had gained their revenge on Antrim in the Ulster final beat the unsuccessful All-Ireland finalists of 1946, Roscommon, 2-4 to 0-6. John Wilson and most of his 1945 colleagues were to play in their second All-Ireland final 3,000 miles away from home and amongst three generations of the Irish diaspora.

In their preparation for the final, Cavan trained much longer than their Kerry opponents. This was because Kerry made the journey by sea whereas the vast majority of the Cavan side went by air. Almost 35,000 people turned up on a hot blistering afternoon in New York's Polo grounds to see the historic All-Ireland football final. The pitch in the Polo grounds, the home of the New York Giants baseball team was bone hard as Mayor Bill O'Dwyer of New York and a native of Bohola in County Mayo, threw the ball in. Simultaneously every household in Ireland with a wireless set was crowded as they listened intently to the wonder of Micheál Ó Hehir's commentary on a game so far away. Radio Eireann had done marvellous work in securing a cable for the broadcast.

The Kerry team, which had taken the precaution of wearing white peaked caps as a protection against the blistering sun, totally dominated the early stages of the game, quickly going into an eight-point lead after only 15 minutes. Kerry scored two goals during that time and had two others controversially disallowed much to the annoyance of the Kerry supporters. As a result, the referee, Wexford man Martin O'Neill, who was Leinster secretary at the time, did not endear himself to the Kingdom followers. At this stage in the game, Bart Garvey who was Wilson's direct opponent was getting a plentiful supply of the ball from his midfield colleagues. His dazzling solo runs, one of which finished in an expertly taken goal, were proving to be a major worry for the Cavan mentors. Necessity demanded that they revamp their side and this they did with almost an immediate positive effect. With PJ Duke now back in the Cavan defence, a totally focused Cavan took the game to their opponents. As Cavan started to mount attack after attack there was also a sudden sea change in the attitude of the majority of the spectators who at the outset were partisan Kerry supporters. Cavan right half-forward Tony Tighe was soloing at speed towards the Kerry defence. He sidestepped a Kerry defender but collided heavily with Kerry captain Jackie Lyne who had anticipated the sidestep. The spectators, not being familiar with the nature of Gaelic football loudly booed the incident, unfairly branded Kerry a dirty team, and thereafter were very vociferous in their support of the Breffni men. Centre half forward, Mick Higgins, who was actually born in New York then dashed through the entire Kerry defence to score a fantastic goal. With their ploy of continually handpassing the ball at speed, Higgins, Tighe, Peter Donohoe and Joe Stafford were causing all kinds of trouble for increasingly nervous Kerry defenders. Only a brilliant save by goalkeeper Danno O'Keeffe prevented another Cavan goal. Still, thanks to a host of frees, scored with consummate ease by full forward Peter Donohoe, the Breffni men went in at the interval leading 2-5 to 2-4.

Just before half-time, Kerry suffered a cruel blow when ace midfielder Eddie Dowling was badly injured after falling awkwardly on the hard ground and had to be replaced. Former Kerry great, midfielder Paddy Kennedy who had lined out at left corner forward with a heavily strapped ankle also had to retire injured in the second half. 'When we recovered so well after the first quarter which had really been disastrous for us there was a very optimistic mood as we left the dressing room for the second half,' Mullahoran's most famous son added.

The second half proved to be a much more dogged contest with very little open play and defences generally on top. The sweltering heat, the unfamiliar humidity and the rock-hard surface all combined to slow down the pace of the game and reduce the quality of the football. With five minutes left in the second half, each side had only added three points to their half-time total to leave the score 2-8 to 2-7. Suddenly

Cavan's apparently superior fitness and youth seemed to allow them to attack at will. The game's three concluding scores all came from the Breffni men. First the unerring boot of Peter Donohoe gave Cavan a two-point advantage before the magnificent Higgins notched two further excellent points after sweeping downfield movements. When the final whistle blew shortly afterwards, Cavan had made history by being the first (and probably only) team to win the All-Ireland senior football final outside of Ireland. They had completed the second leg of the double, having won their first National Football League title when they defeated Cork in the springtime.

The 1947 final was a unique occasion but it was also remembered for Micheál Ó Hehir's pleading for five more minutes of air time as the game reached its concluding stages. The commentary, which was carried over the transatlantic cable had been scheduled to end five minutes before the match actually finished. Luckily O'Hehir's pleas were heeded and listeners all over Ireland heard the game in its totality.

When the match ended, John Wilson looked around him with pride as he savoured what Cavan had achieved. On a personal level he was overwhelmed with joy at having won an All-Ireland medal. Then he thought of all the men who had made this momentous occasion possible. 'Our trainer Hughie O'Reilly, who had captained Cavan's All-Ireland winning team of 1935, had put in a tremendous effort all summer to have us in peak condition. After the first quarter the whole team played very well. Mick Higgins gave a great display of leadership as he continually kept running at the Kerry defence. His interpassing with Tony Tighe at such pace really mesmerised the Kerry players. Peter Donohoe at full forward gave a magical exhibition of free taking. He scored eight of our eleven points. The highest honour that could be paid to him was to be called the "Babe Ruth of Gaelic football" by two leading American sportswriters, Arthur Daley of the *New York Times* and Don Parker of the *Mirror*. PJ Duke, who was a very versatile player, really was a man ahead of his time with his solo running out of defence which was a rare occurrence in those days. Our captain, John Joe O'Reilly gave a truly wonderful performance. I got to know him very well during that summer when we trained together at the Irish army's camp in the Curragh.

My most abiding memory after the game was that I lost my jersey, socks, togs and boots. I was very upset because I wanted to keep my playing gear as a souvenir of our success. However, to my pleasant surprise, a mysterious donor delivered a full set of new gear to my hotel the next morning. After the fantastic celebration in the days immediately following the game I went to visit family relations in Pennsylvania. While there I met a first cousin of Seán MacDiarmada, one of the signatories of the 1916 Proclamation. I was particularly delighted when she greeted me in Irish and especially when the whole family recited the Angelus in our native language. There was a match in Celtic Park between a combined Kerry/Cavan team and a US selection which the visitors won easily. I did not participate in that game but it made its own bit of history as it was the first ever GAA match to be played under floodlights. I then went to visit another cousin, a nun, in Massachusetts before returning to Ireland on the famous liner the "Queen Mary." For all of us, the whole experience was just something that you dream about. The mystery and nostalgia of visiting the United States, the novelty of flying outwards by plane and returning in the prestigious and luxurious "Queen Mary" left us with a lifetime of wonderful memories. Over the years, the spirit of adventure of that football team has not dimmed. As for Mick Higgins, I think it is safe to assume that he will remain the only native-born American to win an All-Ireland in America.'

John Wilson, though only 25 years of age, retired from inter-county football after the following year's All-Ireland final in 1948. Cavan retained their Ulster title that year when they again defeated Antrim before beating Louth in the All-Ireland semi-final. Thus for the third time in four years, John Wilson and Cavan were in an All-Ireland final. That semi-final victory, however, was the last time that John would ever wear the blue and white jersey that he had first worn as a minor seven years previously. In the semi-final, he received a serious shoulder injury which only allowed him to take his place among the subs for the final. Furthermore he had taken up a teaching position in St Kieran's College in Kilkenny where he taught until 1950. Also in 1950, he emigrated to London where he obtained a teaching post at Finchley Grammar School and he also attended the University of London for further studies. Though he returned briefly to captain his club, Mullahoran, to their fourth consecutive county title in 1950, the pressures of travelling and the world of academia meant that his Gaelic football playing days were over. In 1952, he returned to Ireland and took up a teaching post in St Eunan's College in Letterkenny, Co. Donegal. While there, he became involved in coaching the college team as well as the Donegal minor side. In 1956, Wilson was the coach to the first Donegal side to win an Ulster minor title when they defeated Armagh by 2-5 to 0-6. In addition, he was a member of the Ulster Colleges' GAA Council and a very active inter-county referee. He refereed several Dr McKenna Cup, Dr Lagan Cup and Ulster championship games. He maintains that his only refereeing claim to fame is the fact that he holds the dubious distinction of sending off Tyrone centre half back Paddy Corey and his direct opponent, the late Pat Campbell of Armagh, in an Ulster championship game in 1957.

Regarding the games' rules, Wilson would make two minor alterations. 'First of all, I would abolish the handpass. I think that because of the speed with which it is executed it is almost impossible for a referee to decide whether it is legal or not. However, I would retain the fist pass as I feel it incorporates a more definite striking action. The other aspect of the modern game which really annoys me is the present attitude of many referees to a good shoulder tackle which is an integral part of Gaelic football. The best example of this was in the 1999 Ulster championship semi-final between Armagh and Derry. Derry's Henry Downey gave an Armagh player a good hard shoulder yet he was penalised and Armagh scored the equalising point from the resultant free.'

The Mullahoran academic, who had now graduated with a first-class honours MA from the National University of Ireland moved to Dublin in 1960. Here he taught Classics in Gonzaga College until he became a TD (Teachta Dála or Member of the Irish Parliament) in 1973. The busy, full-time, Gonzaga teacher also lectured part time at St Patrick's Teacher Training College in Drumcondra and at UCD.

John Wilson's only reason for entering politics was to play a part in finding a peaceful solution to the political problems of Northern Ireland. 'I felt it my duty as an Irishman and especially as an Ulsterman to do my best along with Fianna Fáil and the other members of Dáil Eireann to work with the British government and the political parties of Northern Ireland for a peaceful resolution of the historic divisions within that community. That could only be achieved in the context of creating political institutions in which both the unionist and nationalist traditions could be accommodated.' So for the following 20 years from 1973 onwards John served as a TD for Cavan/Monaghan. During that time, he held several ministerial portfolios including Tourism and Transport, Transport, Posts and Telegraphs, Defence and Education.

In his opinion, his outstanding achievement as Minister was the breakthrough in teachers' salaries when he served as Minister for Education. 'I had been a teacher for 23 years and knew intimately the inadequacies of the salary structures at all levels within the education system. It was therefore a great source of personal satisfaction when I managed to convince the cabinet of the need to introduce a radical overhaul of pay structures which would reflect salaries commensurate with a modern, well-trained and highly motivated teaching profession.'

In 1992 when Albert Reynolds became Taoiseach he appointed the Cavan man as Tánaiste, a position he held until he retired from politics in 1993. Five years later, in 1998, the Irish Government appointed John Wilson as Victims' Commissioner to head a Commission which had been recommended by the governments of Ireland and the United Kingdom in the Good Friday Agreement. The main terms of reference of the Victims' Commission were to conduct a review of services and arrangements in place, in the Republic of Ireland, to meet the needs of those who have suffered as a result of violence over the past 30 years and to identify what further measures needed to be taken to address the suffering and concerns of those in question. As the report of the commission was being finalised in June 1999, John Wilson was asked to act as joint Commissioner with Sir Kevin Bloomfield (British Government Representative) on the Independent Commission for the Location of Victims' Remains. 'This investigation, which is ongoing, is a very harrowing but necessary exercise. It is really a very sad job, dealing with the very traumatic experiences of the victims' families.'

John P. Wilson has an avid interest both in the world of literature and music. Current affairs, foreign affairs, and biographies are his favourite reading material. He loves listening to classical music, Irish traditional music and Irish ballads. Marching tunes like 'Roddy McCorley' and 'The Dawning of the Day' hold a particular affection for him.

John and his wife Ita (who was born in London of Irish ancestry) have five children, Siobhán, Claire, Lucy, John and Maria. He selected the following Ulster team:

ULSTER (1933-1999)

Séamus Hoare
(Donegal)

Jody O'Neill *(Tyrone)*	Jim Smith *(Cavan)*	Leo Murphy *(Down)*
Comdt. John Joe O'Reilly *(Cavan)*	Big Tom O'Reilly *(Cavan)*	Jim McCullagh *(Armagh)*

Phil Brady
(Cavan)

Jim McKeever
(Derry)

Kevin Armstrong *(Antrim)*	Mick Higgins *(Cavan)*	Alf Murray *(Armagh)*
Peter Donohoe *(Cavan)*	James McCartan (Snr.) *(Down)*	Seán O'Neill *(Down)*

Subs. Ollie O'Rourke (Monaghan), Jim McDonnell (Cavan), Seán Ferriter (Donegal), Anthony Tohill (Derry), Mick Brewster (Fermanagh), Jackie Taggart (Tyrone), Joe Stafford (Cavan), Charlie Gallagher (Cavan), Tony Boyle (Donegal)

Some of the above are not selected in their recognised positions but nevertheless John feels they could adapt very comfortably to their new roles

John Wilson was a central figure in the great days of Cavan county and Mullahoran club football in the 1940s. He was selfless, fearless and totally dedicated in his determination to do his best for his team. These were noble attributes which served him well as he undertook the demands and responsibilities of ministerial office at national, European and world levels. For thousands of people, either with party political affiliation or with none, John P. Wilson represented the efficiency, integrity, decency and honesty so necessary for a fair and equitable democratic system of government.

The fact that he is a learned scholar of Irish, Greek and Latin does not detract from his innate natural ability to mingle among the grassroots of his people in any part of Ireland. Rather it emphasises his true greatness – a statesman who so often in the past stood on the wet, cold terraces of Breffni Park cheering on his beloved Cavan on a Sunday while on the following day he was engaged in intricate political negotiations at the very highest level and in very plush surroundings in Brussels or London – John Wilson is a man who can 'walk with kings nor lose the common touch' – truly, a man for all seasons.

Eddie Keher

IN THE VILLAGE OF Inistioge, near Thomastown, Eddie Keher first saw the light of day. It was in the village square at the age of three and a half that Eddie first remembers hearing the clash of the ash. When his next-door neighbours, who were older, joined the impromptu coaching sessions conducted by Portarlington native Michael Noonan and local man Jimmy Phelan, Eddie was attracted immediately. By the time he started primary school those rudimentary skills, which Eddie had acquired, were supplemented by local teacher Martin Walsh. So good was he that at the age of eight he was selected on his club's U-14 side. – Coincidentally, future star and county colleague Ollie Walsh was the player who actually marked him in this, his first competitive outing. In 1952, at the age of eleven, the then diminutive forward won his first county U-14 medal – a feat that he repeated three years later.

In 1954 Eddie went to one of the GAA's most famous secondary school hurling nurseries – St Kieran's College in Kilkenny city. When the legendary coach Fr Tommy Maher joined the staff of St Kieran's one year later, he at once spotted the exquisite talent that Eddie possessed and he was, though only a second year student, promoted onto the college's senior team. In 1956, Eddie was a member of the college's junior team which won the Leinster title and one year later Keher and St Kieran's won the Leinster senior title, going on to meet St Flannan's of Ennis in the All-Ireland final. Prior to the final, Fr Maher would keep Eddie and full forward Dick Dowling (later to become a TD) back for extra training after the normal squad training sessions were over. With two defenders to mark them, Fr Maher would give the ball to Eddie an incredible 200 times per session. One basic move would be practised. Eddie, having received the ball on the left wing would pass it inside to Dick. If free of his marker, Dick would turn and score. If not, he would pass it to Eddie who would then shoot for a point.

In the colleges' final with eight minutes to go, St Flannan's were comfortably ahead when Fr Maher reminded Keher and Dowling of their rehearsed moves. In those last, pulsating minutes this strategy was singularly responsible for St Kieran's scoring three goals and winning the game by the minimum of margins 4-2 to 2-7. Eddie Keher had won his first All-Ireland medal. St Kieran's reached the following year's decider only to be defeated by St Flannan's. In his third successive senior colleges' final, in 1959, thanks to an inspirational display of forward accuracy from Keher, St Kieran's won another colleges' title when they defeated Tipperary CBS by five points.

Simultaneously Keher was now featuring on Kilkenny county minor teams winning four Leinster medals in consecutive years from 1956 (as a sub) to 1959. In 1957 and 1959 they reached the All-Ireland minor final only to be beaten by Tipperary on each occasion.

1959 was a very special year in the hurling career of Eddie. Having played in both colleges and minor All-Irelands, his big breakthrough came in the replayed All-Ireland senior final between Kilkenny and Waterford. When regular left half-forward Johnny McGovern was injured, Keher was drafted into the attack after only 15 minutes play. Kilkenny, who were beaten in that game by a magnificent Waterford 15, only scored two points in the second half, both of them courtesy of the 18-year-old.

For the following three years, Wexford, Dublin and Wexford again prevented Kilkenny from getting out of Leinster. The majority of the 1957–1959 three-in-a-row Leinster senior winners were either retired or approaching the veteran stage, so it was very much a rebuilding process for the Noresiders. Despite winning his first national senior title when Kilkenny defeated Cork in the 1962 League final, Keher must have wondered if Kilkenny were ever going to succeed in winning the Liam McCarthy Cup in his lifetime.

That was all, however, to change dramatically in 1963 when Kilkenny overcame Dublin easily in the Leinster final and thus reached the All-Ireland final. Some old hands like Ollie Walsh, Denis Heaslip, Billy Dwyer, Johnny McGovern and Seán Clohessy still remained to give the necessary experience to the rising generation of Kilkenny hurling artists such as captain Séamus Cleere, Ted Carroll (St Kieran's winning captain in 1957 and future County secretary), Phil 'Fan' Larkin, Tom Walsh and Eddie Keher. Fr Maher, who had been training the team since 1957, in addition to his St Kieran's duties, was confident that he had the correct blend of youth and experience, of determination and skill.

Their opponents in the final were Waterford, their conquerors of 1959. This was an exceptionally talented team, wonderfully gifted in all the skills of top class hurling. Players such as Austin Flynn, Martin Óg Morrissey, Tom Cheasty, Larry Guinan, Phil Grimes, Séamus Power and Frankie Walsh would have been automatic nominees for any All Stars team if such an honour had then existed. As events panned out Kilkenny gave a truly magnificent performance with their fast, skilful hurling and use of space, making life exceptionally difficult for the men from the Decies. Whereas the whole Black and Amber side gave a fantastic performance, that 1963 final will forever be associated with Eddie Keher. This was the day that he burst upon the national scene with a vengeance, scoring the exceptional total of 14 points. His magical stickwork belied the fact that he had no family hurling background. Indeed his father, Stephen, had not played hurling, as he was a native of Roscommon where football took precedence.

That day in 1963 was to see the fulfilment of Fr Maher's belief in the hurling genius that he had first met eight years previously. However, it was a combination of three distinct factors that made Keher show his true potential. First, he had a naturally skilled first touch. Second, thanks to Fr Maher's coaching he had perfected his ever-so-accurate finishing technique and third, he had a very sharp hurling brain which allowed him to make quick decisions on the field of play. As a free-taker par excellence, with the possible exception of Christy Ring and Jimmy Doyle, he had no peers. Prior to that 1963 final, after finishing work each evening in a Dublin bank, Keher spent at least an hour perfecting the art of free-taking that Fr Maher had so capably coached, both in St Kieran's and with the county senior team. 'I kept thinking back to what Fr Maher had taught me and I kept practising each evening until I developed a successful system of rising and hitting the ball. Fr Maher told me: "You look at the posts. You stand over the ball and say I am going to get you off the ground." When the ball comes up you automatically hit it. You cannot miss it when you take that correct stance and concentrate on lifting the ball. As well as adopting the right technique, the hurley must feel perfectly comfortable in your hand and of course you must have the correct temperament especially when under pressure,' stated Keher who was the first hurler to play in a minor and senior All-Ireland in the one year.

No wonder, having put those techniques and attitudes into action, that Keher contributed 14 points in that fantastic 4-17 to 6-8 victory over Waterford. In that game, as well as his own individual brilliance, the authoritative wing back play of Séamus Cleere and two breathtaking saves by the spectacular goalkeeper Ollie Walsh were highlights of a great game. These were two major turning points in the game. 'Near the beginning of the game he made a wonderful save which gave us a huge psychological boost as well as keeping us in the game. Towards the end, another fantastic stop by Ollie was responsible for us winning,' said Eddie who, in 1997, took early retirement from the AIB Bank in Callan where he served as manager.

The most outstanding hurling side in the first half of the 1960s was Tipperary. Having watched the young pretenders in 1963 gain a first All-Ireland senior title for Keher and company, they were not going to stand idly by in 1964 and allow the mantle of true greatness be passed from Munster to Leinster. So, when the two sides met in the 1964 All-Ireland, Tipperary, then at the peak of their form, gave an exhilarating team performance easily disposing of the Noresiders' challenge on a scoreline of 5-13 to 2-8. Eddie Keher looked upon the Premier county as having a host of outstanding hurlers playing superbly at the one time. 'Tony Wall, Theo English, John Doyle, Mick Burns, Jimmy Doyle, Babs Keating were all stars in their own right. Collectively they were very formidable opponents.'

Keher and Kilkenny's next success was in 1966 when the Cats overcame Tipperary in the home final of the National Hurling League before defeating New York overwhelmingly in a two-leg final. As a result, Kilkenny were expected to win the

1966 All-Ireland but again defeat was their lot when Cork, with the three unrelated McCarthys, Justin, Charlie and captain Gerald to the fore, notched up a 3-9 to 1-10 victory. However, that defeat strengthened Kilkenny's resolve and for the first time in 45 years, in the championship, Kilkenny beat Tipperary in the following year's final. This was a day of contrasting fortunes. For Kilkenny, it was the end of a hoodoo that had become more desperate with each Kilkenny defeat by a Tipperary championship side. On the other hand this was the day that also saw the end of the career of Tipperary's long-serving corner back John Doyle. His shattered dream was the elusive record ninth All-Ireland senior medal won on the field of play. That defeat meant he had to be content to share with Christy Ring the total of eight medals won on the field of play. Eddie Keher's joy was somewhat blighted by the fact that an injured wrist left him sidelined for six months.

Two years later, under the captaincy of Eddie Keher, Kilkenny defeated Cork by six points to enable them claim three All-Ireland titles in the 1960s. Coming from such a small club as his native Rower-Inistioge made him an especially satisfied man when he returned there with the Liam McCarthy Cup. What made it extra special was that three other Inistioge men were there to share that momentous moment with him. Wing half Billy Murphy, corner forward Fr Tom Murphy and substitute Pat Kavanagh, who actually came on in the game, were all members of this homely, tightly knit community.

1971 saw Tipperary avenge their 1967 defeat to the Noresiders when they just edged out Kilkenny in a very high scoring game 5-17 to 5-14. This day, amongst other things, is remembered for an inspirational display by Tipp's Babs Keating who played the whole second half in his bare feet. Just after half time, a nail had protruded up into his boot and, not having any spare ones, the Grange man was forced to shed them. But the outstanding feature of the match was observing one Eddie Keher give one of the most superlative individual displays in any sport in Ireland. In one of the greatest impeccable performances of marksmanship ever witnessed, and from all angles, Keher scored the colossal total of 2-11 and still ended up on the losing side.

Until that season, the legendary Nick Rackard of Wexford had held the scoring record for one year. In 1956 he had accumulated the phenomenal aggregate of 36 goals and 35 points (143 points). Keher, however, outscored him in 1971 amassing eight goals and 141 points (165 points) in the process.

It is often said that the Kilkenny team of that era reached its peak in the 1972 decider against Cork. Ranked as one of the best All-Irelands within the last 50 years, it will always stand out as a snapshot of all that is great in hurling. Tremendous artistry, total commitment and terrific scores were the norm as Kilkenny and Cork sought the ultimate prize. The last quarter display by Kilkenny has justifiably entered the folklore of Gaelic games. As the game entered its final 20 minutes, Cork, inspired by Seánie O'Leary and Ray Cummins, seemed to have an unassailable lead of eight points. Then that swerving sidestep of Keher, ably abetted by Kieran Purcell at full forward and Pat Delaney at centre half forward, swung into action scoring 2-9 without reply. Kilkenny had won their 18th crown by a margin of seven points, 3-24 to 5-11. Again Keher was the dominant scoregetter with a contribution of 2-9 in one of the most amazing comebacks in the history of hurling.

Without the injured Jim Treacy, Kieran Purcell and Keher who had suffered a broken collar bone, Kilkenny succumbed to Limerick in the 1973 All-Ireland but gained their revenge the following year. With the injured trio back on board and only a seemingly lethargic Limerick to contend with, Keher led the Treatymen a merry dance as Kilkenny coasted to their 19th and Keher's fifth All-Ireland. The following year, in the first 70-minute All-Ireland, Kilkenny beat a resurgent Galway side 2-22 to 2-10. In another incomparable performance of wizardry and marksmanship, the man from Inistioge had won his sixth and last All-Ireland senior medal.

In the spring of 1976 Eddie Keher appeared, for the last time, in a major national final when he played against Clare in the replay of the National Hurling League decider. A winning one it turned out to be when Kilkenny overwhelmed the Bannermen by a five-goal margin. A defeat against Wexford in that year's Leinster championship final made Keher ponder his future when the 1977 championship arrived. This was a tough campaign with Kilkenny bowing out to Wexford by a three-point margin in the Leinster final. When his club lost the Kilkenny county final later that year, Keher's mind was made up. After 18 years of inter-county hurling, Eddie's time had come to retire. Spanning three decades, he had given wonderful service to the Black and Amber. For Leinster he had worn the Railway Cup jersey for 17 successive seasons (1961–1977) winning a record nine interprovincial medals. In addition he had garnered three Gaelic Weekly All Star awards (1966–1968) and five successive Carrolls' All Star Awards (1971–1975) as well as being Texaco hurler of the year in 1972.

The measure of the man's greatness is that when hurling icons are mentioned, Eddie Keher's name inevitably surfaces. Hurling has had its quota of great wielders of the ash. Each generation has claimed that its hero was the best. That, however, is both an impossible and unfair statement to make when one looks back over a hundred years of top-class hurling. Great sportsmen in any code can only be measured in relation to the players that they actually played with or against. Nevertheless, one must always respect the judgements of many hurling connoisseurs who have constantly placed three forwards of consummate skill above the rest. The swashbuckling, strong and skilful Mick Mackey of Limerick attracted thousands of people in the 1930s to watch his outstanding exploits. Christy Ring of Cork was a fiercely competitive hurler with a deadly eye for scoring, whose first major game was the 1941 All-Ireland final and whose last was the Railway Cup replay of 1963 – an incredible 22 years. During that time, he had won 18 Railway Cup medals and eight All-Ireland senior medals. The third name is always that of Eddie Keher. Coincidentally, Keher's first Railway Cup campaign of 1963 was Ring's last.

Though not as physically strong as either Mackey or Ring, Keher was able to look after himself when the going got tough. He was, nevertheless, the supreme stylist whose body swerve and eye for goal made him the most feared forward of his generation. In 1984, Mackey, Ring and Keher were selected by the *Sunday Independent*/Irish Nationwide in their hurling team of the century. That alone is an indicator of the superb hurling craftsman that Eddie Keher undoubtedly was.

When he retired, the modest, unassuming Keher turned to coaching and was on the Kilkenny management team that guided the county to another senior All-Ireland success just two years after his retirement in 1979. When under his command Kilkenny lost the 1980 Leinster final to an Offaly side, on the verge of greater things to come, Eddie decided to relinquish his new managerial position. Even though he was to serve as an inter-county selector in subsequent years, to all intents and purposes, Keher's public hurling career ended with that defeat to Offaly who had just broken an 18-year-old Kilkenny/Wexford stranglehold of the Leinster championship. Still involved in club coaching and club administration, Eddie was asked by the then President of the GAA, Dr Mick Loftus, in 1988, to help organise a National Hurling Masters (Over 40s) competition. This he did and for the past number of years he has been actively involved in coaching Kilkenny Masters sides, winning two All-Irelands with them in 1995 and 1997.

Keher, who does not want any more changes or modifications to the hurling rules, feels that there is a great need for more consistency in the implementation of the current rules. One comparatively recent phenomenon in Gaelic Games irritates the man who currently contributes a weekly GAA column for *Ireland on Sunday*.

'I detest the swapping of jerseys after a match by players. I hate to see the winning team, in a final, wearing their opponents' jerseys when they are receiving the cup and standing on the rostrum. It presents an untidy image and more importantly if they had proper pride and respect for their own county jersey they would not do it.'

Looking to the future, Eddie would like all referees to follow the example set by John Moloney of Tipperary in the 1960s and 1970s and for all GAA officials to adopt the dignity and capabilities of past presidents of the GAA. 'John Moloney was a brilliant referee in both football and hurling. His interpretation of the rules was second to none. If he made a mistake he would admit it to the offended team or player just after the game. He was very human in his approach.

'From the moment I met the late Alf Murray, President of the GAA from 1964 to 1967, I have been impressed with both the role of the presidency and how capably and inspirationally that position has been filled, so effectively, by each successive president right up to Joe McDonagh.'

Eddie and his wife, Kathleen, have five children. The eldest, Eamonn, is working in Australia, Clodagh is married and living in Dublin, Deirdre works with AIB in Carlow, Colm is teaching in Clonmel CBS and Catherine is a student in the National College of Art and Design.

When he looks back on his career, he thinks of the great players he was fortunate to play with and against. His period with Kilkenny will always be associated with skill, success, dexterity and determination. Between the provincial final losses to Wexford in 1970 and 1976, Kilkenny just lost two championship games. This was a remarkable record considering the quality of the teams they faced. 'Tipperary, Wexford, Limerick, Cork and Galway were not just opponents. Between them they possessed some of the greatest men ever to lift a hurley. In those years Wexford had Mick Jacob, the Quigleys and Pat Nolan. Tipperary had Mick Roche, Michael Keating and Francis Loughnane. On the Limerick team were such stalwarts as Eamon Cregan, Eamon Grimes and Joe McKenna. Cork had the McCarthys, Ray Cummins and Seánie O'Leary. Galway had stars in PJ Molloy and John Connolly.' When one looks at the composition of those Kilkenny sides between 1963 and 1975 one cannot but be impressed by the number of quality players those teams possessed. Goalkeepers Ollie Walsh and Noel Skehan; defenders Pa Dillon, Jim Treacy and Pat Henderson; magnificent centre fielders Frank Cummins and Liam 'Chunky' O'Brien; dashing Pat Delaney on the '40', the irrepressible Kieran Purcell and of course the unrivalled Eddie Keher, were just some of the stars from many teams of stars.

As well as all those players just mentioned and naturally omitting himself, Keher warms to the task when asked to name the hurlers who impressed him either before, during or after his own hurling career. 'Damien Martin (Offaly) was a fantastic goalkeeper. Billy Rackard, Tom Neville, Jim English, Willie Murphy and Vincent Staples of Wexford, Mick Burns (Tipperary), Eamon Russell (Clare) and Donal Clifford of Cork were excellent defenders. Seán Clohessy (Kilkenny) was both an excellent midfielder and astute forward. Christy Ring (Cork), Jimmy Doyle (Tipperary), Tom Murphy and Tom Walsh (both Kilkenny) were all beautiful hurlers. I have also admired the exceptional skills of DJ Carey (Kilkenny), Nicholas English (Tipperary), Jamesie O'Connor (Clare), Charlie Carter (Kilkenny), John Fenton (Cork), Jimmy Barry Murphy (Cork) and Joe Hennessy (Kilkenny).'

Eddie Keher is also a follower of Gaelic football and numbers among his many friends the great Seán O'Neill and James McCartan who won three All-Ireland medals with Down in 1960, 1961 and 1968. 'I always supported the Down team when they came to prominence. In turn, I have admired the wonderful attacking qualities of the Dublin and Kerry sides of the 1970s and the Meath team of the late 1980s and early 1990s. The most outstanding footballer, in my view, playing the game today is Tyrone's Peter Canavan,' concluded the man who scored the remarkable total of six goals and 45 points (63 points) in five championship games in 1972.

Eddie Keher's contribution to any community associated with him extends beyond that of a normal human being. Having always been concerned with the use and abuse of alcohol in our society, he actively participates in creating an alcohol-free environment for the youth. A founder member of the NO NAME club in Kilkenny city in 1978, Eddie is currently national treasurer of this organisation, which specifically caters for fourth and fifth year secondary school students between the months of October and April. In most major population centres, alcohol-free discos are organised for these age groups on a weekly basis. Transport is organised and each local organising committee supervises the discos themselves. 'On Temperance Sunday in 1977, Fr Tom Murphy, a curate in St John's Parish gave a strong talk on temperance decrying the fact that all entertainment for young people seemed to be drink-orientated. Immediately afterwards, the proprietor of Newpark Hotel in Kilkenny, Bobby Kerr, Fr Murphy, Eamon Doyle came together and made the necessary arrangements for the setting up of the No Name club. We are celebrating our 21st anniversary this year,' Eddie happily added.

When picking his Leinster and Ireland sides Eddie made the following selections

IRELAND

Selected from period 1959 to 1977 (my own era). Players who contested All-Ireland Finals in that period. No Kilkenny players considered.

	Pat Nolan *(Wexford)*	
Nick O'Donnell *(Wexford)*	Pat Hartigan *(Limerick)*	John Doyle *(Tipperary)*
Mick Burns *(Tipperary)*	Mick Roche *(Tipperary)*	Denis Coughlan *(Cork)*
Gerald McCarthy *(Cork)*	Philly Grimes *(Waterford)*	
Jimmy Doyle *(Tipperary)*	Tom Cheasty *(Waterford)*	Babs Keating *(Tipperary)*
Charlie McCarthy *(Cork)*	Tony Doran *(Wexford)*	Eamon Cregan *(Limerick)*

LEINSTER TEAM
Selected from period 1959 to 1977
Players who played for Leinster – No Kilkenny players considered

Damien Martin
(Offaly)

Tom Neville   Nick O'Donnell   Padraig Horan
(Wexford)   *(Wexford)*   *(Offaly)*

Jim English   Billy Rackard   Willie Murphy
(Wexford)   *(Wexford)*   *(Wexford)*

Des Foley   Mick Jacob
(Dublin)   *(Wexford)*

Jimmy O'Brien   Padge Kehoe   Martin Quigley
(Wexford)   *(Wexford)*   *(Wexford)*

Paddy Molloy   Tony Doran   Mick Bermingham
(Offaly)   *(Wexford)*   *(Dublin)*

In *Bliain-Iris Oifigiúl C.L.G – 1965* Eddie Keher wrote as follows. 'We in Kilkenny are fortunate in having a great hurling tradition. But though this tradition is an advantage it is not an essential for the development of hurling in any county. Its advantage, in our case, lies in the fact that the youth of Kilkenny are born and bred, as one might say, with the "ash between their teeth." For most of them "ball" and "hurl" are among the first words in their vocabulary and no doubt a hurley is their first play-toy. It is often said that a hurley in a cot is more important than a baby's bottle. From day to day as they grow to boyhood they hear of the achievements of the Doyles of Mooncoin, the herculean feats of Paddy Larkin, the inspiring displays of Lory Meagher, the deadly accuracy of Jim Langton and the polished and brilliant style of Seán Clohessy. This surely is also true of Tipperary, Cork, Waterford, Wexford and the other hurling counties.'

In that excellent analysis of why Kilkenny people are steeped in such a rich hurling tradition Eddie Keher accurately portrayed the past stars who have perpetuated that glorious legacy. Since that article was written 25 years ago, no sportsman has epitomised so authentically the beautiful and artistic game of hurling as its author has done. Eddie Keher has passed on and continues pass on the fruits of the ancient game of the Gael to another generation of aspiring hurlers.

Paddy Doherty

PADDY DOHERTY WAS BORN in Ballykinlar, County Down in 1934. His father, John played in goals for Down that same year. John encouraged his three sons, Henry, Paddy and Francie to become involved with the local club. In those days, there was no school or underage competitions in Paddy's area so his first experience of competitive football was at minor level. Both in 1951 and 1952, Paddy was selected at left half forward on the Down county minor side. In 1952, Down, with Doherty particularly prominent, reached the Ulster minor final only to lose by two points to a Cavan side which reached that year's All-Ireland final. The following year, Paddy was promoted to the Down junior team which drew with Armagh in the first round of the provincial championship. Paddy's performance had been so impressive that a bus load of supporters from his native parish decided to travel to Armagh to see their new hero. Unfortunately for them and Down, a communications slip-up meant that no taxi collected Paddy. Thus he missed the game and, to make matters worse, they were beaten. Paddy's tally of 1-4 in the drawn game had been in vain.

In 1954, Paddy made his first competitive appearance for the Down senior team when they played Tyrone in a McKenna Cup game in Newcastle. Two months later, he made his senior championship debut but the Mourne men were well beaten by Derry. As nothing of consequence seemed to be happening with regard to the nurturing of Gaelic football in Down, Paddy started to play soccer at local level. In 1956, Paddy's team got to the final of a district competition against a British Army team who were based in Ballykinlar. Played before an attendance of over 2,000 people in Downpatrick, Doherty scored five goals in a marvellous display. Cross-channel soccer scouts heard of Doherty's brilliance and he was invited to join several English clubs. Eventually he signed for Lincoln City but because of homesickness he returned home after only eight weeks. Immediately Irish league 'B' division side, Ballyclare Comrades snapped up the scoring sensation from Ballykinlar. The speedy outside left proceeded to torment opposing defences and amassed the phenomenal total of 33 goals in just over half a season with the Antrim-based soccer team. As Gaelic players were then not allowed to play soccer, Paddy was suspended from the GAA for 12 months. This decision forced Doherty to make a choice between the two codes.

'Even though I enjoyed playing soccer I simply could not bear the thought of standing on the sideline every Sunday watching my GAA club play. So, I decided to quit the soccer scene to be allowed to play Gaelic football. When I made my decision, I had to return to Ballyclare to collect my football boots. Their manager asked me to play just one more game for them. I played under the name of 'Campbell' and scored three goals in that last game of soccer. I remember reading the *Belfast Telegraph's* Saturday night sports paper account of the game. It stated: 'Campbell, who was making his debut, scored two great goals in the first half and ran through the whole defence to complete his hat trick in the second period.'

Even though Gaelic football was always my favourite game, I knew that if I had stayed with soccer I could have made it. Billy McCullough who played with me at Ballyclare later went to Portadown before transferring to Arsenal. He went on to win several caps at international level. He told me that I was very foolish for quitting soccer but I have no regrets whatsoever. When I rejoined Down and we started winning Ulster championships, another Irish league side, Ards, asked me to sign for them. They offered me £250 to sign professional terms. They would also pay me £8 per week. They assured me that they would win the league and that I would get a free trip to America. However, my father persuaded me not to accept the offer and I consoled myself with the thought that Down would win the All-Ireland and that I would get a trip to America with them,' Paddy told me when I met him at his Castlewellan home.

Having missed a lot of Gaelic football in 1957, due to his suspension, Paddy was back as lively and as keen as ever when 1958 began. Not having played in the 1957 Ulster senior championship enabled Paddy to play in the 1958 Ulster junior championship. This he did in style, captaining them to an Ulster title and scoring 34 points in the three games they had played. As the 1958 Ulster senior championship campaign approached there was no outward sign that the fortunes of Gaelic football in Down were about to change dramatically. For the previous two years, one man had planned otherwise.

In 1956, the Town Clerk of Downpatrick, Maurice Hayes, was elected secretary of the Down GAA County board. He immediately brought to the post a new sense of order, innovation, imagination and professionalism. He organised collective and regular training sessions, introduced the concept of tactical awareness and arranged challenge games with the top teams in the country. As a result, players developed in self-confidence. Hayes had convinced them, through these friendly matches, that they were as good as any team in Ireland. When Down, minus Doherty, were trounced by Donegal in the first round of the 1957 Ulster championship, the players were devastated. Hayes' ideas, they felt, were falsely based. It was in the aftermath of that game that Hayes revealed his master plan. Down, he told them, with proper physical preparation and a positive mental attitude would win an All-Ireland within the next five years. 'If you do what we say, we will ensure that medically, socially and workwise we will look after you,' he told the astounded players. 'There will be regular training throughout the year and indoor training when the nights are short and the weather unsuitable.'

Danny Flynn was appointed trainer and Barney Carr team manager. Martin Walshe became the first doctor to be appointed to a senior football county team on a permanent basis. Down's thorough preparation began to bear fruit when they convincingly defeated Donegal in the first round of the 1958 Ulster championship. In the semi-final, they deprived Tyrone of a possible three-in-a-row Ulster titles when the O'Neill county suffered a heavy 1-9 to 0-2 defeat. Down were now in their first Ulster final since 1942. It took a herculean display by Derry midfielder Jim McKeever to ensure a four-point victory for the Oak Leaf county. Down, though disappointed, were far from being despondent. They had started to combine excellently as a team and they now had the irrepressible Doherty back in harness. He was adding that vital scoring power in the forward line. In addition, the Down minor team of 1958 had a potentially great senior player in a brilliant youngster called Seán O'Neill. Year One of the Hayes five-year plan had been very satisfactory.

The following year in the annual Wembley GAA tournament, Down showed the first glimpses of greatness when they overcame Galway in a splendid encounter. The experience of playing before a huge crowd would stand them in good stead. In that year's Ulster championship, Down defeated Antrim and Tyrone (after a replay) to reach their second successive Ulster final against Cavan. In a brilliant display of individual skill and terrific teamwork the Mourne men crushed the Breffni challenge on a 2-16 to 0-7 scoreline. Though Down subsequently lost to Galway in that 1959 All-Ireland semi-final, Hayes and company were not unduly perturbed. They reasoned that the defeat was part of the natural learning process and that, after all, Down had progressed another rung on the ladder to ultimate glory. With Seán O'Neill now a vital cog in the forward line, the concept of playing as a cohesive unit became central to Down's future strategy. What is now known as 'total football' would replace the 'catch and kick' style favoured by so many counties.

Prior to the 1960 Ulster championship, Down had a fantastic league run which culminated in the defeat of Kerry in the semi-final and Cavan in the final. Down had now won their first major national title. They easily coasted through the Ulster championship defeating Cavan in the final. The All-Ireland semi-final would be a much more difficult proposition. Their opponents, Offaly, played brilliantly in the first half of that game to go in at the interval leading by 2-4 to 0-3. Then, in the second half, Paddy Doherty showed the huge crowd his true worth when he, time and time again, ran at the hard-pressed defence creating scoring opportunities both for himself and his colleagues. With eight minutes to go, the deficit had been reduced to three points. The pendulum of fate then swung decidedly in Down's favour. They were awarded a controversial penalty when centre half forward James McCartan was allegedly fouled in the square. Totally oblivious to the pleadings of his late mother in the stand not to take it, ice-cool Paddy strolled up to take the spot kick. The tension was unbearable as many Offaly supporters voiced their disapproval of the referee's decision. Undaunted, Paddy Doherty sent the ball crashing to the corner of the net. Though both sides exchanged further points the sides were level when the full-time whistle blew. Down had snatched a lucky result from the jaws of an imminent defeat. There was no doubt as to who was Down's hero. Paddy Doherty of the unerring boot had notched 1-7 of Down's final tally of 1-10. His mother's initial fears had been utterly dispelled by the magnificence of her son's display. Before the replay, former Meath All-Ireland winning captain, Peter McDermott, had been asked to advise the Down team on the necessary qualities of astuteness and tactics. This instilled a great confidence in Down and they, thanks to a fantastic performance by Joe Lennon, deservedly overcame the midlanders by two points in the replay. The All-Ireland final was to see Down face the might of Kerry who had, down through the years, set such high standards for other counties to emulate. They were going for their 20th title and Down were aiming for their first. Playing scintillating combination football at a blinding pace, Down controlled the first half and went in at the interval leading by 0-9 to 0-5. Kerry, however, fought back after the resumption to draw level. Then came the moment of destiny that was to change the course of Gaelic football. Team captain Kevin Mussen passed the ball to James McCartan 40 yards out from the Kerry goal. Kerry goalkeeper Johnny Culloty allowed McCartan's lob to slip through his fingers to give the Ulster champions a three-point advantage. Shortly afterwards, Paddy Doherty raced towards goal and was pulled down in the square. For the second time in six weeks, the man from Ballykinlar calmly slotted the resultant penalty into the net. Down were now on their way to an historic triumph. Six points ahead, the men from the 'wee six' were about to create one of the greatest outpourings of euphoria ever witnessed in Croke Park. As Doherty's kick nestled in the net, Down supporters spontaneously threw scarves, hats and coats into the air in a gesture of unbridled joy. The players could not ignore the crescendo of noise that enveloped the ground as Doherty's penalty hit the net. Looking round at their delighted supporters spurred the Mourne men to display the full repertoire of their exquisite skills. They seemed to score at will with the immaculate Doherty forcing the white flag to be raised thrice. One minute before the end, thousands of Down fans spilled onto the sidelines. Luckily they were forced back and when the final whistle sounded, Down had won their first All-Ireland title inflicting upon Kerry their heaviest All-Ireland defeat on a 2-10 to 0-8 scoreline.

By this victory, Down had not only won a national football title, they had also brought a new sense of hope and instilled in 'lesser' GAA counties, confidence and self belief. For Paddy Doherty and Down, Maurice Hayes' dream had arrived two years ahead of schedule but no one was complaining. 'I will never forget the feeling when the final whistle sounded. Originally I was relieved because I felt that the crowd pouring onto the pitch could have resulted in the game being abandoned. It was a wonderful feeling for all of us when Kevin Mussen raised the Sam Maguire Cup. The journey home through Dublin and all along the road right up to the border was unbelievable. When we reached the border we all got out of the bus and walked across into County Down with the Cup. Being the first team from the six counties to win the All-Ireland made it an extra special occasion.'

Down were feted throughout the rest of the county for the next few weeks and they were given a civic reception in Belfast's City Hall to mark their achievement. In those days that was a giant step in the field of community relations. That magnificent Down side won the Ulster championship the following year when they defeated Armagh in the final. The All-Ireland semi-final of that year was a case of 1960 revisited. For the third time in two years, Down and Kerry were to meet in a major game. In the eyes of some GAA followers, two important questions had been left unanswered in 1960. Was James McCartan's lucky goal the real reason why Down beat Kerry and had Kerry's traditional catch-and-kick style simply been outmanoeuvred by a team which did not play Gaelic football? These questions were emphatically answered on a Sunday in August in 1961. For Paddy Doherty, that day was extra special. Team captain Kevin Mussen had been sensationally dropped and Paddy was selected to replace him as captain. That mantle of responsibility rested lightly on his shoulders as, in the first minute of the game, he crossed the ball to Seán O'Neill who crashed it to the net. Down dominated the first quarter but Kerry rallied to take control of the second quarter. The half-time scoreline of 1-5 to 0-8 was an accurate reflection of that first period. The second half was to see Down at their majestic best. Jarlath Carey and Joe Lennon nullified the aerial power of Mick O'Connell and Séamus Murphy and their forward line totally mesmerised the Kerry defence with their constant running and pinpoint passing. In the end, Down achieved a 1-12 to 0-9 victory. There were no further doubts or questioning the merits of a truly great footballing side.

In the final, Down again faced old rivals Offaly. The first half of that memorable decider was to see Down again carve incisive openings in the Offaly defence to score three goals. Offaly were not far behind with two goals on the scoreboard. Nevertheless it was the vision, combination and clinical finishing of the Down goals which had such a devastating effect on Offaly. Down's first goal was the result of a passing movement between corner back George Lavery, Jarlath Carey and Paddy Doherty. Doherty sent the ball high to James McCartan. In one movement, he jumped, caught the ball and turned immediately to send it to the net for an inspirational score. Doherty was again the provider when he crossed the ball for Seán O'Neill to notch goal number two. Corner forward Brian Morgan added a third to leave the half time score 3-2 to 2-3.

Six minutes after the interval, Offaly had strong appeals for a penalty turned down when left half forward Tommy Green appeared to be fouled in the square. However, no free was given and Down went on to record a narrow but deserved victory, 3-6 to

2-8. For the second year in succession, the Mourne men had won the All-Ireland. That day's performance finally clinched the stars of the County Down's entry into the GAA's hall of fame. There were no weaknesses in the side. Eddie McKay was a safe competent goalkeeper. Full back Leo Murphy, a prodigious kicker of a ball, ruled the roost and was flanked by two tigerish markers in George Lavery and Pat Rice. Dan McCartan was a commanding figure at centre half back. In 1960, he had Kevin Mussen and Kevin O'Neill on either side of him whereas in 1961 Patsy O'Hagan and John Smith were his half back colleagues. All four were intelligent team players. At midfield Joe Lennon and Jarlath Carey showed that one did not just have to be a good high fielder to control midfield play. Their innate positional sense and their ability to shadow opponents and box the ball away brought a new dimension to midfield play. The whole Down forward sextet were simply magnificent and must rank as one of the most formidable forward lines in the history of the game. The silken skills of Seán O'Neill at right half forward, the playmaker qualities of James McCartan on the '40', and the uncanny accuracy of the fleet-footed Doherty completed a magical half forward trio. Tony Hadden at right corner forward had a penchant for acting as a third midfielder and for fisting points. In the other corner Brian Morgan was a will o' the wisp player whose devastating runs broke the hearts of many defenders. In 1960, the versatile O'Hagan was full forward whereas in 1961 PJ McElroy was an ideal target man.

Paddy Doherty was overjoyed but nervous as he walked up the steps of the Hogan Stand to collect the Sam Maguire Cup. 'As I made my way up I remember Offaly's goalkeeper Willie Nolan asking me for the match ball. I told him that one of Down's back room men, Paddy Fitzsimmons, had it. Willie found Paddy who gave him the ball. I was delighted that Willie got it because he was a very nice man. I did not like making speeches so I made the shortest speech of any winning captain. I just said, "Thanks very much Offaly," and that was that.'

In 1962, Down won the National Football League when they defeated Dublin by a point. They were also rewarded for their All-Ireland successes of the previous two years by being invited on a coast-to-coast tour of the United States. Paddy Doherty often thinks of the Ards soccer manager who had offered him the opportunity of travelling to America with them. When he thinks of all that he had achieved with Down in the interim, nothing or no one could have compensated him for the sheer joy those Down successes brought to the Ballykinlar bricklayer. 'I also got to know very well for the first time, the great commentator Micheál Ó Hehir on that tour. He was one of the nicest and most friendly people I ever met. We both shared a common interest in horse racing and we went to several race meetings.'

When Down returned from their American trip, they beat Fermanagh and Tyrone to reach their fifth consecutive Ulster final. A combination of injuries and tiredness was only partly to blame for Down's heavy shock defeat by Cavan. The magnificent team play of Cavan, capably marshalled by Gabriel Kelly, Tom Maguire, Ray Carolan, Jimmy Stafford and captain Jim McDonnell ended a glorious era in Down football. Still, they contested the next seven Ulster finals which in itself was an enormous feat. They reached the national league finals (home) in both 1963 and 1964 only to lose to Kerry and Dublin respectively. They also lost the 1963, 1965 and 1966 All-Ireland semi-finals.

In 1968, only four of Down's history-making side were still playing. Dan McCartan was now at full back. Joe Lennon was captain and played at left half back. Seán O'Neill was wearing the number 14 jersey and was nationally acclaimed as one of the greatest full forwards in the history of the game. Completing the quartet was 34-year-old Paddy Doherty now manning the centre half forward position.

Down started 1968 in exhilarating style when they defeated Kildare in the national league final by three points. In addition to the four members of the 'old guard' the Mourne side had new stars in Peter Rooney and John Purdy from the St Colman's College/Hogan Cup winning team of 1967; goalkeeper Danny Kelly (brother of television personality Gerry) Jim Milligan and Ray McConville. However, it was the sheer athleticism of 'rookie' midfielder Colm McAlarney who now stole the limelight.

In a tough bruising encounter, interspersed with passages of brilliant football, Down defeated Derry by two points in the first round of the 1968 Ulster championship. Donegal were then overwhelmed to enable Down to reach their eleventh successive Ulster final. For the seventh time in that eleven-year sequence Down met Cavan in the decider. After another superb display, the Mourne men emerged victorious by a five-point margin. Thanks to a wonderful performance by corner back Tom O'Hare, Down defeated Galway in the All-Ireland semi-final by two points. The final was a repeat of the 1960 decider against Kerry. The Kingdom, like their opponents, had just four survivors from that historic occasion; Mick O'Connell, Mick O'Dwyer, Séamus Murphy and Johnny Culloty. After six minutes play, Down were leading by 0-2 to 0-1 when Seán O'Neill scored one of the most unique goals ever witnessed. After corner forward Peter Rooney had hit the post about five feet above the crossbar, the inrushing O'Neill managed to stab the rebound into the corner of the net. If a lesser player than O'Neill had scored, the shot would have been put down as a fluke. However, given O'Neill's tremendous reflexes and his instinctive talent for the impossible, most commentators concluded that O'Neill's goal was the hallmark of a genius. What had legitimately annoyed Kerry was the fact that one of their players appeared to be fouled just before this inspirational goal. Playing with supreme confidence, the Mournemen added another goal by John Murphy and a pointed free by Doherty to leave Down leading by 2-3 to 0-1. Only eight minutes gone and the game appeared to be over before it had begun. With Colm McAlarney fetching superbly and with his trademark long, galloping strides making life extremely difficult for a hard-pressed Kerry defence, the teams retired at the interval on a 2-7 to 0-5 scoreline. Another star in that first half had been captain Joe Lennon. Joe, however, had to retire at the interval with a badly damaged medial knee ligament.

Kerry, to their eternal credit, fought back gallantly in the second half to reduce the deficit to four points. Though Kerry scored a goal in the last minute, the final whistle sounded with the score at 2-12 to 1-13. Paddy Doherty and his three colleagues from 1960–1961 had won their third All-Ireland medal. A new generation of Down stars had now savoured the sweet taste of All-Ireland success.

Paddy Doherty played in his last Ulster final in 1969 when Down were well beaten by old adversaries, Cavan. That game is still remembered for one of the most elegant goals ever scored in Belfast's Casement Park. Gaining possession 30 yards out, 35-year-old Doherty looked up, spotted a gap in the Cavan goal and drop kicked the ball with power and pace into the far corner of the net.

Shortly afterwards, he retired from the game he had graced at the highest level for 15 years. Paddy then became part of the Down management team and he was in that position when Down next won the Ulster championship in 1971. Paddy, who had reluctantly agreed to play against Cavan when he scored three points in that year's Ulster semi-final also made a brief appearance in the All-Ireland semi-final against Galway. The Westerners comprehensively beat the Mourne men on that occasion. Paddy had made his last appearance in the arena where he had thrilled so many for so long.

Doherty also contributed handsomely to Ulster's golden era of Railway Cup successes winning six medals in all, just two short of the record haul of his esteemed playing colleague, Seán O'Neill. As a clubman, he played for Ballykinlar for 19 years winning two senior league medals and losing two county championship finals to Newry Mitchels – the home club of Seán and Kevin O'Neill. In 12 Ulster final appearances between 1958 and 1968, he amassed the amazing total of six goals and 41 points. In 1960, Doherty scored 13 goals and 97 points to head the national scoring charts. On seven other occasions, Doherty finished in the top five in the national scoring stakes. The Railway Cup final in 1965 was to see Doherty score 0-12 and in the same competition the following year, he scored all of Ulster's eight points in their 1-8 to 1-4 success over Leinster in the semi-final. All in all, he scored over 900 points in his playing career with county, province and country – a stupendous feat by any standards.

Paddy, who was an SDLP councillor for many years now lives in Castlewellan with his wife Angela. They have four children, Michael, Patricia, Gary (who lives in Tralee and plays for Austin Stacks) and Fiona. Paddy thinks that there is too much emphasis on physical fitness in the modern game. As a consequence he feels the skills of the game are being neglected. To make the game and its competitions more attractive Paddy would suggest the following alterations:

1. I would abolish free kicks or sideline kicks from the hand as they eliminate the wonderful skill of kicking frees from the ground.
2. I would do away with the provincial championships for a two-year trial period and introduce an open draw. The first round should be held on a two-leg basis. After that, a straight knockout system should apply.
3. If an open draw was not introduced, I would propose that the teams knocked out in the first round of each provincial championship should go into a separate draw for a proper 'B' championship.
4. All medals at provincial and All-Ireland level should be presented to both the winning and losing teams immediately after the finals.
5. Finally, I think there should be a special section reserved in Croke Park on All-Ireland football final day for all previous All-Ireland senior medal winners. We would not mind buying the tickets in order to meet and have a chat about the great times that we had in the past.

Paddy loves to visit Cheltenham for the horse racing festival each year and renew acquaintances with such GAA luminaries as Jack Mahon of Galway and Cork's All-Ireland winning captain of 1990, Larry Tompkins. His favourite present-day players are Mickey Linden and James McCartan of Down, Maurice Fitzgerald (Kerry), Michael Donnellan (Galway), Anthony Tohill and Henry Downey of Derry and Tyrone's Peter Canavan. From the past, he has a special grá for many of his Cavan opponents who, in his estimation, were superb athletes but were unlucky to meet a Down side at their peak. 'Gabriel Kelly, Jim McDonnell, Ray Carolan and Charlie Gallagher were fabulous players. Oddly enough, my most difficult opponent by far was not a Kerry or Offaly player. Colm Mulholland of Derry really had the Indian sign on me.'

In his time, Paddy Doherty has seen and heard about many funny incidents. His favourite concerns himself and a match in which he was playing for Ballykinlar against arch rivals Glen – the club of Dan and James McCartan. 'It was the replayed final of the league. We were finding it tough going. One of their spectators turned to one of our supporters, Joe Redmond and said, "Dan McCartan has Paddy Doherty in his pocket today!" Shortly afterwards I sidestepped Dan and scored a goal and Joe said, "I think there must be a hole in Dan's pocket!"'

When the GAA millennium football side was selected, Paddy Doherty was stunned that Kerry's great Jack O'Shea was not selected. Paddy echoed the thoughts of many when he stated 'How could Jack O'Shea be picked on the centenary team and be replaced on the millennium team by a player who was playing before Jack?'

Paddy Doherty's Ireland and Ulster all-time selections are as follows:

IRELAND

John O'Leary
(Dublin)

| Enda Colleran | Leo Murphy | Jerome O'Shea |
| *(Galway)* | *(Down)* | *(Kerry)* |

| 'Red' Collier | Paddy McCormack | Tom O'Hare |
| *(Meath)* | *(Offaly)* | *(Down)* |

Mick O'Connell   Jack O'Shea
(Kerry)   *(Kerry)*

| Matt Connor | Seán Purcell | Micheál Kearins |
| *(Offaly)* | *(Galway)* | *(Sligo)* |

| Mike Sheehy | Seán O'Neill | Mickey Linden |
| *(Kerry)* | *(Down)* | *(Down)* |

ULSTER

Eddie McKay
(Down)

| Gabriel Kelly | Leo Murphy | Pat Rice |
| *(Cavan)* | *(Down)* | *(Down)* |

| Jim McDonnell | Tom Maguire | Tom O'Hare |
| *(Cavan)* | *(Cavan)* | *(Down)* |

Jim McKeever   Colm McAlarney
(Derry)   *(Down)*

| Seán O'Neill | Ray Carolan | Peter Canavan |
| *(Down)* | *(Cavan)* | *(Tyrone)* |

| PJ Treacy | James McCartan (Snr.) | Mickey Linden |
| *(Fermanagh)* | *(Down)* | *(Down)* |

Like so many people in the 1960s, Paddy Doherty was an ardent fan of many Irish showbands. They brought to the people the music and songs that they could identify with and admire. The Gay Lords from Lurgan and Brian Coll and the Plattermen from Omagh were two of Paddy's favourite bands. On the highest pedestal of all, he placed the legendary Brendan Bowyer and the Royal Showband from County Waterford. Coincidentally, Brendan was an enthusiastic supporter of the Down team of the 1960s. Writing in his autobiography, Bowyer said that if Paddy Doherty was not the greatest footballer in Ireland he would do the 'Hucklebuck' on top of the Hogan Stand. The physical impossibility of that spoke for itself. So did the considered opinions of two of Ireland's most influential Gaelic footballers of that era, one a constant colleague and the other an outstanding opponent, both of whom had seen Doherty at his imperious best. His colleague, Joe Lennon, consistently said that Paddy Doherty's innate genius and natural feel for the game made him his favourite footballer of all time. Kerry's supreme stylist Mick O'Connell came to the same conclusion on the night after Down had given one of their best ever displays in the 1961 All-Ireland semi-final against Kerry. As he rowed across to his island home in Valentia, he paused and outwardly reflected to his boating companion. 'That Paddy Doherty must be the greatest footballer in Ireland.'

Those comments alone prove beyond doubt the instinctive footballing genius that was Paddy Doherty.

Glenn Ryan

JUST 48 HOURS BEFORE the most important day of his life, the captain of the Kildare senior football team – Glenn Ryan – went for a walk with a few friends on his local golf course. It was Friday 25 September 1998 and Glenn was about to fulfil a lifetime ambition of leading out his native county in their first All-Ireland final in 63 years. This relaxing walk was a ritual that Glenn had practised before every game of the 1998 All-Ireland series. As he was strolling across the fairway, he suddenly felt a mysterious twinge of pain in his thigh. Thinking it must be his imagination, the Round Towers clubman continued walking until he realised that there was definitely something wrong. 'I then did a series of stretching exercises which seemed to exacerbate the tightness in my leg. I could not believe it. I returned home, contacted county selector Johnny Crofton who immediately arranged for me to consult the team's physiotherapist. I did not tell anyone except my parents who encouraged me to think positively. I deliberately refused to tell my team colleagues in case I would dampen their spirits and lower their morale for such an important event in all of our lives. The whole build-up to the game and the pre-match hype passed me by as I attended the physio on twelve occasions between that Friday evening and the game on Sunday. Eventually, just before the throw-in, manager Mick O'Dwyer was happy that I was fit to play. My personal trauma appeared to be over and I could now focus totally on Kildare beating Galway to bring the Sam Maguire cup to the Short-grass county for the first time in 70 years,' Glenn told me when I met him at his home in Kildare town.

Twelve years earlier, Glenn had made his county debut with the Kildare U-14 side. Playing at right half back, in a team that included future senior colleagues Niall Buckley and Ronan Quinn, Glenn gave a very impressive performance as he faced Dublin for the first time. Both in 1989 and 1990 Glenn was a star performer in excellent Kildare minor teams only to be beaten by Offaly and Meath respectively. Initially Glenn was happy especially as he had been chosen as captain on the 1990 team. However, a local newspaper report fuelled his indignation when it stated that Glenn was not worthy of his midfield place never mind being team captain. A few months later, someone more important decided otherwise. When Mick O'Dwyer arrived for his first term as county team manager in September 1990 he called the 18-year-old Ryan into his senior squad. Glenn was delighted that the most successful manager in the history of Gaelic football had such confidence in his ability.

At the beginning of the 1990–1991 National Football League, Glenn made his competitive debut against Derry in Newbridge. Having impressed O'Dwyer a few weeks earlier when he came on as a substitute against Meath in a challenge match, the Waterville hotelier selected him at left half forward against the Oak Leaf county.

One of Glenn's heroes growing up as a boy in the 1970s and 1980s was Kerry's outstanding half forward Pat Spillane. Little did he think then that he would ever play against him. However, in O'Dwyer's first year in charge, Kildare had won their way through to the quarter-final of the league where Kildare were drawn against O'Dwyer's native Kerry. Ryan, the rising star, opposed Spillane, the accomplished veteran. Ryan was impressed, not only with Spillane's renowned ability but also his physique. 'I thought Pat was an average sized, moderately built player until I saw him running straight at me. I just could not believe how strong he was physically.'

Anyhow, Kildare defeated Kerry, then accounted for Ulster champions Donegal 0-14 to 0-10 in the semi-final, but were narrowly defeated by Dublin by 1-9 to 0-10 in the final. Though beaten, O'Dwyer was very happy with his new team's performance. The sleeping football giant that was Kildare had awakened. All supporters and players looked forward to a good run in that year's Leinster championship. A mere twelve months since that unfortunate journalistic remark, Glenn Ryan's football career had taken off at the very highest level.

In both 1992 and 1993, Kildare appeared to be on course for, at least, provincial success when they reached the Leinster final in those years. However, the expectation of both players and supporters were considerably dampened, on both occasions, when the Lilywhites suffered convincing defeats at the hands of Dublin. For Ryan there was some consolation when he was Kildare's best player when Kildare annexed the Leinster U-21 title – their first since 1983 – by defeating Dublin comprehensively in the final by 2-12 to 0-9. At senior level, when Kildare were eliminated, Mick O'Dwyer decided to retire as manager. When O'Dwyer, who had come to Kildare amid great publicity and expectant success, left, many pundits forecast that any remote chance of a potential Kildare resurgence went with him. Former Roscommon All Star and Newbridge resident Dermot Earley was then appointed manager. Narrow defeats in 1995 and 1996 in the Leinster championship to Louth and Laois respectively made him decide to relinquish his position. 'Dermot was exceptionally unlucky. A combination of bad luck and injuries contrived to prolong the agony for both players and supporters. Dermot could not have done more. He just did not get the rub of the green. In order to be successful, everything has to go right on the day,' said Glenn.

After Dermot's retirement, the call again went out from the Kildare County board for Mick O'Dwyer to return. The Kerry man was not found wanting as he returned to manage the Lilywhites in the autumn of 1996. The 1997 Leinster championship provided some inspiration and hope for the future when it took Meath three games to dispose of Kildare. Their 1997 performances convinced O'Dwyer that Kildare had now developed a necessary cutting edge to their style of play. O'Dwyer meticulously prepared his team with greater eagerness than ever before. The additional reason for his new-found optimism was the fact that two players of real quality had now joined the panel. Former Tipperary star Brian Lacey was now available for selection in the Kildare defence and his own son, Karl, had also transferred to Kildare. Having obtained a teaching position in Rathangan, he would add both mobility and accuracy to the forward line.

In the first round of the 1998 Leinster championship, Kildare drew with Dublin, their long standing 'hoodoo' team. The replay was to prove a benchmark as a more confident Lilywhite side edged out the Metropolitans on a 0-12 to 1-8 scoreline. They had played superbly and Dublin's late goal by Declan Darcy only made the tally look respectable. For the first time since 1972, a Kildare team had beaten Dublin in the championship. Kildare were on their way. This fact was further emphasised when Kildare played brilliantly to overwhelm Laois, 2-13 to 0-8, in the Leinster semi-final.

The Leinster final matched Kildare with old rivals and neighbours Meath. In a fantastic game the two sides who had not met in a Leinster decider since 1966 served up a thrilling 70 minutes of entertainment. With right full back Brian Lacey outstanding, and forwards Dermot Earley and Martin Lynch equally impressive, Kildare led by three points as the game entered the last quarter. Then, Meath, as always, dug deep and clinically responded with three unanswered points. There were seven minutes left. It was now that Kildare showed their true and new mettle. Following a kick out by Kildare goalkeeper Christy Byrne, young Dermot Earley, son of the Roscommon All-Ireland player of the same name, rose high to fetch the ball and send it down the left wing. An ever alert Martin Lynch secured possession and accurately crossed the ball to substitute Brian Murphy. With poise and confidence, Cork-born Murphy slammed the ball to the net for a wonderful goal. Now, totally dominant, Kildare added further points by midfielder Willie McCreery and right half forward Eddie McCormack. When the full-time whistle blew, Kildare had won their first provincial title since 1956 by 1–12 to 0–10. Though Meath had been reduced to 14 men when Brendan Reilly was sent off, no one disputed the merits of Kildare's achievement. An ecstatic captain, Glenn Ryan held aloft the Leinster trophy. 'It was unbelievable fairytale stuff. I will never forget that moment of joy,' said Glenn who rates former Kildare footballer Christy Moore as his favourite singer.

That night, and for the following week, the whole county celebrated. Being prisoners of their past glory and slaves to years of failure, the Kildare supporters had now something to cheer about. Glenn Ryan and his team of 1998 were now real and accessible heroes with whom they could readily identify. The subsequent All-Ireland semi-final was an exceptionally colourful and tension laden occasion as Kildare supporters packed the stands and terraces of Croke Park in their thousands. For Mick O'Dwyer it was a time of personal conflict. Here he was, managing Kildare against his native Kerry with whom he had played in six All-Irelands as well as successfully leading them to eight All-Irelands as a manager. This man, who had served his county for an incredible span of 36 years (1954–1990) was now plotting its downfall.

Immediately prior to the commencement of the semi-final, Kildare's brilliant midfielder Niall Buckley failed a fitness test. The inspirational All Star, who had been truly magnificent throughout the campaign, especially in the replay against Dublin when he scored two majestic points, would be a major loss. His withdrawal resulted in left half forward Dermot Earley being switched to midfield and Ken Doyle being drafted in to Earley's position.

During the game itself, Kildare played exceptionally well. With Brian Lacey, Glenn Ryan, Eddie McCormack, Dermot Earley, Martin Lynch and especially roving full forward Karl O'Dwyer being particularly outstanding, Kildare won 0–13 to 1–9. The final scoreline did not really reflect Kildare's dominance but O'Dwyer was not worried as he prepared, for the first time since 1986, to return as manager to Croke Park on All-Ireland final day. As for Glenn Ryan, he simply could not believe that the fates of history had decreed that he would be the chosen one to lead out the Lilywhites in an All-Ireland senior final. Seventy years previously in 1928, a Kildare man, Bill 'Squires' Gannon had been the first man to lift the then new Sam Maguire Cup. Only time would tell whether Glenn Ryan would be the second.

When the game began, Galway seized the initiative and scored three points without reply. Playing fast, direct football it appeared, at first, that they were going to completely demolish Kildare. However, with Glenn Ryan feeling no obvious effects of his thigh injury and giving a masterly display in his centre half back position, Kildare fought back. With midfielder Willie McCreery coming more and more into the game, Kildare scored an unanswered 1-2, the goal coming from a fisted effort by Dermot Earley. This goal seemed to ignite the whole team out of their apparent lethargy. Using their short passing game effectively the Lilywhites seemed to own the ball as half time approached. However, the half-time scoreboard did not truly reflect their outfield dominance. At half-time the score read: 1-5 to 0-4.

Before the All-Ireland final began, O'Dwyer had a player who failed a fitness test. Regular full back Ronan Quinn had to withdraw and usual right half back John Finn was switched to full back. Veteran corner back Sos Dowling was dovetailed to fill Finn's position.

When the second half commenced, Galway played like a team truly transformed. During the first half, Glenn Ryan's opponent, Jarlath Fallon, had been largely anonymous. Now, he really seemed psyched up as he raced ahead of Ryan for the ball from out on the touchline. 'I did not want to foul him and I felt that Ja would not score from that distance. Reckoning that if Ja attempted to score and put the ball wide it would put him off his game I played for safety, just shadowing him. However, he cleverly turned inside and kicked the ball straight over the bar. That really boosted his and Galway's confidence. I believe that was the turning point in the game. There was nothing else I could have done. It is impossible to legislate for such a wonderful score,' Glenn honestly admitted.

For the remainder of the game Galway took control. Being more assured on the ball and hitting long, defence-splitting kick passes they upped their performance. With speedster Michael Donnellan nominally positioned at right half forward, but picking up the ball in the half back line and making deep surging runs into the heart of the Kildare defence, Galway had an alternative attacking option. The whole Galway team had come alive and with Fallon and Donnellan especially prominent, the Tribesmen went on to deservedly win their first senior All-Ireland title since 1966. The final scoreline of 1–14 to 1–10 showed that the west were no longer asleep. However, Glenn Ryan and his team mates were absolutely gutted. 'I just wanted to go away and hide,' said the man whose all-time hero in other sports was former Chicago Bulls basketball player Michael Jordan.

Though defeated, Kildare had contributed much to what had been an outstanding game of skill, speed and sportsmanship. On the day, an excellent Galway team had played exceptionally well and had prepared away from all the undue glare of publicity. On the other hand, Kildare had been made firm favourites and were constantly under the spotlight of unprecedented publicity. Perhaps those contrasting scenarios affected one or other of the teams. No one will ever know nor does it matter. What is important is that history will record that a wonderful Galway performance eclipsed seven decades of Kildare hopes.

One must credit Kildare with all they achieved during 1998. Overcoming the three most recent All-Ireland winners, Dublin, Meath and Kerry in one season was no mean feat. With players such as Karl O'Dwyer, Brian Lacey, Niall Buckley, Willie McCreery, Dermot Earley as well as Ryan himself to form the nucleus of their team, Kildare should have every right to feel optimistic about the future. Glenn, who led his club, Round Towers, to their first county championship title for 35 years, in 1995, possesses the necessary leadership qualities to steer the Lilywhites to the promised land of All-Ireland success. Given the law of averages, that should come sooner rather than later. After all, he led Kildare from the wilderness into the league of that elite group who are genuine contenders for top honours.

A few weeks after the All-Ireland, Glenn played for Ireland in the Compromise Rules series with Australia. Ryan thoroughly enjoyed this experience. 'The pride of playing for one's country along with the top players from the other counties was a tremendous personal honour. I hope the series has a future because it provides an ideal extra outlet for players to perform at a higher and different level.'

Glenn, despite criticisms from some quarters, is a great advocate of the proper use of the short passing game. 'It is a great team game as opposed to the "catch and kick" game. Every player wants to touch the ball as often as possible. There is no greater spectacle than watching the ball being short passed, at speed, from the full back line up to the forwards. I realise it requires a lot of skill, fitness and courage, but constructive handpassing is beautiful to watch as well as improving team spirit and eliminating selfishness.'

Glenn Ryan, whose favourite referee is Galway's Mick Curley because he keeps talking to the players and is not dogmatic in his attitude, admires many players in the modern game. Séamus Moynihan (Kerry), Trevor Giles, Tommy Dowd and Darren Fay of Meath, Peter Canavan (Tyrone), Anthony Tohill (Derry), Michael Donnellan and Jarlath Fallon of Galway are particular favourites.

Having respected the views and dedication of all the managers that he has played under at club, county, provincial and national levels, Glenn has a special admiration for Mick O'Dwyer. 'Being with a living legend is great in itself. He commands great respect from the players, has fantastic commitment to the betterment of Kildare football and his enthusiasm is simply unbelievable.'

The Round Towers Club stalwart, whose brothers, Kieran and Liam, are also very good footballers, believes that all GAA managers should be paid a fixed salary sanctioned by Croke Park. Though defeat was again Kildare's lot when they were beaten by Offaly in the first round of the 1999 Leinster championship, Glenn Ryan still yearns and hopes for that All-Ireland senior medal. The star centre half, who was selected as an All Star in both 1997 and 1998 and has represented Leinster in the Railway Cup from 1991–1998 is still young enough to fulfil that dream.

When picking his Ireland and Leinster sides Glenn made the following selections.

IRELAND (1990–1999)

Christy Byrne
(Kildare)

Davy Dalton   Mick Lyons   Kenneth Mortimer
(Kildare)   *(Meath)*   *(Mayo)*

Paul Curran   Henry Downey   Anthony Rainbow
(Dublin)   *(Derry)*   *(Kildare)*

Jack O'Shea   Anthony Tohill
(Kerry)   *(Derry)*

Trevor Giles   Larry Tompkins   James McCartan
(Meath)   *(Cork)*   *(Down)*

Peter Canavan   Maurice Fitzgerald   Mickey Linden
(Tyrone)   *(Kerry)*   *(Down)*

LEINSTER

Christy Byrne
(Kildare)

Davy Dalton
(Kildare)

Mick Lyons
(Meath)

Robbie O'Malley
(Meath)

Paul Curran
(Dublin)

Keith Barr
(Dublin)

Anthony Rainbow
(Kildare)

John McDermott
(Meath)

Niall Buckley
(Kildare)

Trevor Giles
(Meath)

Declan Kerrigan
(Kildare)

Brian Stynes
(Dublin)

Kevin O'Brien
(Wicklow)

Tommy Dowd
(Meath)

Bernard Flynn
(Meath)

Kildare have a proud past in the GAA. They have won four All-Irelands – 1905, 1919, 1927 and 1928, and contested other All-Ireland finals in 1903 (home final), 1926, 1929, 1931 and 1935 and 1998. Those teams, particularly in the golden era of the 1920s had a great following just as today's Kildare teams have. In the 1903 final, inspired by Joe Rafferty of Clane, the team wore Clane's all-white jerseys and the players painted their boots to match. The public loved the all-white strip so much that the county decided to adopt it as their colour. Thus, the Lilywhites were born.

During the period 1919–1935, Kildare introduced to the game of Gaelic football some of the most talented players the GAA has ever seen. That wonderful athlete, Larry Stanley who captained the 1919 side was the first man to compete for Ireland in the Olympic Games of 1924. The three A's high-jump champion who competed in that event was also a champion long jumper. Other outstanding Gaelic footballers who adorned the Lilywhite jersey were Paul Doyle who played in Kildare's six successive Leinster championship winning teams (1926–1931); Mick Buckley, captain in 1927, Bill Gannon, captain in 1928 and Jack Higgins, captain in 1929.

With such men and such teams of the past to inspire them, there is no logical reason why the men under the command of an equally talented leader such as Glenn Ryan should not emulate the accomplishments of Stanley, Buckley and Gannon. An expectant Kildare following confidently awaits the men of today to find that place in the sun. Glenn Ryan will do his utmost to achieve the Holy Grail.

Mick Loftus

MICK LOFTUS' MOTHER DIED when he was just six years old. His Garda father encouraged Mick and his brothers Marty and Vinnie to become interested in Gaelic football by listening to Micheál Ó Hehir's radio commentaries. Though then living in Elphin, Co. Roscommon Mick who was born in Kiltoom instantly became imbued with a love of Mayo football as they then had a very good side. He remembers clearly listening to the radio when Mayo won their first senior All-Ireland title in 1936. Players such as Henry Kenny, Tom Burke, Paddy Moclair and Josie Munnelly became instant heroes.

In 1939, the Loftus family moved to Crossmolina, Co. Mayo. At that time there was no active club in his new town but when Fr Davis came to the parish as a curate, he re-established the dormant club. Mick Loftus the spectator began to play the game in earnest. When Roscommon won successive All-Irelands in 1943 and 1944, Mick's football education was considerably enhanced. More accessible heroes such as Roscommon's Bill Carlos, Jack McQuillan, Donal Keenan, Brendan Lynch, Phelim Murray and captain Jimmy Murray made Mick want to play the game at the highest level.

His dedicated apprenticeship was finally recognised when he was selected at right half forward on the Mayo minor team that won the 1947 Connacht minor championship. Beating Sligo by four points, they eventually went on to contest the All-Ireland final against Ulster champions, Tyrone. In that game Mayo led at half time by eleven points only for Tyrone to stage a sensational second-half comeback to snatch a one-point victory, 4-4 to 4-3. A devastated Mick still refers to that match as the greatest disappointment in his playing career. He does concede, however, that the superlative display of Tyrone captain, Eddie Devlin, essentially paved the way for the Northerners' success. But there was some consolation. Mick won his first county medal when a flourishing Crossmolina annexed the Mayo junior championship in the same year.

As a supporter, Mick returned to Croke Park for the following year's All-Ireland senior final between reigning All-Ireland champions Cavan, and Mayo who were in their first senior final since they won their initial title 12 years earlier. In the weeks prior to the game, Mick had helped a local farmer with the seasonal chores of saving hay and clamping turf. The farmer, who had a taxi, offered the medical student at UCG a lift to the game. On the way to the match, they had no fewer than three punctures which naturally delayed their journey. Eventually, the ticketless fans reached Croke Park and scaled a wall at the Hill 16 end. Their spectacular ringside view was brought to a hasty conclusion when a concerned Garda sergeant told them to get down. Mick then had a brainwave. He would run the half mile back to Barry's Hotel where the Mayo officials were having lunch. 'There I met the county chairman Fr Eddie O'Hara who had remembered me from the minor team of the previous year. Telling him of my plight, he immediately put his hand in his pocket and gave me his own ticket for the Cusack Stand. I recall excitedly running back to Croke Park, having a bottle of orange and a sandwich. There was not a happier man in Ireland,' Mick recollected when I met him in his home in Crossmolina.

Meanwhile, his own playing career was progressing nicely. Playing for the UCG Sigerson Cup team and an integral part of the Crossmolina team which won their first senior championship in 1949, Loftus soon attracted the attention of the Mayo senior selectors. Though he did not make the squad which won Mayo's second All-Ireland in 1950, he was a substitute when they repeated their success a year later in 1951. A senior All-Ireland gold medal now adorned the Loftus household. Six years later, in 1957, the greatest moment in his football career occurred. Giving his best-ever individual display Dr Mick Loftus, captained Mayo to a junior All-Ireland victory over Warwickshire. Incidentally that team had a legendary figure in its ranks. Josie Munnelly, who had won an All-Ireland senior medal 21 years earlier and who had retired in 1946, made a dramatic comeback at the age of 42 to claim a second All-Ireland medal, albeit at junior level.

As his playing career entered its twilight years, Mick, who acknowledges Paddy Cox of Ballina, Christy Garvey of Roscommon and Patsy Harkan of Castlebar as his most difficult playing opponents became interested in coaching. He was influenced by the coaching techniques of the late Gerald Courell and Jackie Carney who co-trained Mayo's All-Ireland teams of 1950 and 1951 and by the double-winning captain of those sides, the late Seán Flanagan TD who coached the junior All-Ireland team of 1957. For the next few years, Mick spent endless hours coaching his own club's U-14s and U-16s junior and senior teams. 'To be a good coach it is not necessary to be a good player. However, it certainly helps as an ex-player generally understands the game better, knows how to motivate them and pinpoint their strengths and weaknesses. I attended many coaching courses and found them very helpful, especially the residential courses organised by Down's Joe Lennon at Gormanston in the 1960s.'

As Mick's club playing career finally ended he, like many others, became somewhat fortuitously involved in refereeing. 'It happened quite simply. The official referee failed to turn up, I substituted for him and my alternative GAA career took off. Numerous Mayo minor, junior and senior finals soon came my way. Subsequently the Connacht Council and GAA headquarters asked me to officiate at inter-county games both at championship and league levels.

'I'll never forget my first big game – the All-Ireland minor final of 1964 between Offaly and Cork. Before I received official notification of my appointment, I had already booked a family holiday with my brothers in the US. So I went to New York, as planned, the week prior to the game and then got a return flight to Dublin on the Saturday before the final. Unfortunately, the only return flight back to New York on the Sunday was scheduled for 3 p.m., the same time as the minor final was due to end. A great friend and fellow clubman, however, came to my rescue. John Nallen who had played inter-county football with Mayo, Meath, Cavan and Galway was the Ulster Bank manager at Dublin Airport. He succeeded in persuading the pilot to delay the flight until I arrived, in my prearranged taxi after the game, from Croke Park. Slipping a pair of trousers over my refereeing gear in the taxi I arrived at the airport, happily thanked John and was in the plane at 3.30 p.m. Over the Atlantic, I heard that Galway had won the senior game. When I arrived in New York, I showered and quickly togged in six hours after the match! I will never forget John Nallen for all that he did for me on that day. From an inter-county perspective, John was most unfortunate. Mayo, Meath, Cavan and Galway all had won All-Irelands just a few years either before or after his tenure with each of them.'

The following year, 1965, Loftus refereed his first All-Ireland senior final between Galway and Kerry. That game, in some people's minds, is best remembered for the fact that the Mayo referee sent off three players, two from Kerry and one from Galway. Mick does not concur. 'I think, in common with the vast majority of people who saw the game, the great majority of players from both teams played within the rules. Definitely, there was some tension as Galway and Kerry had already played against each other in three major games within a relatively short space of time. I had no option but to send off the players who seriously transgressed the rules. But when I look back on that game there were many redeeming factors. Galway gave a truly wonderful display of team football and the majestic fielding and intelligent long kick passing by Kerry's Mick O'Connell, in the third quarter, was a sight never to be forgotten. The positive aspects of the game, from both teams, far outweighed the negative.'

Mick Loftus, the referee, always trained daily whether or not he had an important game coming up. Every evening, whether he was at home in Crossmolina or abroad on official GAA duties in America or Australia, Mick went for his regular mile run with a series of jogging and stretching exercises included. To this day, he continues his daily routine. It is no wonder that his figure and demeanour belie the fact that he is now 70 years of age.

With such consistent dedication to training and his constant reading of the GAA rules, it came as no surprise that so many top games came his way during an inter-county refereeing career that spanned the years from 1962 to 1976. At the height of that career, in 1968, Mick took charge of the senior All-Ireland final between Down and Kerry, the National Football League final between Down and Kildare, the World Cup final between Down and New York, in Gaelic Park, as well as the All-Ireland colleges final between Coláiste Chríost Rí of Cork and Belcamp OMI of Dublin. 'The World Cup game which was played over two legs brought me into conflict with John "Kerry" O'Donnell who was furious that I had sent off a New York player in the first leg. He wanted to withdraw New York from the competition but he eventually relented and Down went on to win it. Having seen so much of Down that year made me observe closely the sheer quality of their team play and the individual talents of some of the best footballers I ever saw. Full back Dan McCartan, left corner back Tom O'Hare, right half back Ray McConville and captain Joe Lennon were exceptional defenders. Colm McAlarney, with his long galloping stride broke the heart of defenders and Paddy Doherty was one of the most accurate forwards of all time. But the greatest of them all was full forward Seán O'Neill. He was simply a genius with the ball. No defender could ever judge properly what he was going to do with it. He was always thinking and conjuring up moves.'

For a further six years, Mick continued to referee at inter-county level. 'I enjoyed the games and the players who, while not always agreeing with my decisions, nevertheless respected them. One unusual incident provided me with my most difficult game. In a league game involving Offaly, one of their players asked me to mind his dentures for him. I found it extremely hard to concentrate fully on the match in case the dentures would fall out of my pocket and be smashed to smithereens!'

Mick decided to finally opt out of inter-county refereeing. However, this multi-talented GAA man found another position taking up most of his spare time. Early in 1968, Mick began a 12-year stint as chairman of his home club Crossmolina Deel Rovers. Through his vision, a new pitch was developed with ancillary facilities, a pitch and putt course, tennis courts and a swimming pool. Already chairman of the Mayo Grounds Committee, the County board further acknowledged his administrative and organising skills when he was selected, in 1972, as a Mayo representative on the Connacht Council of the GAA. He served on this body until 1984 and was chairman from 1979 onwards.

Having proven himself as an extraordinarily capable and innovative chairman at club, county and provincial level, no one was shocked when Mick's name was announced as a nominee for the presidency of the GAA in 1984. The rest of the GAA counties wanted to share what the cool, thinking, indefatigable Loftus had to offer. As a consequence he was selected as president elect at the Annual Congress in Belfast in 1984, taking over presidential office for the term 1985-1988. His late father would have been proud. His positive encouragement all those years ago had led to his unassuming and genial son becoming the Gaelic Athletic Association's first citizen. 'Those three years were very special in my life. Visiting all the clubs nationwide, officially opening new pitches in both urban and rural areas as well as presenting all the cups on All-Ireland final days have bequeathed to me a litany of wonderful memories. Going to Australia for the Compromise Rules series in 1987 made me realise what our games meant to the exiles abroad. To see the Irish side under the expert management of Kevin Heffernan and brilliant captain Jack O'Shea give their all for their country was just great. The team distinguished themselves, not only on the field of play, but as courteous and dignified ambassadors at receptions and social functions. In the games they were all tremendous but Niall Cahalane of Cork was an especially inspiring player. It was good to see players from the so-called weaker counties getting an opportunity to play at this level. Men such as Noel Roche of Clare and Pat Byrne of Wicklow showed great skill and commitment.'

Mick Loftus has seen many exciting and marvellously skilful games of football over the past 60-odd years. The Galway side of 1964 to 1966, the Down teams of the 1960s and the Kerry teams of the 1970s and 1980s were particular favourites of the doctor who is coroner for North Mayo. John Joe O'Reilly of Cavan, Tony Hanahoe of Dublin, Micheál Kearins of Sligo, Seán O'Neill and Joe Lennon of Down, Jim McKeever of Derry, Pakie MacGarty of Leitrim, Paddy O'Brien and Peter McDermott of Meath, Páidí Ó Sé and Mick O'Connell of Kerry and Seán Purcell and Frank Stockwell of Galway were just some of the wonderful exponents of Gaelic football whose contributions remain imprinted in his memory.

Preferring a blend of the long, accurate, kicking game and short passing only as a system of support play, Loftus decries what he terms the overuse of short passing in today's game. 'Players are now afraid to give away possession so they handpass ad infinitum, to the detriment of the game itself. To counteract this obsession I believe handpassing should be curtailed to three successive handpasses. Having been a referee myself I do not think that the introduction of this new rule would provide any problem for the referee to implement.'

Loftus, who would like to see a round robin series adopted in each province for the All-Ireland championships and a radical restructuring of the current National Football League, believes that Gaelic Games should become an integral part of the school curriculum. 'This should be done in a positive manner and not in a negative way to prevent the promotion of soccer and rugby. It should be instituted under the umbrella of Celtic Studies and should include the Irish language, history, music, song and dance as well as the games themselves. After all, this was one of the primary reasons why the GAA's first secretary, Michael Cusack, helped to found the GAA in 1884.'

On Sunday 30 May 1999, the Pioneer Total Abstinence Association celebrated the centenary of its foundation in 1898 by Fr James Cullen SJ. Forty thousand people attended Croke Park on this gala day of commemoration and thanksgiving. The PTAA or the Pioneers, as they are more popularly known, is an international spiritual organisation which promotes temperance. Through the abstinence of its membership (there are over 250,000 members in Ireland alone) from consuming alcohol they hope, by their example and prayer, to curb the excessive use of alcohol and thus create greater stability in the home, in the workplace and in society as a whole. One of its most prominent members is lifelong Pioneer Dr Mick Loftus who was invited by the PTAA's Central Director, Fr Bernard McGuckian SJ and his assistant, Mayo man Fr Micheál MacGreil SJ to be part of the organising committee for the centenary year's mammoth event in Croke Park. 'For the past 42 years, I have been a GP in Crossmolina. I have noticed how families have been destroyed, jobs lost and moral values diminished by the abuse of alcohol. Twenty per cent of all blood pressure cases and 70 per cent of all road accidents, many of them fatal, are drink related. The subtle advertising of alcohol products in the media inculcates a belief in young people that there is no such thing as enjoyment or entertainment unless one constantly drinks alcohol. Therefore I have been annoyed in recent years when the GAA sanctioned the sponsorship of Guinness for the All-Ireland hurling championships. Promoting drink with sport is not only destroying the true ethos of sport but leads to contradictions. For example, Limerick county teams were sponsored by an anti drugs campaign. This was laudable in itself but when one saw the advertisements for alcohol products in the grounds in which they were playing, logic was thrown out the window. I know there is a popular and justifiable reaction to the use of drugs. Nonetheless it seems to me that there is a certain hypocrisy here. Some leaders of our society love to be anti-drugs but do not, at the same time, even mention the devastating effect the abuse of alcohol has on our whole society. Drink ads should be banned from television in the same way as cigarette ads are. Both the government and the GAA must be consistent in their efforts to eliminate both alcohol and drug abuse. It must be remembered that the abuse of alcohol in Ireland is greater than the misuse of all other drugs combined. As a result of the GAA's ambiguity in this regard and as a personal protest I have not attended an All-Ireland hurling final since Guinness started their sponsorship of it. With regard to myself and my part in the Pioneer celebrations, I would like to compliment them on their marvellous work, often against the tide, for the past 100 years. The Pioneers' Central Director Fr McGuckian, who is a former Antrim county minor football captain is a very able and imaginative leader. His talent could be used along with the government, the GAA, and any other interested body to stamp out this indifferent attitude to the worst evil in our society. I would love to see a concerted effort by the government and others to initiate this immediately. If that were done, the family unit would be healthier and stronger and this society would be better, stronger and thriftier,' concluded Dr Loftus.

When Mick selected his Ireland and Connacht teams he emphasised that his selections were based mainly on the players that he saw most often giving consistently outstanding performances. Roscommon's Bill Carlos and fellow clubman John Nallen were decidedly unlucky not to make his final 15.

IRELAND

Johnny Geraghty
(Galway)

Enda Colleran *(Galway)*	Joe Keohane *(Kerry)*	Seán Flanagan *(Mayo)*
Jim Brosnan *(Kerry)*	John J. O'Reilly *(Cavan)*	Seán Murphy *(Kerry)*

Mick O'Connell *(Kerry)*   Pádraig Carney *(Mayo)*

Seán O'Neill *(Down)*	Seán Purcell *(Galway)*	Mickey Kearins *(Sligo)*
Frank Stockwell *(Galway)*	Tom Langan *(Mayo)*	Kevin Heffernan *(Dublin)*

CONNACHT

Johnny Geraghty
(Galway)

Enda Colleran *(Galway)*	Paddy Prendergast (Mayo)	Seán Flanagan *(Mayo)*
Jimmy Duggan *(Galway)*	Gerry O'Malley *(Roscommon)*	Martin Newell *(Galway)*

Pádraig Carney *(Mayo)*   Mattie McDonagh *(Galway)*

Mickey Kearins *(Sligo)*	Seán Purcell *(Galway)*	Joe Corcoran *(Mayo)*
Frank Stockwell *(Galway)*	Tom Langan *(Mayo)*	Pakie MacGarty *(Leitrim)*

Mick Loftus, player, coach, administrator and referee has served the GAA with tremendous honour and total dedication for the last 60 years. The enormous amount of time spent in all those varying capacities and different challenges would not have been possible without the total support of his wife, Edie, and family Michael (Jnr), Orla, Patrick and Joseph. Despite having a very busy medical practice, the affable doctor found time for both his GAA activities and professional duties. It is hard to visualise how one human being could fit so much into one lifetime. A deeply religious man who has been a daily Mass-goer all his life, he has great trust in God and his fellow man.

'Since my early years, I have been heavily involved in the GAA. It has been a most rewarding and satisfying experience for me. Edie (née Munnelly) came from a strong GAA family, both her father and her brother, Ambrose, having played for Crossmolina and Mayo. At club level I met such great administrators as Fr Davis,

Jack Judge and Jack Coen; with the County board there were excellent men like Fr Leo Morahan, Johnny Mulvey, Paddy Muldoon and PJ McGrath; at Provincial council I worked with people of outstanding calibre especially Brendan Nestor (Galway), Tom Kilcoyne (Sligo) and Frank Kenny (Roscommon). On the national scene, there were great men like Directors-General Seán O'Síocháin and Liam Mulvihill as well as all the presidents including Seán McCague, who takes up office in the spring of 2000.

I also have had the opportunity to represent the GAA officially in the US, Canada, Australia, England and Scotland. The GAA has been very good to me. I only hope I have helped it a little,' Mick concluded.

The GAA has been established successfully on a voluntary ethos in which an innate love of Irish games and the fostering of a parish-oriented community spirit are vital components. This has been achieved, in an all embracing manner, from club level right through its hierarchical structure to Central Council level. No man exemplifies more this unique communal accomplishment than Dr Mick Loftus. It is through the commitment of people like Mick that the GAA has continued to flourish and prosper. The kind, caring doctor from Crossmolina has served his club, county, province and country exceptionally well. Many others will enjoy the fruits of his labour.

Matt Connor

LATE ONE FRIDAY NIGHT after Offaly had lost both their Leinster and All-Ireland crowns to Dublin, in the 1983 Leinster final, Garda Matt Connor went to investigate an accident on Tullamore's main street. A man had fallen off his bicycle and was in a very distraught state. He appeared to be very badly injured. With his face totally covered in blood, he lay motionless, his body crumpled on the hard surface. Just as Matt approached, the injured man looked up at him through his blood stained face. 'Why did you miss that blasted penalty?' As Matt witnessed the man's rapid recovery and the reprimand for his display the previous Sunday, he smiled to himself thinking of the serious impact that a Gaelic football match can have on all of us.

Matt Connor's Gaelic football pedigree was of the highest calibre. His father Jim won six county senior championship medals with his native club, Walsh Island, in the 1930s and 1940s. His brother Murt was a member of the Offaly squad which won successive All-Irelands in 1971 and 1972. As well as that, his first cousin Willie Bryan was captain of the 1971 side and had been selected as a Carrolls' All Star in both of those historic years for Offaly football. Being a young and impressionable schoolboy at the time of those fabulous successes made every Offaly boy want to emulate such stars as goalkeeper Martin Furlong, centre half back Nicholas Clavin, midfielder Willie Bryan and 1972 captain Tony McTague. Through his family's GAA background Matt felt the urge to wear the Offaly colours greater than most.

Matt, whose skill developed in tandem with both his enthusiasm and age, made his debut in goals for the Offaly U-14 team in 1973. However, it was 1977 that was to prove a benchmark in his rising status as a footballer of note. At this stage, his ball skill was already mind-boggling, as was his ability to score from every angle. In that season, Matt played minor, U-21 and senior football for Offaly. In fact, he actually played on the senior side before he played on the U-21 team, making his debut in a National League game against Meath in March 1977 in which he scored a point. Two weeks later, in another league game, against Limerick, his sheer football wizardry, fleetness of foot and unerring simply pulverised the Treatymen's defence. The star left corner forward's three goals and two points bore testimony to his magnificent talent.

Matt's elevation to the senior team was at the behest of Eugene McGee who had arrived the previous year to manage Offaly. Even though Offaly were then in Division Two South of the League, McGee had watched the outstanding, young talent that was available to Offaly and on that basis had decided to accept the managerial position. Given Eugene's impressive track record in managing, starting with UCD's Sigerson Cup sides, the potential for an Offaly resurgence, under his leadership, was great. Young men such as Matt's first cousin, Tomás Connor, Liam Currams, Johnny Mooney and Padraig Dunne along with the experienced existing county players such as Martin Furlong, Seán Lowry, Séamus Darby, Matt's cousin Liam Connor and his brother Richie were to form the nucleus of McGee's future plans. It was Matt Connor, however, who was to become the most influential figure in McGee's attacking strategy.

Simultaneously, as McGee was hatching his future senior championship plans, Offaly were experiencing a good run in the U-21 championship, winning Leinster titles in 1977 and 1979. Matt made his senior championship debut in 1978 against Longford. Having overcome this hurdle, Offaly were beaten in the Leinster semi-final against the then All-Ireland champions, Dublin. McGee was not unduly unhappy, as Offaly had been promoted in that year's League and his side was starting to play an attractive brand of fast, open football. In the 1979 Leinster championship, Offaly made further progress when they reached the Leinster final only to lose to a last-minute goal by Dublin. Still, McGee's blend of experienced players and young talent were gaining in confidence. The Longford man had brought organisation and tactical knowhow to his adopted county. The players could see that McGee's implementation of a strict training programme plus his overall dedication to the task in hand was worth reciprocating. This they did with fervour and a willingness that had been missing for some time.

In 1980, Offaly progressed a step further when they annexed the Leinster title for the first time in seven years. Giving a superlative performance of excellent fetching and long, accurate passing Offaly were worthy of their 1-10 to 1-8 victory over their old rivals Dublin. Matt Connor's wonderful goal, and a personal tally of 1-7 eventually clinched a deserved victory for the Faithful County. Now, Matt Connor was due to play in his first All-Ireland football semi-final.

Facing possibly the greatest side in the history of Gaelic football – Kerry – did not particularly faze the astute McGee. Though Offaly suffered a five-point defeat in that game, McGee came away from it convinced that Kerry were beatable and if given an opportunity Offaly would be the team to do it. In addition, he had witnessed his star forward Matt Connor display all the repertoire of his outstanding skills at the highest level in scoring a phenomenal 2-9 against the best team in the land.

The 1981 season was to portray Matt Connor again at his deadly best, as Offaly sought to do what the team of 1971–1972 had achieved. In the 1981 quarter-final, he notched 0-9 from the centre half forward position, against Westmeath, 1-5 in the semi-final against Wexford and 0-5 as they overcame Laois in the Leinster final. When Offaly met Down in the All-Ireland semi-final, great memories were revived of their exciting tussles in the 1960s when Down won two successive All-Irelands in 1960 and 1961.

In 1960, Down only advanced to the final after a replay with Offaly and then by only two points (a controversial penalty in the drawn game had allowed Down to equalise). Both teams met in the following year's All-Ireland final with Down deservedly emerging victorious on a 3-6 to 2-8 scoreline.

Now, 20 years later, Offaly were determined to break this psychological barrier and defeat the Mourne men. For three quarters of the game, both teams were evenly matched but in the final quarter Offaly moved into overdrive and scored an impressive 0-12 to 0-6 victory. Again Matt Connor displayed his undoubted class when, with consummate ease, he pointed a remarkable sideline kick 45 metres out on the left-hand touchline.

Having reached the All-Ireland final, McGee was delighted with his team's gradual advancement in the All-Ireland championship over the previous four years. Again, in the final, Offaly were pitted against the might of Kerry. Offaly matched Kerry in the first half of the 1981 final and were contented when half time came with a score of 0-5 each. In the second half though, the Offaly backs marked the much-vaunted Kerry forward line very well, but their own forwards failed to score for the first 24 minutes of the second half. It took, nevertheless, a fabulous goal from Jack O'Shea five minutes from the end to kill off the Offaly challenge on a rather flattering winning margin of 1-12 to 0-8.

The ageing profile of the Kerry team, in football terms, plus the exceptional improvement in his own side made Eugene McGee realise that if the sides were to meet in the following year's championship then Offaly could claim the Sam Maguire Cup. So, McGee left no stone unturned as he diligently prepared his team for the 1982 championship. To build up morale and to create a bonding of spirit amongst his team, McGee brought Offaly for a two-week break to Spain in the spring of 1982. Being the first manager to initiate such an exercise, McGee, conducted full-scale daily training sessions during their continental sojourn. Repeatedly, he informed his team that individually and collectively they could beat Kerry to win the All-Ireland if that was the way the championship would pan out. He reminded them that Kerry themselves would be under immense strain as they attempted to be the first team in the history of the game to win five All-Irelands in a row.

In that year's Leinster championship, Offaly won their third successive provincial title when they beat old rivals Dublin, 1-16 to 1-7. This was the biggest defeat the Metropolitans had ever suffered in a provincial decider. Kerry after a replay, meanwhile overcame Cork in the Munster final. Kerry then easily accounted for Armagh in the first All-Ireland semi-final whereas Offaly were decidedly lucky that their opponents Galway missed two scoreable frees in the latter stages of the second semi final. This profligacy allowed Offaly to hold out for a 1-12 to 1-11 victory.

However, as far as Offaly was concerned the pressure was off them and very much on the Kingdom's search for GAA history. The media concentrated on the probability of Kerry winning an unprecedented five titles in a row, whereas Offaly were able to prepare in relative secrecy. Meanwhile, McGee and Offaly planned conscientiously as a major tactical alteration was made to the normal team formation. To prevent the powerful Kerry centre half back, Tim Kennelly, dictating the pace of the game as he had done so capably in the 1981 final, McGee decided to place his team captain Richie Connor at centre half forward. In addition, the usual centre half back was a very versatile player who could create scoring opportunities for his fellow forwards.

Matt Connor was exceedingly nervous as he stood to attention during the playing of the national anthem on All-Ireland final day. Like all great athletes, the anxiety disappeared, to be replaced by a spirited determination, when the ball was thrown in. During that first half, Offaly played fantastic football with their halfback line particularly prominent. Each member of that line, Pat Fitzgerald, Seán Lowry and Liam Currams (a real inspirational score in the sixth minute) raised the white flag before both sides retired at half time with Offaly leading 0-10 to 0-9. During the interval, despite the fact that Offaly were now playing against a heavy, rain-laden wind, McGee was satisfied that Offaly could win. He told them merely to go out and finish the job.

In the third quarter, a determined Kerry put the Offaly defence under severe pressure with John Egan and Mike Sheehy being especially effective. The Kingdom had taken a 0-12 to 0-11 lead when they were awarded a penalty in the 17th minute. Retrospectively, the game was in its defining moment. If the normally reliable Sheehy scored the penalty, Offaly's resistance might be broken. On the other hand, if he missed it, the psychological pendulum could swing decidedly in Offaly's favour. As it happened, long serving goalkeeper Martin Furlong, brought off a tremendous save and the Kingdom siege was lifted. Offaly equalised for the ninth time through Johnny Mooney a few minutes later. Then followed a spell of absolute Kerry brilliance when they scored four unanswered points between the 19th and 26th minutes. Kerry, it appeared, were on course for their name to be entered in the history books. 'At that stage, I feared that we were going to lose,' an honest Matt Connor told me when I met him in his beautiful new residence at Cappincur, just two miles outside Tullamore.

Within the course of the next ten minutes, Offaly had made two significant changes. Firstly, Richie Connor and Gerry Carroll were brought to midfield to try to curb the masterly Kerry duo of Jack O'Shea and Seán Walsh. Secondly, veteran Séamus Darby was introduced at left corner forward. As the game entered its final two minutes Offaly had reduced the deficit to two points thanks to frees, both of them expertly taken by the inimitable Matt Connor. Then in a counter attack, a threatening Kerry movement broke down and Eoin Liston fouled his man. The huge crowd were about to witness one of the most dramatic endings ever witnessed in an All-Ireland final.

Corner back Mick Fitzgerald quickly took the resultant free kick and passed it to Richie Connor. He quickly transferred the ball to full back Liam Connor who had come storming up through the centre. Liam lobbed a high ball into the left corner forward position where Kerry's Tommy Doyle appeared certain to gain possession as Séamus Darby seemed to push Doyle in the back and the ball broke free into his hands. In the twinkling of an eye, Darby turned and sent a blistering shot past the despairing dive of Kerry goalkeeper, Charlie Nelligan, into the net.

Notwithstanding the dispute about the legality of how Darby won the ball, there was no doubt about the goal that followed. Sensationally, Offaly were now leading by a point and that is how it remained until the full time whistle blew. Offaly were the 1982 All-Ireland champions on a final score of 1-15 to 0-17. Matt Connor could not believe it. It was only long afterwards that he fully appreciated the magnitude of Offaly's achievement. It had been an outstanding game of Gaelic football, played at a tremendous pace all through. Over a period of six years, Eugene McGee had brought lowly Offaly to the pinnacle of success. There was, it must be said, a lot of justifiable sympathy that a truly great Kerry team had not accomplished their dreams of five titles in a row. Nevertheless, that should not detract from the magnificence of Offaly's achievement and the fact that its most gifted footballer, Matt Connor, had won a senior All-Ireland football medal.

Matt Connor did not know it but unfortunate circumstances were to dictate that he would only play for his beloved Offaly for a further two years. In 1983, Offaly adopted a too-casual mental attitude when they lost the Leinster final, by five points, to old adversaries Dublin. A tame exit in the following year's championship 0-13 to 0-5 in the Leinster semi-final put paid to any immediate hopes of further championship glory. Having achieved his initial objective, manager Eugene McGee decided to retire. Ironically, that semi-final encounter turned out to be Matt Connor's last championship game.

Though he played in the league under new manager, John Crofton, up to the Christmas break, fate took a cruel hand in the blossoming career of one of the most naturally gifted footballers of all time. Driving home from work on Christmas Day in 1984, Matt was involved in a very serious car accident. Family, friends and the whole GAA community were equally stunned when it was discovered that Matt's resultant injuries would confine him to a wheelchair. Undaunted, the positive-thinking Matt has brilliantly readjusted his schedule of life, is happily married to the charming Siobhán and continues to contentedly serve the community through his clerical work as a member of the Garda Síochána in Tullamore. Dispirited and shocked he and all of us may have been initially, but now life has taken on a new and meaningful challenge to him. At the age of 25, a football career had ended but an era which showed all the talents of Matt Connor, the person, had begun.

'I had a great time with Offaly. Eugene McGee was a very influential manager. He took a very personal interest in my football development and in my progress as a human being. In football he was ahead of his time. His preparation of teams was outstanding. Eugene had the ability to unite the County board, the team and the supporters. Many in the GAA opposed us going on that trip to Spain in 1982 but Eugene knew it would be invaluable for team spirit. Now, thanks to him and others, I have retained a great interest in the GAA. I was a minor selector for many years and still go to as many matches as I am able to manage,' stated Matt.

Matt, who believes that the introduction of the quick free was the best rule to be implemented in recent years because it speeds up the game considerably has great sympathy for referees today. 'People think that they are inconsistent in the application of the rules but one must take into consideration that with so many changes taking place, it will be some time before everyone can be adjusted to them.'

Connor believes that the National Football league should consist of four groups of eight with straightforward promotion and relegation each year. He would recommend that the top two teams in Division One and Two and the top teams in Divisions Three and Four should qualify for the play-offs with the winners of Division One and Two going directly through to the semi-finals. In his opinion, the introduction of an open draw championship would make Gaelic football more exciting and less predictable.

Matt is full of praise for the role the media play in the promotion of Gaelic games. The quality of journalists' articles and the inclusion of top-class colour photographs have added to the glamour of our games. The professionalism of Colm O'Rourke and Pat Spillane in their analyses on 'The Sunday Game' impresses the Walsh Island native. His favourite journalist is Con Houlihan, formerly of the *Evening Press*, and now of *The Sunday World*. 'Con could analyse everyone and everything very accurately while retaining your interest. As well as that, he never is nasty in his writings.'

Matt has very frank views on the All Star selection system. 'After the provincial finals take place each year, the selectors should pick the best provincial 15 based on that year's league and championship form. The final All Stars should be picked only from these 60 nominations. Naturally there would be extra marks awarded to those who starred in the All-Ireland semi-finals and final.'

Matt, whose greatest disappointment was losing the 1983 Leinster final, also had outstanding success at club level with Walsh Island. In 1978, he won his first county championship medal when they defeated Rhode in the Offaly final. This was the start of six successive titles (1978-1983). Matt, his brother, Richie and his double first cousins Tomás and Liam, shared in that success as well as winning two Leinster club titles in 1978 and 1979 to add to their many joint county achievements.

When it came to discussing wonderful football teams and exceptional exponents, Matt has many reminiscences. 'The whole Kerry team of the 1970s and 1980s but especially the full forward line of the skilful Mike Sheehy, the ideal target man Eoin Liston and the opportunist John Egan were fantastic. There was no atmosphere to compare to playing Dublin in Croke Park. Their supporters really added to the occasion. But, of all the talented players that I met, Kerry's John O'Keeffe was the best. He was very skilful, exceptionally strong on the ball and he was very fast. In today's game I would love to play alongside Offaly goalkeeper Padraig Kelly, and defenders Séamus Moynihan (Kerry), Glenn Ryan (Kildare). Anthony Tohill (Derry) and Niall Buckley (Kildare) would be my ideal midfield combination whereas up front I would select Maurice Fitzgerald (Kerry), Peter Canavan (Tyrone) and Trevor Giles (Meath).'

Matt also admires the colossal effort that current management teams put in to prepare county teams so well. 'Luke Dempsey, John Maughan, John O'Mahony and Tommy Lyons are examples of men who have achieved tremendous results with so called less glamorous teams. They have made the players in those counties develop a belief in themselves as well as providing them with top class coaching and man management skills.'

Since 1970, Matt Connor has been a keen follower of English Premiership soccer team Tottenham Hotspur. Former stars Martin Chivers, Clive Allen, Argentinian World Cup star Ossie Ardiles, Paul Gascoigne and Sol Campbell are all particular favourites, but, in the number one spot he places Glen Hoddle whom he feels was hard done by when he was forced to resign as manager of the English international team in 1998. Matt, a self-confessed sports fanatic likes watching all major athletic events and applauds Eamon Coghlan, Sonia O'Sullivan and Catherina McKiernan for their outstanding performances in World Athletics. However, in his opinion, the greatest athlete in his living memory was American track star, Carl Lewis who won nine Olympic gold medals in several disciplines over a long period of time.

GAA man to the core, a true sports fan, Matt Connor loves hurling and the men who have made it a wonderful spectacle of distinctive Irishness over the years. DJ Carey (Kilkenny) and Nicholas English (Tipperary) epitomised for Matt the whole range of skills that hurling possesses. Naturally he is especially proud of what his native Offaly have accomplished since they won their first All-Ireland senior hurling title in 1981. Coming from such a small hurling base, Offaly must be the success of modern times in Gaelic Games. Added to the fact that the footballers' catchment area is also relatively small, one must conclude that when great GAA counties are discussed, Offaly must be placed at the top of the tree. In the eyes of Matt Connor, men such as Pat Delaney, dual star and former footballing colleague Liam Currams, Joachim Kelly, Padraig Horan, Johnny Flaherty, Brian Whelehan, Kevin Kinahan and Johnny Dooley deserve the highest of accolades.

Matt selected the following Ireland and Leinster teams:

IRELAND

Billy Morgan
(Cork)

Robbie O'Malley   John O'Keeffe   Paudie Lynch
(Meath)   *(Kerry)*   *(Kerry)*

Páidí Ó Sé   Henry Downey   Tommy Drumm
(Kerry)   *(Derry)*   *(Dublin)*

Brian Mullins   Jack O'Shea
(Dublin)   *(Kerry)*

Peter Canavan   Larry Tompkins   Pat Spillane
(Tyrone)   *(Cork)*   *(Kerry)*

Colm O'Rourke   Eoin Liston   Mike Sheehy
(Meath)   *(Kerry)*   *(Kerry)*

LEINSTER

Paddy Cullen
(Dublin)

Robbie O'Malley   Mick Lyons   Robbie Kelleher
(Meath)   *(Meath)*   *(Dublin)*

Tommy Drumm   Glenn Ryan   Colm Browne
(Dublin)   *(Kildare)*   *(Laois)*

Brian Mullins   Gerry McEntee
(Dublin)   *(Meath)*

Tom Prendergast   Larry Tompkins   Willie Brennan
(Laois)   *(Kildare)*   *(Laois)*

Colm O'Rourke   Jimmy Keaveney   Bernard Flynn
(Meath)   *(Dublin)*   *(Meath)*

Subs: Kevin O'Brien (Wicklow), Brian Stafford (Meath), Trevor Giles (Meath), Paddy O'Donoghue (Kildare), Kevin Moran (Dublin), Niall Buckley (Kildare)

Matt Connor's senior inter-county career just lasted from March 1978 to December 1984. The thrice All Star amassed 82 goals and 606 points (852 points) in a total of 161 games during that time at inter-county and provincial level. The people of Offaly and the country at large often stood in awe at his wonderful displays of exquisite skill and unerring accuracy either from play or placed balls. Matt, according to himself, did not like physical training *per se* but would train all day every day if a ball was part of the training routine. One facet of Matt's personal skills training highlights the man's innate ability and focused mental approach. After a county training session formally ended, Matt Connor would place the ball at the corner flag. Then with that familiar, slightly arched stance he would step back a few paces looking first of all at the goal posts. After this he would amble up and kick for a point. This routine would be repeated nine more times before Matt would retire for the evening. On average, eight of those ten kicks would inevitably and incredibly sail over the bar, all scored from a virtually impossible angle of 180°. The beautifully balanced player whose sheer football elegance, ballet like athleticism and inherent class, was a master craftsman.

Matt Connor – footballer extraordinaire – will always be considered for automatic selection when any team of all time great Gaelic footballers is being picked. Those of us who saw him in action are grateful for the privilege.

"Why did you miss that blasted penalty?" asked the blood-stained victim as Garda Matt Connor came to investigate an accident one week after the 1983 Leinster final.

Jimmy Barry Murphy

ONE OF THE GREATEST hurling goals of all time was scored in Croke Park on Sunday 7 August 1983. The occasion was the All-Ireland senior hurling semi-final between Cork and Galway. Cork scored five superb goals as they comprehensively defeated the Tribesmen – one of them bore the hallmark of a hurling genius. Elegant midfielder John Fenton sent a long, high, probing ball into the Galway goalmouth. All Star full back Conor Hayes and Cork full forward and captain Jimmy Barry Murphy dashed out to meet the dropping ball. As they jumped together, high in the air, with hurleys at the ready there was a distinct clash of the ash. The Corkman was marginally ahead as the falling sliotar approached them. He instinctively swivelled his hips and with a deft wrist movement and precision timing turned his hurley, connected with the ball and sent an unstoppable shot to the corner of the Galway net. 'I often tried it before but it rarely came off. I do not remember what happened exactly. It was just a reflex action, I suppose. What I do not forget is what a Cork supporter told me after the game. "Jimmy, that was a great goal that John Fenton scored!" I just smiled to myself and agreed with him.'

Twenty-nine years earlier, in 1954, Jimmy Barry Murphy was born in Cork city. When it comes to a background steeped in hurling, none come any better endowed than Jimmy. His grandfather Finbarr Barry Murphy was a sub on the Cork hurling team that defeated Dublin in the 1919 All-Ireland final. His grand uncle Dinny Barry Murphy was on the next Cork team to win a senior All-Ireland in 1926 against Kilkenny. Jimmy's father John won a junior All-Ireland hurling medal in 1940 against Galway.

At the age of 16, Jimmy achieved his first ambition when he obtained his place in the St Finbarr's senior club hurling side. In both 1971 and 1972, the blossoming star played on both the Cork minor football and hurling teams. 1971 was to see him win his first All-Ireland medal when Cork defeated Kilkenny in the minor hurling final and the following year he was again back in the winners enclosure, this time collecting an All-Ireland minor football medal when Cork defeated Tyrone in the decider. The dual full forward's career had certainly taken off in style. The aplomb with which he mastered both codes was a foretaste of much greater things to come.

1973 was to prove an even more illustrious one for the multi-talented Barry Murphy. At U-21 level he was a member of the Cork side that claimed the Munster hurling title when they beat Limerick before going on to defeat Leinster champions Wexford in the All-Ireland final. However, it was the unexpected success of Cork's senior football team that was to provide Jimmy with his greatest triumph in that year. Prior to this, Cork football had been very much in the doldrums. They had last won a senior All-Ireland title in 1945 and it was said, in many quarters, that Cork football rated a very poor second, in official GAA circles, within the county. Now, however, that was all changed. A tremendous underage structure in the county had delivered seven of the previous ten Munster minor football titles. In addition, four All-Ireland minor titles had been won in that period. The general administration of the game had improved immensely and an excellent football management team under the expert direction of coach Donie O'Donovan was in place.

Jimmy Barry Murphy made his senior football championship debut in the 1973 Munster final against Kerry. The interchanging tactics of Murphy and the nominated full forward Ray Cummins totally mesmerised the Kerry defence and Cork scored a very impressive victory, 5-12 to 1-15.

In the All-Ireland semi-final against Tyrone, Cork continued with their high scoring when they chalked up another five goals in a 5-10 to 2-4 win over the Ulster champions. Cork were now in their first All-Ireland since they were beaten by Meath six years earlier. This time they faced Galway in what turned out to be a fantastic game of free-flowing football. From a Cork perspective, they intended to move the ball as quickly as possible to their lethal full forward line of Jimmy Barry Murphy, Ray Cummins and Jimmy Barrett. Galway opened the scoring with a point from a free but, almost immediately, Cork sent a long clearance deep into the Galway danger area. The ever-alert Jimmy Barry Murphy leapt highest and judiciously palmed the ball out of reach of the Galway defence and into the net for a sensational, opportunist, early goal. With Cork midfielders Denis Long and another dual star Denis Coughlan, playing superbly, the Cork attack constantly received a good supply of quality ball. As a result, Cork retired at the interval leading the Westerners by seven points 1-10 to 0-6.

A tremendous rally by Galway after half time produced three unanswered points by the ninth minute. However, Cork soon regained their midfield supremacy and by the 59th minute in this 80-minute final, they had restored their seven point advantage. Still, a determined Galway came back to score a goal and a point to reduce the deficit to three points. When Cork's centre half back John Coleman had to retire injured the mentors switched Declan Barron from the half forward line. This proved a master stroke as Barron proceeded to blot the hitherto impressive Galway captain Liam Sammon out of the game. Consequently, the siege was lifted and Cork regained the initiative. The clever Cummins pointed twice before another piece of Murphy magic finally clinched the game in favour of the Rebel County. Corner forward Jimmy Barrett gained possession, passed to Cummins who spotted the unmarked Jimmy Barry Murphy close to the Galway goalmouth. Despite being fouled, Murphy kept his cool and with supreme confidence broke clear, toe tapping the ball like a professional juggler. Then, much to the chagrin of the Galway defence and much to the delight of Cork supporters, he nonchalantly slotted the ball to the corner of the net. It was a goal worthy of any great occasion. In essence, though Galway came back with a consolation goal, it was the defining moment of the game. Just before the end, Jimmy Barrett added a third Cork goal to leave the final score 3-17 to 2-13. Cork had won their first All-Ireland senior football title in 28 years and Jimmy Barry Murphy had, for the third successive year, won an All-Ireland medal.

'Of all the great days that I experienced as a player with club and county this was my favourite because it was the year that I won my first senior All-Ireland medal,' Jimmy told me when I met him in Fitzpatrick's Silver Spring Hotel in Cork. In terms of quality football, it was an excellent contest dominated by the fact that Cork's full forward line contributed the massive total of 3-11 out of their final tally. For Cork football followers, years of frustrating defeats had been replaced by a highly skilled performance of positive football which resulted in a famous victory. The tall rangy player with the close-cropped hairstyle was now a sporting idol by the banks of the Lee.

Though Jimmy won both Munster U-21 and senior provincial football medals in 1974, Cork were surprisingly beaten by Dublin in that year's All-Ireland senior semi-final. It is generally accepted that Cork totally underestimated Dublin who had not won a Leinster title since 1965. In hindsight, they had not reckoned with the massive organisational skills that new manager Kevin Heffernan had brought to the Dublin set-up. One story told by Cork's captain Billy Morgan, against himself, vividly illustrates the ultra-confidence of Cork. 'In the week before the All-Ireland semi-final, Dublin star Jimmy Keaveney was in Cork visiting Frank Cogan and myself. We went to Frank's house, brought out the Sam Maguire Cup and said to Jimmy, "Take a good look at it because you will never get any closer to it!" Jimmy then told Kevin Heffernan about the incident. Heffernan used our comments as a huge motivating factor against us.'

That 1974 All-Ireland semi-final, as turned out, was Cork's last semi-final championship appearance for nine years. In the intervening time, they were unfortunate to come up against an extraordinary Kerry side – one of the greatest in the history of Gaelic football. Without any prospect of further provincial football success, and the physical and mental demands of playing football and hurling at the top level Jimmy decided, in 1980, to concentrate on hurling. His county football days were over.

Meanwhile, the hurling skills of Jimmy Barry Murphy were attracting national attention. In 1976, Cork beat Tipperary and Limerick to win the Munster final and reached the All-Ireland final against Wexford. With centre half back Mick Jacob dictating matters, Wexford appeared to be on their way to success. In fact, so dominant were the Slaneysiders that, with ten minutes to go, only four Cork players were in their original positions. Then the Cork mentors pulled a master stroke which changed the course of the game. Jimmy Barry Murphy was switched from the wing to centre half forward. This proved decisive in two ways. Firstly, it curtailed Jacob's dominance and secondly it allowed Murphy to exert his own influence on the game. Giving a superlative display of immaculate positional sense and accurate marksmanship, the St Finbarr's man inspired Cork to record a 2-21 to 4-11 victory. For the second time in three years, in two different codes, Jimmy had turned a possible defeat into a glorious win. For Cork's management team of coach, Fr Bertie Troy, trainer Kevin Kehilly and selectors Frank Murphy, Christy Ring and Jimmy Brohan it was a fitting reward for a season of meticulous preparation. For captain Ray Cummins it was a moment to savour as he had given up his football commitments to concentrate on bringing the Liam McCarthy Cup to Cork.

The following year, Cork retained the Munster crown and defeated Galway in the All-Ireland semi-final to reach their second successive hurling final against Wexford. Captained by Martin O'Doherty, Cork again took the honours. In a team of heroes, Cork had three new stars, Tim Crowley, Tom Cashman and Dermot McCurtain, who had not even been on the panel the previous year. It was a very special, historic occasion for Crowley who became the first player from west Cork to win an All-Ireland senior hurling medal while playing with a west Cork club – Newcestown.

Jimmy Barry Murphy and Cork won three All-Ireland titles in a row when they successfully defended their Munster and All-Ireland titles against Waterford and Kilkenny respectively. It took a powerful performance by Tim Crowley when he was switched from left half forward to midfield to counteract the dominance of Kilkenny's Frank Cummins in that area, to finally swing the game Cork's way. As a result, he was voted 'Man of the Match' by RTE. Another distinguished Cork Gael, GAA President, Con Murphy, will never forget those three years of Cork hurling brilliance. During his term of office, he had the distinction of presenting the Liam McCarthy Cup to three Cork men – Ray Cummins, Martin O'Doherty and 1978 captain Charlie McCarthy.

In 1979, Jimmy Barry Murphy won another Munster senior medal only to suffer defeat to an up-and-coming Galway side in the All-Ireland semi-final. However, it was 1982 before Cork were again to win a Munster title and for the following four years, Cork retained the provincial crown, with Jimmy a central figure in all those triumphs. In 1982 and 1983 he had the honour of captaining his native county but unfortunately for him, Cork were beaten by Kilkenny on each occasion in the All-Ireland final. 'Considering how fortunate I was in achieving so many successes it would be rather churlish of me to complain about not winning those finals. Nevertheless, human nature being what it is, it would have been nice to captain a winning Cork side.'

Having scored six goals in the 1976–1978 championship campaigns, Jimmy was back at his goalscoring best in 1984. In the opening round, he scored a fine goal against Limerick. The Munster final against Tipperary was to see Cork's longest serving All-Ireland medallist at his deadly best. Not only did he notch two magnificent goals but he was the chief architect in Cork's 4-15 to 3-14 victory. Cork captain John Fenton, Tony O'Sullivan, Seán O'Leary and John Crowley were the other stars as Cork secured the McCarthy Cup in the GAA's centenary final against Offaly. It was held in Thurles to commemorate the founding of the GAA there in 1884. Like 1973 in football and 1976 in hurling, it was Jimmy Barry Murphy who featured in the goal that clinched the 1984 title. After 26 minutes of the first half, the Cork-based financial consultant gained possession and sent a lovely weighted pass to corner forward Seánie O'Leary who dispatched the sliotar to the Offaly net. Thereafter Cork controlled the game to emerge comprehensive victors 3-16 to 1-12. Jimmy had won his fourth All-Ireland senior hurling medal.

The next year, Cork won their fourth Munster title in a row but were beaten by Galway in the All-Ireland semi-final. When 1986 came along, Jimmy decided that if Cork were to win that year's All-Ireland he would retire. The Rebel County beat Clare in the Munster final and Antrim in the All-Ireland semi-final. Now, Jimmy Barry Murphy was in his seventh All-Ireland senior hurling final and a winning one it proved to be when Cork gained revenge for Galway's win the previous year. When his friend and colleague of many years standing, Tom Cashman, raised the Liam McCarthy Cup, Jimmy knew that he had played his last major game in Croke Park. Though still only 32 years of age, Jimmy knew his time had come. So he stopped playing both at county and club levels.

With his club, St Finbarr's, Jimmy accomplished much both in hurling and football, winning six county hurling championships and five county football championships. In early 1975 the 'Barrs defeated Newmarket on Fergus and Ballycran of Down before overcoming The Fenians of Kilkenny in the All-Ireland club hurling final. Again, Murphy, with another inspirational goal, and a commanding performance by dual star Donal O'Grady paved the way for a famous victory. Three years later, St Finbarr's won their second All-Ireland hurling title when they beat Rathnure of Wexford. The route to that year's final began with an enthralling win over fellow Corkonians Glen Rovers in the Cork county final before an estimated crowd of 34,000 – one of the biggest ever attendances at a club fixture in any code in Ireland. After a replay, they beat Sixmilebridge of Clare in the Munster final and O'Donovan Rossas of Antrim in the All-Ireland semi-final. True to form, Jimmy Barry Murphy – the man for the big occasion – secured the victory over Rathnure in the final with another brilliantly taken goal.

1980 was a historic year in the St Finbarr's club which can trace its existence back to 1875. They became the first club to win an All-Ireland club title in both codes when they defeated, amongst others, Kilrush of Clare and Scotstown of Monaghan on their path to the All-Ireland final with St Grellan's of Ballinasloe. In the decider, Murphy was at his scintillating best as he bobbed and weaved his way through the St Grellan's defence to set up all three goals for his colleagues in a thoroughly convincing 3-9 to 0-8 victory. They successfully defended their title the following year when they again disposed of Scotstown in the semi-final before they conquered Meath champions Walterstown in the final. By the time St Finbarr's had won their third All-Ireland football title (and their fifth in all, including hurling) in 1987, the Gaelic Games genius that was Jimmy Barry Murphy had retired from the game. However, along with stars such as Christy Ryan, Donal O'Grady, Gerald McCarthy, Charlie McCarthy and the evergreen John Allen, Jimmy had left an amazing legacy of contribution to St Finbarr's. In the process, he had accumulated another four All-Ireland medals to add to his eventual haul of six senior All-Ireland medals at county level (one in football and five in hurling). As a player, Jimmy was now totally fulfilled. Now it was time for the selfless star to put something back into the game that had served him so well for so long.

Immediately after his retirement, he became very involved with underage coaching at St Finbarr's. In 1993, the Cork County board asked him to manage the county minor team. Later that year, Jimmy brought them to a Munster final which they lost to Tipperary. The following year, Cork won the Munster title and were only narrowly beaten in the All-Ireland final by Galway. It was third time lucky when Jimmy successfully steered Cork to All-Ireland glory in 1995. The convincing 2-10 to 1-2 win over Kilkenny was Cork's first national minor success since 1985.

Cork's lack of hurling championship honours at senior level since they won the 1990 All-Ireland against Galway had been attributed to an absence of accomplishments at minor level. Prior to the autumn of 1995, Cork had only won one senior championship hurling game in the previous three years and that victory was over a county – Kerry – which was more renowned for its footballing prowess. So after that 1995 triumph, a tidal wave of emotion ran through Cork almost begging Jimmy to take on the task of hurling saviour. As a result, Jimmy agreed to manage the senior side initially bringing in former colleagues Tom Cashman and Tony O'Sullivan as fellow selectors.

To say that Jimmy had a rough first year in his new managerial role would be to severely understate the problems. First, they suffered the utter humiliation of relegation in the National Hurling League. Second, and much more significant they lost their first round championship game to Limerick by the incredible margin of 16 points. Worse still, this was Cork's first home defeat to Limerick in over 70 years of championship hurling. In 1997, defeat was again the Rebel County's lot when they succumbed to a four-point defeat to Clare in the semi-final of the Munster championship. However, by the end of that season, though naturally disappointed,

Jimmy was optimistic on two fronts. Their Munster conquerors, Clare, had gone on to record a resounding All-Ireland win and more important, from a Cork perspective, their U-21 side scored a highly impressive victory over Galway in the All-Ireland final. In spite of these limited successes, the cynics were bemoaning the fact that Cork had not been in an All-Ireland senior semi-final since 1992. Given Cork's traditional and unrivalled status as a premier hurling county, the fact that they had not even reached a Munster final for five years was a particularly contentious issue.

As Cork entered the 1998 season, Jimmy knew that Cork would have to achieve something of importance if they, as a management team, were to retain their credibility. His team responded in style as they overwhelmed Clare by eleven points in the league semi-final and then went on to easily defeat Waterford in the league final. But again the Leesiders disappointed in the championship. Though they narrowly defeated Limerick in the first round they once more suffered the ignominy of defeat as Clare convincingly beat them in the provincial semi-final.

Jimmy and company faced a do-or-die scenario in 1999 as Cork faced the rigours of a fourth Munster championship campaign under his stewardship. With this in mind, the management team boldly decided to give youth its fling. Six newcomers were introduced for the championship semi-final game against Waterford. The fact that Cork had won both the minor and U-21 All-Ireland hurling titles in 1998 was a huge psychological boost as they embarked on this brave but imaginative youth policy. Cork played well to defeat the men from the Decies by six points and thus reach their first Munster final in seven years.

The previous three years, untimely exits to Limerick and Clare (twice) were forgotten as they diligently prepared for the Munster final against Clare. Though Clare had to field without the injured Jamesie O'Connor, they nevertheless played magnificently only to be beaten by a superior and hungrier Cork side 1-15 to 0-14. Cork had convincingly won their first Munster championship since 1992.

The All-Ireland semi-final against Offaly was a thoroughly exciting and evenly contested encounter with the Midlanders leading by two points as the game entered its last ten minutes. Then Cork, inspired by a truly wonderful centre half back display by Brian Corcoran upped the tempo considerably. In the last seven minutes, Cork scored five points without reply to run out winners by 0-19 to 0-16.

In the final, Cork were pitted against Kilkenny for the 18th time in a decider. Their record versus the Cats in finals was not very impressive. They had only won seven of those major contests. Also, Kilkenny had deprived Jimmy of captaining a winning Cork side in 1982 and 1983. In the view of many pundits, Cork, though possessing players of immense skill, were too light in build and too inexperienced in big game situations. Furthermore, as the match approached, it was clearly apparent that the weather conditions were deteriorating. This development appeared to lessen the hopes of the Rebel County. However, despite speculation from some quarters that there would be changes in the starting 15 for the final, Jimmy and his fellow selectors Tom Cashman and Seánie O'Leary kept faith with the same side that had served them so well all summer. That meant that all six championship debutantes, Donal Óg Cusack (long-serving goalie Ger Cunningham, retired in February), Wayne Sherlock, Mickey O'Connell, Timmy McCarthy, Neil Ronan and Ben O'Connor were retained. The selectors were not going to change their youth policy (the average age of the team was 22) at this late stage.

Cork opened the scoring in the final with a point by captain Mark Landers in the eighth minute. This was closely followed by two other Cork points by the impressive right half forward Timmy McCarthy. Kilkenny scored their first point in the 20th minute courtesy of a Henry Shefflin free. The Kilkenny midfielder Andy Comerford and Cork corner forward Joe Deane exchanged points to leave the score 0-4 to 0-2.

Kilkenny, who clocked up an incredible eight wides in the first half, then seized the initiative and sent over three unanswered points to lead at the interval by the minimum of margins 0-5 to 0-4. When the game restarted, Cork's Alan Browne who had replaced the out-of-form Neil Ronan scored a neatly taken point, with his first touch of the ball, to leave the sides level. Despite this encouraging start by Cork, it was Kilkenny who proceeded to dominate the game with Andy Comerford being particularly impressive in the centre of the field. The net result of this period of Kilkenny control was that the 'Cats' led by 0-9 to 0-5 with just 16 minutes of the second half gone. After this, Mark Landers, who had not been fully fit coming into the game, was replaced by Kevin Murray who scored a very valuable point just after he entered the fray. During the next five minutes, the sides exchanged two points each to leave the score 0-11 to 0-8 in Kilkenny's favour with 57 minutes gone. The defining moment, in most viewers' opinions, of the 1999 senior hurling final had come three minutes earlier. With his side three points to the good, Charlie Carter found himself clear in front of the goals with only the goalkeeper to beat. Instead of going for a goal which could have clinched the game for Kilkenny he took the safer option and put the ball over the bar to give Kilkenny a four-point cushion. Encouraged by this, Cork upped their performance considerably as each player displayed a tremendous resolve to focus totally on the task in hand. Two players in particular played a key role in the Leesiders' revival. Timmy McCarthy, who had moved to midfield, played terrific hurling to break the stranglehold that Andy Comerford had been exercising in that sector. Livewire wing forward, Seán McGrath who had been inconspicuous in the first half suddenly found his real form. His electrifying pace and soloing skills continually tormented the retreating Kilkenny defenders. For the next eight minutes McGrath, twice, Ben O'Connor and Joe Deane with two pointed frees during that purple patch of Cork brilliance left the Rebels leading 0-13 to 0-11. Three minutes from the end, the hardworking Shefflin pointed a free to reduce the arrears to a single point. The closeness of the scoring, with the possibility of a Kilkenny goal, kept the packed stadium on tenterhooks as the minutes ticked away. When the final whistle eventually sounded there had been no further scores and for the first time in nine years, Cork were All-Ireland senior hurling champions.

As in all their games during the 1999 campaign, it was Cork's ability to display a great fighting spirit in the last quarter that finally swung the game in their favour. The whole defence was especially outstanding Fergal Ryan, Diarmuid O'Sullivan and John Browne in the full back line kept the much vaunted and talented Kilkenny full forward line of Ken O'Shea, Henry Shefflin and Charlie Carter at bay. Wayne Sherlock, Brian Corcoran and dual star Seán Óg O'hAilpín increasingly imposed their will on proceedings as the game progressed. (Ó hAilpín was in line to add his name to an illustrious band of Cork men to win All-Ireland medals in both codes. Unfortunately for him, even though he gave a very competent performance at full back, Meath spiked his double chances when they defeated Cork two weeks later in the 1999 All-Ireland football final). Centre half back, Brian Corcoran, strode the field like a proverbial colossus and deservedly received the Man of the Match Award. In the forward line, centre half forward Fergal McCormack, a nephew of Mick O'Connell of Kerry football fame, put in a hard 70 minutes. Timmy McCarthy, first of all at wing forward and later at midfield, made a particularly telling contribution with his fetching and incisive runs and must have run Corcoran close for the Man of the Match honours. His gaining of vital possession especially in the second period, allied to the intricate skills of the penetrative runs of Seánie McGrath ultimately paved the way for Cork's success.

Jimmy Barry Murphy's views on the game, its great players and his hopes for the future of Ireland generally are well thought out and concise. While acknowledging that the so called 'back door' system in championship hurling has appreciably raised the profile of the game, he maintains that teams like Galway and Antrim require some type of round-robin method before they enter the championship proper. 'As it is, they are coming into the championship cold compared to the beaten provincial finalists who have played two or three games at least.'

When it comes to the game's great players, Jimmy stresses that the following are only an example of the many talented hurlers he has seen in his lifetime. 'Ger Cunningham (Cork), Noel Skehan (Kilkenny), Tommy Quaid (Limerick) and David Fitzgerald (Clare) have been outstanding custodians. My most difficult opponent was Phil 'Fan' Larkin (Kilkenny). Seán Stack and Ger Loughnane of Clare and Eamon Cregan of Limerick were fantastic defenders. Eamon was the complete hurler as he was equally good in defence and in attack where he was a prolific scorer. John Connolly of Galway was a fabulous midfielder. Eddie Keher of Kilkenny, Ray Cummins, Charlie McCarthy and Seánie O'Leary of Cork, Olcan McFetridge and Terence McNaughton of Antrim, Nicholas English and Pat Fox of Tipperary were just some of the more talented forwards that I had the pleasure of playing with or against.'

The man who is a financial consultant and senior partner with Southern Business Finance Ltd has great admiration for the work that John Hume and Gerry Adams have done to restore peace to Northern Ireland. 'First of all, one must credit John Hume for initiating the whole peace process. In spite of much opposition he was unwavering in pursuing his talks with Gerry Adams in order that an IRA ceasefire would become a reality. One must also give tremendous praise to Adams for persuading the men of violence towards the path of peace. All of this has implications for Gaelic games. If the Good Friday agreement is implemented in full, if true peace extends amongst everyone on this island and if political institutions with which all sections of the people can identify with are created then there will be no need for any bans within the GAA.'

The new All-Ireland winning manager is himself an avid soccer fan who follows the careers of individual Irish soccer players regardless of which club they play for. He makes an exception with one well known soccer side – Glasgow Celtic. Jimmy who played soccer for Cork Celtic during the 1971 League of Ireland season has a particular liking for the 'Bhoys of Paradise.' I have followed them since they won the European Cup final in Lisbon in 1967. I was always conscious of their historical roots based mainly on poor immigrants from Donegal. Jimmy Johnstone, Bobby Lennox, Willie Wallace, Billy McNeill and Bertie Auld are men I will never forget from that era of Celtic success when they totally dominated Scottish soccer.'

In essence Jimmy Barry Murphy is a sports fanatic who can, at will, name players, teams, horses or dogs of any period during the last 30 years. 'Many people do not understand why I am so interested in so many sports. For example I could watch test cricket and listen to commentator Richie Benaud all day, everyday.

Jimmy has a particular passion, which he inherited from his father, for greyhounds and up to recently he trained quite a few of them. He has visited all the leading greyhound stadia both in Ireland and in England. One of his most abiding memories is a visit to see the English Greyhound Derby in 1973. 'It was held at the now-derelict White City stadium in London. Apart from enjoying the race I was taken up with the whole ambience of the place mainly because the Olympic Games were held there in 1908.'

A lover of music, particularly Irish traditional music, Jimmy bows to no one in his admiration for the music of Christy Moore. 'He is a fabulous singer, is very funny and is a marvellous all-round entertainer. I never miss his concerts when he comes to Cork.'

Jimmy and his wife Jean, who were married in 1976, have four children. The eldest, Brian, was a highly promising underage hurler and footballer before he decided to concentrate on playing soccer with Cork City. In August 1999, Brian was granted leave of absence by Cork IT where he was a student, so that he could sign a one-year contract with English soccer club Preston North End. The other members of the family, Deirdre and Anne are secondary school students whereas the youngest, Orla, is still at primary school.

When the All-Ireland hurling champions of 1999 arrived home to Cork's Patrick Street on the Monday following the game, one of the largest crowds ever assembled in this sports-loving city gathered to give a tumultuous homecoming to Jimmy Barry Murphy and his team. Those capital celebrations were to spark off a series of similar scenes of adulation and exultation throughout the rest of the county in the ensuing week. In the towns, villages and parishes from where the individual players came, that euphoria reached unprecedented levels of exuberance. One village in particular encapsulated that scene of unbridled joy and celebratory enthusiasm. The picturesque east Cork village of Killeagh had not produced many star hurlers for the county team but the sustained dedication of their officials led by the indomitable Tom Seward supplied three players for the 1999 winning side. This intermediate club had given team captain Mark Landers, scoring will o' the wisp Joe Deane and sub goalie Bernard Rochford. More than anywhere else, Killeagh exemplified the breadth and depth of Jimmy Barry Murphy's vision.

It is often said that Nice Guys finish last. On this occasion the Nice Guy, and they do not come any nicer than Jimmy Barry Murphy, deservedly stood at the top of the podium of Irish sport. For four years he calmly ignored the pleadings of lesser mortals to do things differently. When the final whistle sounded on the evening of Sunday 12 September 1999, all Cork knew that Jimmy had done it his way. Outwardly he possessed an excellent blend of diplomacy, determination and discernment. Inwardly there was a silent, steely single-mindedness. Together they dovetailed perfectly to return the Liam McCarthy Cup to the banks of the River Lee county. Jimmy Barry Murphy, the manager, had at last come first.